# ADVENTURES ON SEVEN CONTINENTS... AND OTHER ESSAYS

- SPORTS
- MEDICINE
- BOOKS AND WRITING
- PEOPLE
- TRAVEL AND PLACES
- FAMILY

## JOHN DAVIS CANTWELL, M.D.*

*For May Scott —
with my best wishes for
good health & happiness
John Cantwell MD 1/5/04*

\* Clinical Professor of Medicine, Morehouse School of Medicine and Emory School of Medicine. Director of Preventive Cardiology and Cardiac Rehabilitation, Piedmont Hospital, Atlanta, Georgia.

© 2003 by John Davis Cantwell, M.D.
All rights reserved.

No part of this book may be reproduced, stored in a retrieval system, or transmitted by any means, electronic, mechanical, photocopying, recording, or otherwise, without written permission from the author.

ISBN: 1-4033-8428-2 (e-book)
ISBN: 1-4033-8429-0 (Paperback)
ISBN: 1-4033-8430-4 (Dustjacket)

This book is printed on acid free paper.

1stBooks – rev. 02/05/03

# FOREWORD BY HANK AARON

I've enjoyed having Dr. Cantwell as my physician. We share a number of common interests, including a love of baseball and of family.

This book of essays has something for everyone, ranging from sports to medicine, travels to unusual places, an appreciation of good books and talented writers, and heartfelt comments to his children. I know you'll enjoy it.

*Hank Aaron*

# ACKNOWLEDGMENTS

Chapters 5, 52 and 53 appeared in The American Journal of Cardiology and are reproduced with permission. Chapter 50 was originally published in Clinical Cardiology and Chapter 65 in JAMA, both used with permission. Chapter 12 appeared in The New York Times, who granted permission to reprint it. Chapter 23 is from Cardiovascular Reviews and Reports.

Chapter 10 was co-authored with the late Roger Cantwell. Ryan Cantwell co-authored chapter 41.

The photo in chapter 14 is courtesy of Walter Victor, Jim Schultz and the Atlanta Braves. Mark Silverman, M.D., took the photo in Chapter 25 and provided the picture of J. Edgar Paullin, M.D. The pictures of Byron Herbert Reece in chapter 37 are courtesy of Roger Kintzel and the Atlanta Journal-Constitution, and the one of Margaret Mitchell in Chapter 40 is courtesy of Durwood McAlister and the Atlanta Journal-Constitution. The Georgia Tech Sports Information Department kindly provided the figure in chapter 47. I thank Fred and Willa Deane Birchmore for use of the figure in chapter 53. Walter Victor provided the photo in chapter 67. John Griffin, M.D., took the millennium photo in chapter 73 and the Everest photos. Mark Thompson from MT Publishing Co. gave permission to use a picture of pilot John Powers and his plane, reproduced from "Helton's Hellcats."

Fred Boyer and Anne Morgan did the transcription work and their fine efforts are greatly appreciated. Melissa Connor prepared the figures.

## DEDICATION

To Marilyn

To me, fair friend, you never can be old,
For as you were when first your eye I eyed,
Such seems your beauty still."
                            Shakespeare
                            Sonnet 104

    ...and to

Sarah Carson Myers
  Cameron Davis Cantwell
    Blair Sullivan Myers
      Hannah Christine Cantwell
        Ashley Davis Myers

You light up my life.

# CONTENTS

SPORTS ............................................. 1
1. THE SUMMER OF '49 ....................... 3
2. YOU CAN'T STEAL MEMORIES ................ 8
3. WHATEVER HAPPENED TO MIKE GOLIAT? REFLECTIONS ON THE 1950 "WHIZ KIDS" .................................... 11
4. GLORIOUS SEASONS - THEN AND NOW ....... 22
5. CARDIOLOGIST IN THE DUGOUT ............ 27
6. OLYMPIC VISIONS ........................ 34
7. THE OLYMPIC SPIRIT - AND A LEGACY ..... 41
8. THE 1996 OLYMPIC MEDICAL EXPERIENCE .............................. 47
9. THE FIVE OLYMPIC PASSIONS IN SPORTS AND MEDICINE .................... 52
10. A LEAGUE OF HIS OWN .................... 57
11. THE BOYS OF WINTER ..................... 62
12. SEASONS ................................ 66
13. A GATHERING OF LEGENDS ................ 72
14. Maddux ................................. 76
15. The Ultimate 10K: John Colter's Run For His Life ....................... 82

MEDICINE .......................................... 85
16. MEMORIES OF MEDICAL SCHOOL ............ 87
17. TO A SON ENTERING MEDICAL SCHOOL ...... 94
18. I WAS A YOUNG DOCTOR THEN ............. 99

19. GLOBAL ASPECTS OF CORONARY HEART DISEASE AND LONGEVITY .................. 103
20. HIPPOCRATES REVISITED ................ 110
21. AN EXPLOSION IN CENTENNIAL OLYMPIC PARK ................................... 115
22. THE HORSE AND BUGGY DOCTOR .......... 121
23. CARDIOVASCULAR MILESTONES IN THE 1900s .................................. 129
24. APRIL AND MURRAY ..................... 137
25. Why Cows Walk Backwards: Reflections on J. Willis Hurst, M.D. .................................. 140
26. A DIFFICULT PATIENT? ................. 145
27. Searching for Calcutta ............... 152
28. To A Son Entering Medical Practice ... 157

BOOKS AND WRITING ......................... 161
29. BOOKS I'LL NEVER PART WITH .......... 163
30. Tales of a "Best-Selling" Author ..... 176
31. The Lost Diary of Agnes Von Kurowsky ............................... 181
32. Olive Ann Burns: A Fond Remembrance ........................... 189
33. Six Physicians And Their Common Mistress .............................. 195
34. Chekhov's Journey .................... 207
35. Wallace Stegner: A Life Remembered ... 216
36. Encounters with James Dickey ......... 222
37. Byron Herbert Reece: The Mountain Poet .................................. 230
38. The Six Flagraisers on Iwo Jima ...... 239

39. AN "AFFAIR" WITH EMILY DICKINSON ...... 246

40. Margaret Mitchell: Her Life and Works .................................. 255

PEOPLE ................................................. 271

41. William Heberden: His Life, His Times, and His Book .................. 273

42. PARKINSON'S DISEASE IN A MASTER SURGEON ............................. 279

43. The Legacy of James Edgar Paullin, M.D. ............................... 284

44. Shackleton's Heart ..................... 295

45. RENOIR'S RHEUMATISM .................... 307

46. THE ADVENTUROUS ELISHA KENT KANE, M.D. ............................... 311

47. THE PHYSICIAN WHO HELPED CAPTURE GERONIMO ............................. 318

48. OSLER: A ROLE MODEL FOR TODAY'S PHYSICIAN ............................ 325

49. AN ENCOUNTER WITH PAUL DUDLEY WHITE ................................. 329

50. WILLIAM STOKES, M.D. ................... 335

51. AN EVENING WITH DUTCH ................. 342

52. LEILA DENMARK, M.D.: PRACTICING MEDICINE AT AGE 103 .................. 349

53. A LIFETIME OF FITNESS ................. 354

TRAVEL AND PLACES ..................................... 359

54. WANDERING LONELY AS A CLOUD: AN ODYSSEY IN MID-CAREER ............... 361

55. MEDICINE AND ADVENTURE IN THE HIMALAYAS ............................. 373

56. ON THE INCA TRAIL TO THE LOST CITY OF MACHU PICCHU .......................... 382

57. STALKING HEART HEALTH MYSTERIES IN KENYA ....................................... 391

58. TO ANTARCTICA: A JOURNEY INTO THE SELF ......................................... 395

59. FROM RUSSIA WITH LOVE (OR AT LEAST GOODWILL) ................................... 403

60. SEARCHING FOR NOAH'S ARK ............... 414

61. ADVENTURES OF A HARVARD DROPOUT ....... 424

62. THE CITY TOO BUSY TO HATE ............. 429

63. FROM EVEREST TO ANTARCTICA - TRAVELS ON SEVEN CONTINENTS ........... 435

64. SEARCHING FOR VAN GOGH IN THE SOUTH OF FRANCE ......................... 444

FAMILY ....................................... 451

65. BRAD .................................... 453

66. A VERY SPECIAL OLYMPIAN ............... 460

67. LETTER TO A YOUNG SON ................. 466

68. TO A TEENAGE DAUGHTER ................. 470

69. LETTERS FROM A YOUNG MAN AT WAR ....... 473

70. THE MAN AT THE WINDOW ................. 486

71. MR. MAGOO .............................. 491

72. A FAMILY OF NURSES .................... 496

73. REFLECTIONS ON A 38TH WEDDING ANNIVERSARY ............................ 502

74. A FATHER'S FAREWELL TO HIS SON ........ 506

*Adventures on Seven Continents And Other Essays*

# SPORTS

*John Davis Cantwell, M.D.*

# 1

## THE SUMMER OF '49

David Halberstam was 15 years old in the summer of 1949, the year his father died. The family had moved to a new home in Connecticut. The boy didn't feel accepted in his new environment, so immersed himself in the New York Yankee-Boston Red Sox pennant race as a means of coping.

Forty years later he wrote a book about that season (*Summer of '49*), and, in so doing, met "men I had once admired as heroes."

That is, all except one - Joe DiMaggio - who was uncooperative. The author was philosophical about the latter:

*"So be it; if there is a right under the First Amendment to do books such as this, there is also a right not to be interviewed. I'm sorry he didn't see me; he still remains the most graceful athlete I saw in those impressionable years."*

The main characters are DiMaggio, injury-prone and nearing the end of his career, and Ted Williams, in mid-career, convinced that he is the game's greatest hitter. Some of the Boston sportswriters took exception to this and delighted in trashing Williams in print.

Halberstam reminds us what baseball meant back in 1949, and still does today:

*"Baseball was rooted not just in the past but in the culture of the country; it was celebrated in the nation's literature and*

*John Davis Cantwell, M.D.*

*songs. When a poor American boy dreamed of escaping his grim life, his fantasy probably involved becoming a professional baseball player. It was not so much the national sport as the binding national myth."*

The anecdotes enliven the text. We are told of the encounter Red Sox manager Joe McCarthy once had with slugger (and boozer) Hack Wilson, when both were with the Chicago Cubs. McCarthy lectured Wilson on the seriousness of drinking, illustrating his point by pouring a shot of whiskey into a glass filled with worms. The worms quickly died. "What did you learn from that?" has asked Wilson. "That if I drink I won't have worms," the slugger answered.

The teams seemed evenly matched. The Red Sox may have had more talent, but the Yankees thought they lacked mental toughness. They were also devoid of a natural leader. Shortstop Johnny Pesky was feisty enough, but on the small side physically. Second baseman Bobby Doerr was too laid back. Ted Williams "wanted no extra responsibilities - striving to be the best hitter in the game and living up to the expectations of the fans and his teammates was quite enough."

The Yankees, as outfielder Gene Woodling recalled, were a tough team:

*"It was a team where everyone demanded a complete effort. It was not a team where anyone ever said 'nice try' when you made a long run after a fly ball and didn't get to it…you weren't supposed to try, you were supposed to <u>do it</u>."*

The different personalities of the players were what I found to be the most interesting part of the book. Vic Raschi, the Yankee pitcher, was practically unapproachable on days he was to pitch. Photographers quickly learned to avoid him, or have tobacco juice sprayed over their shoes. He even disliked having his catcher or infielders come out to the mound to visit during the game.

Ellis Kinder, his counterpart on the Red Sox, had his own approach to the game. He was "an old-fashioned, unreconstructed carouser, cavalier in the extreme about training rules and curfews…He believed that baseball and alcohol mixed…He could drink hard all night and pitch hard the next day without any signs of deterioration or fatigue. In fact, carousing was an essential part of his pregame preparation." A young bonus player, Paul Hinrichs, once asked him if he had any tips. Kinder asked him if he smoked, if he chased women, and if he drank. The answer was no to all three. "I'm afraid you will never make it," he said, and walked away (the lad pitched only three innings in the major leagues in his career).

The character of Dom DiMaggio (the Red Sox center fielder and brother of Joe) shines forth. Early in his career he was bothered by the constant comparison with his brother. Dom was a consistent .300 hitter, but was made to seem lacking when compared with Joe:

*"But gradually he overcame it. The war years helped. In the service he learned that there was a good deal more to life than baseball, and slowly he learned to ignore other people's expectations. That was his greatest victory -*

*John Davis Cantwell, M.D.*

*to accept his own talents and limitations and to live happily with them."*

In the epilogue, Halberstam tells us what happens to the boys of summer in later years. Junior Stephens, the Red Sox shortstop, "robust, powerful, and seemingly indestructible as a player,…keeled over on a golf course and died of a heart attack at the age of 48." Johnny Pesky, the third baseman, seemed on the verge of death until diagnosed as having an allergy to wheat. Second baseman Bobby Doerr was a hitting instructor and coach for a number of years before moving back to rural Oregon, where he could enjoy hunting and fishing. Ted Williams lived in Florida, where he approached fishing with the same precision as he did hitting a baseball. In his world, you either do things well or you do them poorly. If you chose that latter approach, "he wanted no part of you." Williams never tipped his hat to the crowd after hitting a home run. In his last major league at bat, a home run no less, the crowd begged him to come out of the dugout for an encore, but no avail. As John Updike wrote, "Gods do not answer letters."

For the Yankees, third baseman Bobby Brown became a successful cardiologist (not heart surgeon as the author states) and was President of the American League. Ace reliever Joe Page ran a tavern in the coal-mining region of Pennsylvania, until his death from throat cancer. The intense Vic Raschi also operated a liquor store and died of a heart attack at 69. Shortstop Phil Rizzuto keeps close to the game as an announcer for the Yankees.

And Joe DiMaggio has made a career of being - well, Joe DiMaggio. He retired in 1951, as he didn't want the fans to remember him struggling. His marriage to Marilyn Monroe has been the subject of a book by Roger Kahn. He enjoyed old-timers' games but was too proud to play. When appearing at such outings, Halberstam claims that DiMaggio requested to be introduced last, and as the game's greatest living player. This may be true, but one wished that DiMaggio had granted an interview so he could say "it ain't so" about this rumor or unnecessary vainness. The lingering image I prefer is of a man who supposedly never threw to the wrong base, or got thrown out dashing from first to third…an athlete who carefully studied the sky ("the ceiling of his stage"), "planning what to do when a high fly disappeared momentarily in a patch of sun-dazzled blue." According to Robert Lipsyte, DiMaggio "rehearsed every move, under every sky." He was a master of his trade, one who not only <u>knew</u> what he was doing, but who <u>cared</u> about what he was doing. DiMaggio died of lung cancer in 1999. Ted Williams' body was frozen on July 5, 2002.

*John Davis Cantwell, M.D.*

# 2

## YOU CAN'T STEAL MEMORIES

My dad was quite a guy. A hardworking country doctor, he set aside ample time to be with his children and to share their interest in sports. I was the youngest son and expressed a desire to work my way through medical school by playing major league baseball, a la Bobby Brown, the Yankee third baseman. After hearing that Bob Feller had once credited his success to his father, who taught him how to pitch behind the barn, Dad rushed out and purchased a catcher's mitt.

Now Dad wasn't in the best of shape. His idea of exercise was to ride horseback for several hours. Nonetheless, he crouched down (with some difficulty) behind the makeshift home plate and told his 10-year-old son to fire away. I zipped a high hard one on the inside corner; it caromed off Dad's chest and he retreated to the house for repairs, never to return.

That summer, I became a rabid Philadelphia Phillies fan, even though we lived near Green Bay, Wisconsin. The "Whiz Kids" captured one's imagination with their come-from-behind rush to the pennant. Using a rake handle for a bat, I spent countless hours blasting small stones over the barnyard fence. Del Ennis had 26 home runs, but I had over 5000 - and in just one week. Occasionally I would take to the mound, usually in the person of Robin Roberts, the Phillies' *stopper!* Sometimes I would pretend to be Curt Simmons, depending upon how many left-handed batters the Dodgers were packing into the lineup that day.

One weekend Dad took me to Chicago. The Phillies were in town to tangle with the Cubs. We just happened to stay at the old Edgewater Beach Hotel, the same place where the Phillies headquartered. All this had been secretly arranged behind my back, thanks to my father and a patient of his (who was related to Richie Ashburn, the Phillies' centerfielder).

I was in ecstasy, hobnobbing with the likes of Willie "Puddin' Head" Jones and Granny Hamner. I treasured an autographed ball that they gave me.

A half century has passed. Dad died of a heart attack in 1970. Robin Roberts is now in the Hall of Fame, Mike Goliat disappeared, and I now attempt to crouch behind the plate for my grandchildren.

I never did make professional baseball, although I once had a tryout with the Braves in Milwaukee County Stadium. There were at least a hundred of us, attired in garb ranging from spiffy American Legion uniforms to bib overalls. The Iron Mike fired six pitches to each candidate and we swung away under the watchful eye of Braves' hitting coach Paul Waner. Of my six pitches, three came at my head and two others were low and in the dirt. The last pitch was on the outside corner and I punched a soft liner to right field. Waner shook his head: "You don't move your belly button fast enough when you swing, son." With that as my benediction, I left the tryout camp shortly thereafter, contemplating my navel for the remainder of the day. Fortunately, one didn't need a fast belly button to get through medical school.

*John Davis Cantwell, M.D.*

    I kept the autographed baseball from the Phillies in my medical office, only to have someone abscond with it. Let 'em have it, I thought, they would never be able to steal the memories I cherish of a loving father drawn close to his young son during a memorable baseball weekend long ago.

# 3

## WHATEVER HAPPENED TO MIKE GOLIAT? REFLECTIONS ON THE 1950 "WHIZ KIDS"

Heroes, unlike mentors, are often viewed via a child's perspective and from a distance. As William Oscar Johnson once wrote, "they have feet neither of gold nor of clay, but only of flesh." As such, they face the same obstacles we mortals do - bad habits, interpersonal and financial problems at times, aging, and ill health - and often emerge less heroic in the process, but sometimes even more so, as in the case of Philadelphia Phillies pitcher, Jack Brittin, who successfully battled multiple sclerosis for 38 years.

I was interested in a followup on the heroes of my tenth year, the 1950 Phillies. What had become of them, nearly a half-century after their playing days? What health problems have they encountered? How many are still living?

Like the Atlanta Braves of 1991, the Phillies electrified the baseball world that year by emerging from the cellar to challenge for the National League championship. The "Whiz Kids" as they were called, won on the last day of the regular season. Robin Roberts won his 20th game and right fielder, Dick Sisler, hit a dramatic home run in the 10th inning.

Although the Phillies were a relatively young team, many had been battle-tested veterans. Left fielder, Del Ennis, had been in the South Pacific. Reserve catcher, Stan Lopata, had won the Bronze Star and Purple

*John Davis Cantwell, M.D.*

Heart. The third catcher, Ken Silvestri, won three battle stars and a Bronze Star in the Pacific. Pitcher, Jocko Thompson, a paratrooper, had fought in the Battle of the Bulge. Twice wounded, he won seven battle stars, a Bronze Star, and a Silver Star. Reserve outfielder, Dick Whitman, was also in the Battle of the Bulge. Jack Brittin had taken part in the invasion of Okinawa.

To find out what had become of the Phillies, I met with Richie Ashburn, their Hall of Fame center fielder, then a Phillies broadcaster.

**Richie Ashburn**

Ashburn was generous with his time, very friendly and candid, still radiating heroic qualities 45 years after our first meeting, when he had autographed a ball for me.

I also met with Sharon "Babe" Talley, the daughter of shortstop Granny Hamner, who was born in 1950. In addition, I communicated with Dean C. Paul Rogers, of the SMU Law School, who wrote a book about the Phillies, in collaboration with Roberts, the Phillies' other Hall of Fame player.

I was especially interested in the whereabouts of Mike Goliat, the second baseman, who had disappeared from my radar screen after the 1950 season.

**THE VETERAN**

The catcher, Andy Seminick, was a 30-year-old veteran in 1950. The youngest of 10 children of a coal miner, Seminick left the mines at age 19 to pursue a baseball career. A tough guy, he played the last part of the 1950 season with an ankle fracture.

After his playing career ended, Seminick worked as a coach, manager and scout in the Phillies organization. He lives in Melbourne, Florida, and keeps involved with the Florida Tech athletic programs. Their baseball field is named after him.

**THE NATURAL**

The first baseman was Eddie Waitkus. In 1949, Eddie had been shot by a deranged 19-year-old woman who had lured him to her hotel room in Chicago under the pretense that she was from his hometown and had an important message to deliver. The bullet passed through

*John Davis Cantwell, M.D.*

his chest and lungs and lodged near his spine. The woman did have sense enough to call the front desk for help. Five operations were required. Thanks to vigorous off-season rehabilitation, Waitkus played in 154 games the following year and hit .284. He was never quite the same healthwise. He subsequently worked as a floor manager in a Massachusetts department store and married one of the nurses who had cared for his gunshot wounds. He died of abdominal cancer at age 53. His shooting inspired Bernard Malamud to write *The Natural*. Robert Redford starred in the movie.

**PUDDIN' HEAD**

Willie "Puddin' Head" Jones, the third baseman, was a "charmer," says Ashburn, "but you wouldn't want him marrying your daughter." Jones had spent three years in the Navy, returning to baseball in 1946. A power hitter and a good fielder, he had a solid career with the Phillies and later went into automobile sales, living in Cincinnati. He died of throat cancer at age 59. He had been a cigarette smoker.

**GRANNY**

The shortstop, Granny Hamner, was tough as a street kid who "might have been in prison if it hadn't been for baseball," laughed Ashburn. The Phillies captain, Hamner was a "cocky firebrand who battled and clawed every step of the way." He had signed a bonus out of high school in 1944, at age 17, and was soon inserted into the Phillies lineup.

Hamner became an instructor and a coach in the Phillies minor league operations after his playing days, and was considered an excellent judge of baseball talent. A drinker and a smoker, he died of a heart attack at age 66.

## BIG DEL

The left fielder, Del Ennis, was a native of Philadelphia, where his father worked for the Stetson Hat Company. Ennis had been an all-state fullback in high school. As the cleanup hitter for the Phillies, he hit .311 in 1950, with 31 home runs and 126 runs batted in.

Ennis owned and operated a bowling alley in Jenkintown, Pennsylvania, after his playing days and invested well. He also raised greyhounds, naming many for his Whiz Kid teammates. He lost a leg due to diabetes complications. He also had a family tragedy - his wife (his childhood sweetheart) hung herself, as had her mother. Ennis died of a bleeding ulcer at age 70.

## PUTT-PUTT

Ashburn, the center fielder, was nicknamed "Putt-Putt" by Ted Williams, who observed that he ran "as though he had twin motors in his pants." Ashburn was 23 in 1950, and in his third season. He played 12 years for the Phillies, was an All-Star for four years, and won batting titles in 1955 and 1958, and was one of the handful of Phillies to have his number (#1) retired. He was voted into the Hall of Fame. He worked as a Phillies broadcaster and also as a sports columnist for the *Evening Bulletin*. He developed insulin-dependent diabetes at age 50. A torn rotator cuff limited the tennis, golf and squash that he enjoyed for many years.

*John Davis Cantwell, M.D.*

**HALL OF FAMER'S SON**

Dick Sisler, the right fielder, was the son of Hall of Famer, George Sisler. His father was the Dodgers' head scout and instructor in 1950 and was at that final game when Sisler belted his three-run home run in the 10th inning to give the Phillies the National League Championship.

Like a number of his teammates, Sisler had been a Navy veteran. In 1950, he batted .296, hit 13 homes runs and batted in 83 runs.

After his playing days, he coached for several major league teams and once managed the Cincinnati Reds briefly.

He resided in a nursing home in Nashville in his 60s and died of Alzheimer's disease.

**THE STOPPER**

Robin Roberts was the Phillies "stopper" throughout his career, the man you wanted on the mound at the most crucial times. He grew up in Springfield, Illinois, where he was a three-sport athletic star. One of six children whose parents had immigrated to the United States from Wales, Roberts played basketball at Michigan State and was once voted the top college player in Michigan.

Over a 19-year career, he won 286 games and made the All-Star team seven times. He is a member of the Hall of Fame. Extremely durable, he once completed 28 straight games, unthinkable in the present era.

The crucial last game against the Dodgers of 1950 was Roberts' third start in five days. It was his sixth attempt at reaching the coveted 20 wins in a season.

*Adventures on Seven Continents And Other Essays*

At age 41, Roberts tried a brief comeback with the Phillies, but he had lost his great skills by then. He became a stockbroker and a color commentator on the Phillies home radio network and wrote sports columns for the *Wilmington News-Journal*. In the mid-1970s, he became the head baseball coach at the University of South Florida, and held that position for eight years. He currently resides in Tampa, where he remains active in golf. He co-owns a golf course with Curt Simmons in Limekiln, outside Philadelphia.

**LEFTY**

Curt Simmons, the star left-handed pitcher, was a native of Egypt, Pennsylvania. As a school boy, he pitched his American Legion team to two state championships and once struck out eleven Phillies in an exhibition game in his home town. In 1947 when he was 18, the Phillies signed him to a $65,000 bonus, at the time a considerable sum. In 1950, his season was twice interrupted by military obligations, yet his record was an impressive 17-8. He missed the end of the season, and the World Series against the Yankees, a significant loss to the Phillies.

In 1953, Simmons lost part of his left great toe in a lawnmower accident, which may have affected his performance momentarily, but he did make a comeback. His record was 18-9 in 1964 and he pitched in the World Series that year for St. Louis.

His 20-year big league career ended in 1967.

He presently manages the golf course in Limekiln, aided by Robin Roberts, Jr.

*John Davis Cantwell, M.D.*

**THE MVP**

The National League's Most Valuable Player in 1950 was the Phillies' relief pitcher, 33-year-old Jim Konstanty. He appeared in 74 games. An all-around athlete while at Syracuse University, Konstanty lettered in soccer, basketball, boxing and baseball.

He mixed speeds well on his pitches and had a great slider and palm ball, in addition to excellent control. His personal pitching coach was an undertaker and neighbor, Andy Skinner, who caused the regular coaching staff some chagrin when he came around, but was generally effective in straightening out Konstanty's mechanical problem at the time.

Konstanty owned a sporting goods store in Oneonta, New York, for many years and was also a minor league pitching coach for the Cardinals and the Yankees. For four years he served as athletic director at Hartwick College in Oneonta.

He retired at age 59 and died the next year of lung cancer. He had never smoked, nor had he used alcohol to any extent. The funeral director for his final service was none other than his personal pitching coach and friend, Andy Skinner.

**THE SKIPPER**

The manager of the team was Eddie Sawyer, a former science professor at Ithaca College. At Ithaca he had been a football halfback and an excellent student. Sawyer had been described as "dignified, scholarly, tolerant, unflappable, witty and tough, when necessary." A shoulder injury had limited his own career.

He lost some of his magical touch after the 1950 season. Seminick and Sisler were traded in 1951 when the team finished in fifth place. Midway during the 1952 season, they were mired in sixth place when Sawyer was replaced by Steve O'Neill. He did return as the Phillies manager in 1958, but quit after the first game in 1960, saying that at age 49 he "wanted to live to be 50."

He later worked as a distributor for the Plymouth Golf Ball Company, and died after a brief illness at age 87.

**GOLIAT**

And what about Mike Goliat? The least well-known of the Phillie regulars, the second baseman was also the son of a coal miner from Pennsylvania, one of nine children. He had injured his knee the day before the Phillies called him up from their triple A farm team. He agreed to have it x-rayed only when the team doctor promised to let him play irrespective of the findings.

Goliat hit 13 home runs in 1950 and had 13 game-winning hits. His performance trailed off shortly thereafter. He had married during the 1950 season and, perhaps due to his wife's good cooking, was 25 pounds overweight when he reported to spring training the next year. He was send down to the minor leagues and was out of the majors by 1952. He subsequently went into the trucking business and presently lives outside Cleveland.

Goliat was unavailable when C. Paul Rogers tried to interview him for his recent book on the team. I tried to contact him by telephone, but his number was unlisted. I did manage to

*John Davis Cantwell, M.D.*

get his address, and wrote to him, but never got a reply.

**REFLECTIONS**

In reflecting on the team over 50 years later, several impressions come to mind. The salaries then were relatively low, such that the players had to find "real jobs" after their playing days. Today, if players manage their money well, most will be financially secure for life.

Cigarette smoking and alcohol abuse were problems in 1950, as they are today, leading to premature deaths from heart and lung disease and other types of cancer. Several of the Phillies developed diabetes, still a major problem in 2003, but more effectively managed now than previously. Alzheimer's disease afflicted the batting star of that final National League championship game, and still is a heartbreaking problem to thousands of families today. Small therapeutic breakthroughs have been made, but much progress remains.

What will become of the present day Atlanta Braves' players, the "Whiz Kids" of 1991, who captured the fancy of the baseball world with their performance that season and, unlike the Phillies, have continued to succeed? There are no guarantees, even with prudent lifestyle habits, as Jim Konstanty exemplified. However, one can certainly decrease the risk of premature heart attacks by avoiding cigarettes, keeping dietary and blood cholesterol levels low, maintaining a desired weight and blood pressure level, and engaging in regular life-long endurance exercise (not just golf). Avoiding cigarettes and restricting alcohol to no more than two standard-sized drinks daily, if at all, can minimize the risk of certain cancers, as can regular blood prostate specific antigen (PSA) tests, rectal examinations, and colonoscopy evaluations. The electron beam CT scan is an new test which helps detect significant coronary disease before clinical symptoms become manifest.

**POSTSCRIPT**

On September 9th, 1997, Barely 10 weeks after my interview with him, Richie Ashburn summoned the Phillies trainer at 5:30 a.m. because of chest pain. By the time the trainer and the paramedics arrived, he was dead, from cardiac arrest.

In reflecting on his life, I recalled a lot of fond memories including an incident late in his career, when he was with the hapless New York Mets. The Venezuelan-born Mets shortstop would periodically collide with Ashburn on fly balls to short left- center field. Ashburn decided to shout "I got it" - in Spanish. The next occurrence he did so again, hollering "Yo lo tengo." The shortstop veered off at the last moment, but Ashburn was flattened by left fielder, Frank Thomas. Thomas didn't speak Spanish and the ball dropped for a double.

*John Davis Cantwell, M.D.*

# 4

## GLORIOUS SEASONS - THEN AND NOW

The Atlanta Braves' baseball season of 1991 began with a new general manager and a multitude of new players, including the little munchkin, Rafael Belliard. By the All-Star game they seemed to be sinking in the standings, as has been the case so often in the past. To sustain my interest in baseball I read two very fine books, Robert Creamer's *Baseball in '41* and David Lamb's *Stolen Season*.

Creamer recounted the glorious season 50 years ago, when Ted Williams batted .406 and Joe DiMaggio hit in 56 straight games. He writes of the pennant battle, between the Cardinals (with rookie, Stan Musial) and the Dodgers, and carries us through the World Series, wherein the Yankees beat the Dodgers, aided by a third strike passed ball by Dodger catcher, Mickey Owens.

David Lamb is about my age. When he was a teenager, his beloved Boston Braves moved to Milwaukee. His loss was my gain, as I grew up in Wisconsin, and soon became a loyal fan of the Milwaukee Braves. Lamb wrote the sports editor of a Milwaukee newspaper, asking if they'd be interested in publishing periodic articles on the team from the perspective of a "deserted" teenager. The articles were accepted, and I recall reading them with great interest in the late 1950s.

Years later, David Lamb (now a newspaper correspondent for the *Los Angeles Times*) was sent to Beirut, "to cover Lebanon's orgy of national suicide." He had previously covered the Vietnam war, the overthrow "of both Idi Amin and Haile Selassie, the war in Somalia and another in Zaire." Along with a dozen other journalists, Lamb had taken cover from "the thundering artillery of the attacking Lebanese army" in an abandoned nightclub in the basement of the Commodore Hotel. Amid the deafening explosions of direct hits to the hotel, Lamb told a colleague that if they survived, he (Lamb) "would find something to write about that's a million miles from Beirut. Like baseball."

He kept his vow, taking an unpaid leave from the *Times* and purchasing a secondhand mobile home and made baseball his reentry ticket to a country "I had been gone from too long." He concentrated on the minor leagues, wandering "from California to Tucson, El Paso and Chattanooga, into Florida and up the Eastern seaboard to Elmira, New York, across the Midwest, through Montana and the Northwest and back to California." What he found was "baseball as I remembered it, played on real grass and in a time when the teams we cherished were ours for life." He also found many of the heros of his youth, such as Warren Spahn and Eddie Mathews, telling of their various successes (and failures) since their playing days.

I suspect that David Lamb followed the escapades of the 1991 Braves, ensconced in Atlanta these past 35 years. For me it was the culmination of 16 years as a team physician, often frustrating years in which either talent was lacking or potential unfulfilled. I didn't need to read books on baseball to sustain my interest after the All-Star game, for the Braves were living out their own field of

*John Davis Cantwell, M.D.*

dreams. The team was kind enough to include all the physicians (Drs. Bob Wells, David Watson, Bob Crow and Joe Chandler) and their spouses on the Delta charter flights to Pittsburgh and Minneapolis, a magnificent 14 games in less than three weeks. Memories that come to mind include the following:

- The appreciation of a team effort, including Jerry Willard and Francisco Cabrera.
- Dr. Watson's reflex hammer tomahawk.
- The beautiful view of Pittsburgh, as one emerges from the tunnel leading to the city. I had expected smoke-stacks and haze. Instead I saw the confluence of three rivers, fountains and parks, and fine neighborhoods such as Oakland and Shadyside.
- The devilish grin of disabled pitcher, Mark Grant, who deserved a full World Series share for his enthusiasm and encouragement.
- Looking down on Pittsburgh from the LaMont restaurant, high on the bluffs, and a waiter who drove us back to our hotel when we had trouble getting a taxi.
- Testing my pitching speed (a pitiful 58 mph) at the Carnegie Science Center and seeing the movie, *To The Limit*, which was what the Braves took themselves to.
- Shopping for baseball ties.
- Trying to stay towards the back of the player's bus (a coach chastised us for lack of "seat etiquette").
- "Chase," the obnoxious Pirates fan, who took issue with our cheers.
- The sparkling personality of Telly Peña, and the quiet heroics of her husband,

Alejaaandro!! (as my daughter Kelly cried at the top of her lungs, when he advanced to the mound).
- The itinerary for the final trip to Pittsburgh ("after winning games 6 & 7 we will depart directly to Minneapolis").
- Steve Avery, inhaling helium from balloons and responding to mock interviews by teammates with his Donald Duck-type voice.
- Lisa Olson, cheering hard for "Greg-O," our catcher.
- Trying to avoid a champagne soaking, in the locker room after the Braves won the National League Championship.
- The celebration on the Delta L-1011, taking us from Pittsburgh to Minneapolis, contrasted with the quietness on the final return flight.
- Lonnie Smith, asking me (a mere mortal) to autograph his team bat. I will forgive his base running mishap for that thoughtfulness.
- The anguish on the faces of Charlie Liebradt (a delightful guy) and his wife as Kirby Puckett took him deep in game 6.
- The cheers of the 5000 or so, at 5:00 a.m., when we finally arrived back in Atlanta, culminating in the great victory parade.

Yes, it was a great season. Perhaps 50 years from now someone like Robert Creamer will write a nostalgic review or a David Lamb-type will track down today's heros, such as David Justice and Mark Lemke, in their baseball afterlives. I wonder what he'll find?

Back in my medical office, I had yet to find a patient who wasn't touched by the Braves

*John Davis Cantwell, M.D.*

effort. One man, doing business in a remote part of Spain, had his office fax daily accounts of the playoffs and World Series games. A cardiac patient got so excited she had to stop watching the live action on television, opting instead to record the ending and play it back after reading about it in the morning paper.

Few events can capture the imagination and ignite the spirit of young and old, rich and poor, the sick and the well. Baseball is one such event, but is only a metaphor of life itself. We need to plumb the depths of the latter for other events, perhaps community efforts to help the less fortunate, to keep the enthusiasm and goodwill ever flowing.

# 5

## CARDIOLOGIST IN THE DUGOUT

> "Some baseball is the fate of us all. For my part,
> I am never more at home in America than at a baseball game."
> Robert Frost

At first glance, it might seem strange for a cardiologist to serve as the team physician for a major league baseball club. Indeed, the Atlanta Braves are about the only team to have one. On further inspection, however, it may be appropriate.

All cardiologists have a background in general internal medicine, so are qualified and capable of dealing with a myriad of general medical problems that players experience, ranging from migraine headaches to upper respiratory infections. Cardiologists are well versed in the merits of coronary risk factor modification in baseball players who have generous allowances for lavish meals and time on their hands to pick up habits like smokeless tobacco and cigarette smoking. Teams also have managers, coaches, trainers and office staff who are often older and may already have cardiovascular diseases such as hypertension and coronary atherosclerotic problems, all appropriately treated by the team cardiologist. The cardiologist can also advise the team management as to the value of using automatic external defibrillators for the stadium as an integral part of the trainer's medical kit, along with the

*John Davis Cantwell, M.D.*

potential merits of screening higher-risk coaches for underlying coronary disease, using the electron beam computed tomography scan and the exercise test when appropriate.

**BEGINNINGS**

Shortly after Ted Turner purchased the Braves in 1976, I was asked to join the medical staff. Dale Murphy was a rookie catcher that year. Phil Niekro was one of the established stars. My duties would include an annual trip to the spring training headquarters in Florida for the preseason physical examinations. During the season, I would work every third home game, providing medical care for our team, the visiting team and the umpires. Other volunteer physicians are responsible for the spectators.

On game days I arrive at the stadium about an hour before the first pitch, for sick call. The team orthopedist typically handles the musculoskeletal problems, which are the most numerous. The symptoms I usually see are general medical ones, often upper respiratory in nature, with colds and allergic rhinitis heading the list. Chest pain is an occasional problem, as are palpitations, the latter especially in those who are heavy caffeine users. I was once summoned to see a relief pitcher who had developed severe left anterior chest pain. Upon questioning him I learned that it began right after a bout of hysterical laughter, in response to another player's joke. He was reassured that it was just an intercostal muscle strain. Anther player was removed from a game with palpitations and tachycardia. An electrocardiogram revealed atrial fibrillation, and probably triggered by the 10 cups of coffee he was imbibing several hours before the game. I've had to go onto the field only once, when the Dodgers' Steve Garvey flattened our catcher, Bruce Benedict, in a vicious home plate collision. As the young Benedict drifted in and out of consciousness on our ambulance ride to the emergency room, he repeatedly asked me if (1) he had hung onto the ball (he did), and (2) if we were still ahead (we were, 2 to 1). He never once expressed concern about his own condition.

Among my finest memories have been the trips to spring training, always accompanied by my youngest son, Ryan. In my first trip to West Palm Beach, the Braves stayed at the Sheraton Hotel. We would usually arrive on a Thursday and spend a day or so at the beach, flying kites, bicycling and unlimbering our throwing arms. The team physicals were Saturday and Sunday mornings. Ryan was too young initially to leave alone, so I took him along to the doctor's office and positioned him in a corner of the examining room, with his back to the patient. The first morning he stayed busy, but did ask me on the way out why I put medicine in all of the players' bottoms (his interpretation of the rectal examination). Midway during the physicals on the next day I heard him whisper my name. I turned around and saw a giant rubber rectal glove filled with water, waving at me, and a devilish grin on a little boy's face.

The next year I left him in our hotel room with instructions to keep the door locked and also on how to call room service for his breakfast (or me in an emergency). When I returned shortly after noon he was on the verge of tears. There had been a power failure in the hotel and he was never able to use the phone to order food, or even to call me.

**TURNER'S MANDATE**

In the 1980s, noting that a number of the players were overweight, used tobacco and appeared less than fit for professional athletes, I advised the management to do more thorough fitness assessments, to include body composition analysis, exercise testing with oxygen uptake measurement, and muscle strength testing. This proposal was finally enacted when David Letterman and various other media personnel began to make fun of several Atlanta players, calling one "a tub of goo." Owner Ted Turner mandated that the team physicians do extensive testing and provide nutritional consultation.

Each player had the tests noted above, along with blood lipid analyses. Serum cholesterol readings included levels of 320, 305, 280, 264, 263, 253, 247, 243 and 242 mg/dl. The dietician counseled every athlete when body fat was in the overweight or obese category, and those with hyperlipidemia. One player refused to discuss his dietary habits with the dietician, but said he would visit with her about any other topic of her choice. Ten years later I read where he had undergone coronary angioplasty.

We designed off-season conditioning programs for each player, and provided a facility and supervision for such. Only one player took advantage of this. Most claimed that they had their own exercise equipment at home.

## THE 1990s

The Braves became successful shortly after John Schuerholz took over as general manager and Bobby Cox as manager, reaching the World Series five times and winning it once. They added a conditioning coach, who travels with the team and works individually with the players. The players are noticeably more fit. Cigarette smoking is now rare, and smokeless tobacco use is declining. Serum cholesterol levels have dropped, with the average reading in 2002 being 177 mg/dl. Each player is given a copy of his laboratory data, along with information on ideal blood lipid levels and the recommended amount of dietary cholesterol and saturated fat.

The physicians travel with the team during the playoffs. It was a special thrill in 1991 to visit Pittsburgh, trailing 3 games to 2 for the National League championship and see John Smoltz and Steve Avery pitch back-to-back shutouts, propelling us into the World Series against Minnesota. The miracle win the following year, also against the Pirates when Francisco Cabrera lined a hit to left field and a lumbering Sid Bream just beat the throw to home plate, is another cherished memory, as was the win in game 6 of the 1995 World Series to give Atlanta the title. A 5-game spurt in St. Louis and New York, where the Braves outscored opponents 49 to 2, will never be forgotten, nor will a visit to Yankee Stadium, walking around center field, once the domain of Ruth, DiMaggio and Mantle, and meandering through Monument Park.

It helps me as a team physician to have once been a baseball player, for I can better comprehend the agony of a batting slump, the pain of a foul tip off the shin, and the

*John Davis Cantwell, M.D.*

difficulties of competing at a high level in the presence of an illness.

I try to keep a low profile in the locker room, not bothering players for autographs or special favors and visiting with them before the game only as they wish. When working Sunday afternoon games, I like to attend their pregame chapel service, and have even been a guest speaker. I once threw batting practice to the pitchers, trying to get a knuckleball past Phil Niekro and a sidearm changeup by our closer, Gene Garber, ducking behind the protective screen to keep from seeming decapitation from line drives up the middle.

Athletes have a need to "stay within themselves" during games, doing what they do best and not trying to hit a home run if a walk will keep a rally going. Team physicians need to do likewise, staying within their own area of expertise and not trying to do something in a locker room (like injecting a joint) that they don't ordinarily do in their offices. Strict confidentiality is also mandatory when dealing with a player's health and personal problems. It might make good conversation with friends, but it violates the standards we ascribe to.

I am sometimes asked who my favorite player or players have been. Dale Murphy ranks at the top, two-time National League Most Valuable Player and a man of great moral strength and character. Hall-of-Famer Phil Niekro also impressed me with his blue-collar work ethic, and ability with his arm, glove or bat to make something happen that would put his team in a position to win. Some favorites were never superstars. I admired reserve shortstop Darrel Chaney for his professionalism, always keeping himself mentally and physically primed to fill in if the need arose.

Of the current players, Greg Maddux amazes me. An unimposing physical specimen, the bespectacled Maddux combines a winner's mental toughness with late-breaking, seemingly laser-guided pitches, a Golden Glove (13-time award winner), and a deceptive feistiness at bat that can deliver a triple down the right field line or a blooper that scores the go-ahead run.

Robert Frost was right. Some baseball <u>is</u> part of us all, and I am no exception. Players may earn considerably more than the small salary team physicians receive, but we have a definite advantage - our careers are much longer. It has been a joy for me to be involved with the sport for over 25 years, and I hope to continue for many more, until I hang my stethoscope next to my college baseball spikes. Perhaps I will turn the job over to my son, Ryan, who already knows firsthand how much joy his father has experienced in a career longer than even Hank Aaron's.

**With son Ryan at a Braves' game**

*John Davis Cantwell, M.D.*

# 6

## OLYMPIC VISIONS

Where else but the Olympic Games can you see the president of one nation and the vice president of another enthusiastically doing the wave, watch a Russian speed skater urinate while discussing the latest novel he has finished (*Gone with the Wind,* no less) and dine on imported Italian pasta and wine with Albert Tomba's physician. I was in France to begin a four-year term on the International Olympic Committee (IOC) Medical Commission. Before departing, I reflected upon the history of this magnificent event.

In 1980 I had the opportunity to visit the ruins of Olympia. Positioning my feet in the starting blocks, I tried to imagine that I was Coroebus, a young cook from the nearby village of Elis, attempting to win the 200-yard dash over 2700 years ago. I also saw the site where the Olympic torch is lit and visited the monument containing the heart of Baron de Coubertin, the Frenchman who dedicated his life to reviving the Olympic Games in 1896 (about 1500 years after they were stopped). I was impressed with how much a single, determined person can accomplish, as evidenced in recent times by Billy Payne in Atlanta, whose drive brought the Games to his home area.

*Adventures on Seven Continents And Other Essays*

**Tunnel to the track at Olympia**

Over 40,000 spectators attended the ancient Olympic events including the likes of Socrates, Herodotus and Pindar. The only woman allowed to view the spectacle was the priestess of Dimetra. Any other who tried faced the death penalty. The latter was waved for Pheronice of Rhodes who, while embracing her victorious boxer son, Pisidores, had her robe slip off. The officials spared her life, but deemed that, in the future, athletes had to compete naked to prevent further problems of this nature. In 724 B.C., a 400-yard run was added and, in 720 B.C., a three-mile event. In the following century, the games were expanded to include other activities such as boxing and wrestling. Around the time of Hippocrates, the Olympics were increased from one to five days.

*John Davis Cantwell, M.D.*

A hero in the 6th century B.C. was Milo of Croton, a six-time Olympic wrestling champion. His typical meal was said to include seven pounds of meat, seven pounds of bread and up to five quarts of wine. He once ate an entire bull in one day. Such eating habits deviated from the athletes of earlier times who ate only fresh cheese and drank water.

Athletes trained for 10 months in their local area during the Olympic year. One month before the games they congregated in the village of Elis and trained before Olympic judges who whacked them with rods when their efforts were deemed unsatisfactory.

The champions received an olive wreath and various gifts along with large sums of money, a free home and meals, and a city street named after them. This has changed little through the centuries.

One of the early cheaters was the Emperor Nero who, with 5000 bodyguards, entered several events and "won" them all. He was also "voted" the best singer and musician. Had there been a prize for pyromania, I'm sure he would have won that, too.

The games were abolished in 394 A.D. by the Roman Emperor Theodosius who, as a Christian, was opposed to pagan spectacles. A year later, the 40-foot statue of Zeus was hauled away. In the 6th century A.D., earthquakes leveled the temple of Zeus. The games had ceased for 1502 years.

The were revived by a diminutive public educator, Baron de Coubertin, who had started an organization to encourage physical education programs in French schools and colleges. De Coubertin was stimulated to revive the Olympics after visiting the ruins in Greece, which had been excavated by German archaeologists between 1875-1881. The Panathenaic stadium in Athens, originally built in 330 B.C., was restored to a seating capacity of 70,000, and the first modern games were held on April 6th, 1886, the 75th anniversary of Greek independence from the Turks. The 13 Americans who competed had to first cross the Atlantic Ocean in a ship, transverse Italy by train, spend 24 hours on a boat to Patras, and then cross Greece by train. They arrived in Athens one day before the games, were marched about and advised to drink the local wine. Little wonder that events such as the marathon were won, not by an American, but by the little Greek shepherd Spiridon Louis.

The inevitable questionnaire was added to the Olympics in 1900. Among the penetrating questions were: 1) Were you reared as an infant naturally or artificially? 2) What is the color of your beard? 3) How strong was your grandfather?

**IOC MEDICAL COMMISSION**

As alluded to, it was a unique opportunity to join the IOC Medical Commission for the 1992 winter games. The Commission, chaired by a Belgian prince, encompasses a mix of physicians and former Olympians, including Sebastian Coe (twice Olympic gold medalist in the 1500-meter run) and Dame Mary Glen-Haig, a participant in the fencing competition in the Olympic Games from 1948-1960.

The commission meets twice daily during the Olympic Games, at 7:30 a.m. and 10:00 p.m., to discuss medical issues, usually concerning doping control and use (and possible abuse) of certain medications. A member of the

*John Davis Cantwell, M.D.*

Commission is present at each venue and supervises the urine collection of all medal winners, the 4th-place finisher, and others chosen at random. About one percent of the tests will reveal banned substances. Other items discussed at the twice-daily sessions included 1) the possibility of blood testing in future games [in hopes of detecting those who do blood doping, use erythropoietin (EPO) and human growth hormone], 2) eligibility of HIV-positive athletes, and 3) the relative merits of buccal smears versus physical examinations in gender testing.

**THE ATLANTA OLYMPIC MEDICAL SUPPORT GROUP (OMSG)**

The purpose of serving on the IOC Medial Commission was to gain experience for helping coordinate the 1996 games in Atlanta. With the input of my colleague, Dr. Bill Cleveland, and that of the Atlanta Committee for the Olympic Games (ACOG), we assembled a team of 240 health care workers who were instrumental in organizing the event. The members faced a monumental task, one involving long hours, no pay, absence of perks (such as free tickets for distant relatives) and definite termination once the job was completed.

The proposed team was a talented and diverse one including an internist who once competed in the Miss America contest, a Fulbright scholar, a GI specialist who was a linebacker on Notre Dame's national championship football team, a former Olympic 10 km runner, and team physicians from the Braves, Falcons, Hawks and Georgia Tech. The bulk of the members, however, were medical personnel who, with quiet competence through the years, had won the admiration and respect of their patients and their peers and the honor of representing their city and state in this endeavor.

The overall goals of the AOMSG were threefold:

1. To provide top quality medical care for Olympic athletes, spectators, and the Olympic family of officials.
2. To build bridges between individuals and groups, not just in Atlanta but throughout the region.
3. To leave a legacy behind that will benefit people long after the Olympic flame has been extinguished. An example is the Olympic Village Polyclinic which will serve Georgia Tech students in the years to come.

I love the city of Atlanta, the virtual explosion of pink, white and red in the spring, Indian summer, the Sunken Garden Park and the Nature trail in Morningside, the talents of William Fred Scott, Tall Tales Bookstore, the homeless, the vision of John Portman, the Peachtree Road Race and the pregame banter in the Braves clubhouse. In my 30th year of medical practice here, I have the utmost admiration and respect for my medical colleagues. With their help and support, we achieved our Olympic goals and visions and had a grand time in the process.

Are the Olympics worth all the effort? Centuries ago the Greek satirist Lucian addressed a skeptical visitor from Scythia;

*"My dear Anacharis. If it were time for the Olympic Games...the events there would themselves teach you that the energy we*

*John Davis Cantwell, M.D.*

*give to athletics is not wasted. But telling you how delightful the games are will not really convince you. You should sit there yourself, among the spectators, and see the fine contestants, how beautiful and healthy their bodies are, their marvelous skill and unbeatable strength, their daring, and ambition, their firm resolve and their desolate will to win. I know quite well that you would never stop praising them, clapping and cheering."*

# 7

## THE OLYMPIC SPIRIT - AND A LEGACY

Several years ago I stood in front of the Academy in Athens, an institution steeped in tradition and perpetuated by the efforts of succeeding generations. It was on this site that Socrates taught Plato, Plato taught Aristotle, and Aristotle helped educate Alexander the Great, who nearly conquered the world by the age of 33.

With the Greek tradition in mind, I thought the Academy of Medicine in Atlanta an appropriate place to hold the charter meeting of the Olympic Medical Support Group, as we planned for the Centennial Olympic games. The Academy of Medicine is young by Greek standards, only 50 or so years old. The institution housed within, the Medical Association of Atlanta, dates back almost a century more, still a relative neophyte, but nonetheless an institution that has built on the efforts of each succeeding generation to improve medical care in this city. We saluted the efforts of our predecessors, and were cognizant of the unique opportunity we had before us, our "one moment in time," to provide a medical legacy of our own that future generations will benefit from.

**OLYMPIA - AND THE BARON**

After visiting the Academy in Greece, I ventured into the Peloponnesus and walked about the ruins on Olympia, uncovered in the 1870s. Baron de Coubertin did likewise, in

*John Davis Cantwell, M.D.*

1895. He could sense the "skeletons of former Olympic victors," communicating to each other in the "mute language of the dead," the astounding news that the Olympiads would begin anew after a hiatus of 1500 years. It would be as if Major League Baseball went on strike in 2003 (which it could) and recommenced in the year 3500!

Coubertin was a man of high ideals, a Billy Payne type, who could look above the din of political infighting and focus on the Olympic spirit. His motto was as follows:

> *"The important thing in the Olympic Games is not to win but to take part, the most important thing in life is not the triumph but the struggle. The essential thing is not to have conquered but to have fought well. To spread these precepts is to build up a stronger and more valiant and, above all, more scrupulous and more generous humanity."*

Coubertin had one characteristic "that stood out above all others," something that helped those of us entrusted with the medical leadership of the 1996 Olympics, when the going got tough. Coubertin had the ability "...to seize the Olympic banner when his cause appeared to be hopelessly lost and rally around it individuals who would give it new life and new hope."

**THE 1896 GAMES**

Back in Athens, I ventured to the Olympic stadium, originally built during the reign of Hadrian, and renovated for the 1896 games. I could almost picture the Greek peasant,

Spiridon Louis, bursting into view "between the marble colonnades," to win the marathon. He had trained during his work hours, "jogging twice a day beside his water-bearing mule the nine miles back and forth between his village and Athens." The evening before the race he had spent in fasting and in prayer. Louis's victory helped perpetuate the Olympic Games, for the excitement it engendered seem to snuff out opposition to the contests. As in modern times, Louis was tempted by overzealous fans:

> "As he left the stadium...grateful countrymen fought to give him whatever they had of value, littering his path with gold watches, watch chains, and silver cigar cases. A tailor offered to make him suits for the rest of his life, a barber promised him free shaves forever, a restauranteur said he could always eat for nothing at his place."

He resisted such rewards, but did acquire a cart and horse to replace his mule.

There were difficult and challenging times in preparing the Olympic medical plans for Atlanta. Certain decisions had to consider gender, race, religion and politics. Egos were taxed, and friendships tested.

**THE OLYMPIC SPIRIT**

The Olympic spirit I seek is best exemplified by former gold medalists Abebe Bikila, Emil Zatopek and Jesse Owens. William Johnson once wrote:

John Davis Cantwell, M.D.

> "Olympians carry no marks of identification once the victories are won, the medals given out. Nothing is predictable except that their lives are never the same again. As a group, the only thing can be said of them: their feet are made of neither gold nor of clay, but only of flesh."

It was evident that Abebe Bikila's feet were made of flesh, for he ran barefoot when winning the gold medal in the marathon in 1960. He repeated as gold medalist four years later. Some years after, he was severely injured in an automobile accident, and paralyzed from the waist down. A reporter once asked him if he was bitter. Bikila responded that men of success might meet with tragedy. He felt that it was God's will that he had won the marathon, and that it was the will of God that he had his accident:

> "I was overjoyed when I won the marathon twice. But I accepted those victories as I accept this tragedy. I have no choice. I have to accept both circumstances as facts of life and live happily."

Emil Zatopek, from Czechoslovakia, ran "as if he had scorpions in his feet." In 1952, he won the 5000 meter, 10,000 meter and marathon events, a feat never before accomplished, nor since. Ron Clarke, of Australia, competed a few years later and became a close friend of Zatopek's. Despite setting 21 world records in his own career, Clarke encountered various obstacles which kept him from winning but a single bronze medal in the Olympics. Years

*Adventures on Seven Continents And Other Essays*

later Clarke visited Zatopek in Czechoslovakia, and found that things had not gone well for his friend and mentor. Zatopek had opposed the communists and, accordingly, was stripped of his comfortable lifestyle, relegated to collecting garbage. At one point, however, people would recognize him and refuse to let a former Olympic champion carry their trash, doing it themselves.

In an emotional farewell, Zatopek gave Clarke a small package, and asked that he not open it until airborne. The gift was one of Zatopek's gold medals, with the following note:

*"Dear Ron*
*You are the greatest runner ever and should have won an Olympic gold medal. I have four, and that is too much. I want you to have one of mine.*
*Your dear friend,*
*Emil"*

The final example of true Olympic spirit was the friendship of rivals, Jesse Owens and Lutz Long. It was 1936, in Berlin. Long was the epitome of Hitler's master race: blond, blue-eyed, a gifted athlete. Jesse Owens was an Alabama sharecropper's son, also blessed with tremendous athletic talent.

In the qualifying heat of the long jump, Owens faulted twice. Once more and he would be disqualified. Long walked over to him, told him he had had similar problems several months before, and suggested that he start his jump on an imaginary line, several inches behind the official one. Owens did so, qualified for the Olympic finals, and beat out Long for the gold medal.

*John Davis Cantwell, M.D.*

They remained close friends. During World War II, Long saw that the battle was going poorly and wrote a note for Jesse Owens in the event of Long's demise, asking Owens to one day come to Berlin, seek out his son, and "tell him of their friendship and of their competition in the 1936 Olympics."

Long was killed in action shortly thereafter. Years later Jesse Owens did as he was asked, taking young Karl Long to the Olympic Stadium in Berlin and showing him the bronze names of Owens and Long, next to each other, hammered deep in marble on the stadium gate. You could still see the bullet holes all around.

# 8

## THE 1996 OLYMPIC MEDICAL EXPERIENCE

Over 4000 medical personnel (including 664 physicians) gave unselfishly of their time and talents towards the 1996 Olympic medical effort. Over a 30-day period physicians treated 10,723 patients. Ancillary medical personnel saw an additional 18,000.

Two lives were saved, thanks to prompt medical action during cardiac arrests. Thirty-eight athletes were hospitalized, as were 22 Olympic family members. The medical response to the Centennial Olympic Park bombing was exceptional: 111 patients were evaluated in 11 area hospitals. The on-site medical team performed with cool efficiency, as 30 ambulances transported all the patients in 32 minutes.

In February 1994, I was appointed Chief Medical Officer (CMO) for the Games. Dr. Jim Ellis replaced me as co-chair of the OMSG. In my role on the IOC Medical Commission (IOC-MC), I attended the Games in Albertville (1992), Barcelona (1994), and Lillehammer (1994), all invaluable learning experiences for the CMO role.

Elizabeth Martin was hired as Director of Medical Services in 1992. She led a team of ACOG medical planners in day-to-day planning and operations. The team gradually expanded to 15 members as the demands dictated. Thanks to Ms. Martin's drive and efficiency, I was able to maintain a part-time outpatient cardiology practice until shortly before the Olympic Village opened.

*John Davis Cantwell, M.D.*

The Olympic medical staff were almost all volunteers, except for those of us who were on loan from hospitals, organizations such as the Red Cross, or corporations. The amount of time volunteers spent in planning sessions exceeded all of our predictions.

Medical care during the 30-day Olympic period went very well. Personnel from the Centers for Disease Control and Prevention (CDC) did an excellent job in providing daily medical reports to me, which I presented to the IOC-MC in our late evening meetings. The reports were of such high quality the subsequent Games in Nagano and Sydney used the system as a model.

What did I learn from this experience? Early on, I realized that the Olympic effort was like a giant ball rolling towards a destination. I had to keep up with the ball, lest I be run over by it, and could steer its course only a little bit. Mostly, however, I had to practice patience. The various Olympic factors, such as security, transportation and medical, were intertwined. The momentum of one was tied to that of all others.

I was not surprised that the medical care was so exceptional, because I had great confidence in the medical personnel and hospitals we used. Despite our flaws, American health care is the best in the world, and we demonstrated that under the microscope of the world's scrutiny.Although my days were long, I tried to see one event per day, coupled with a visit with the medical staff at that particular venue. My 10 highlights were as follows:

1. Carl Lewis winning his fourth consecutive gold medal in the long jump, joining Al Oerter as the only Olympian to accomplish that feat.
2. Michael Johnson's first-ever double golds in the men's 200 and 400 meter dashes.
3. Dan O'Brien (whom I had met in Barcelona) redeeming himself as the "world's greatest athlete" in the decathlon.
4. Donovan Bailey and Gail Devers becoming the world's fastest man and woman, respectively.
5. Fatuma Roba winning the women's marathon and giving credit to her inspiration, the late Abebe Bikila, also from Ethiopia.
6. Noureddine Morceli, the world record holder in the mile, easily winning the 1500-meter event.
7. Jan Zelezny's repeat as the gold medalist in the javelin throw, and later getting a tryout as a pitcher by the Atlanta Braves.
8. The super heavyweight Greco-Roman wrestling match between Alexandre Karelin and Matt Ghaffari (a.k.a. "Rocky").
9. The men's gold medal doubles badminton match between Indonesia and Malaysia.
10. The teamwork of the U.S. women's basketball squad, as contrasted to the lack of cohesiveness of the men's "dream team."

*John Davis Cantwell, M.D.*

**At the Olympic Stadium in Atlanta**

I was greatly impressed with our Olympic medical team, who worked long hours with no pay and few (if any) perquisites. Their smiling faces and helping hands carried the Olympic spirit of goodwill and fellowship to new heights.

On a personal note, as one who enjoys sports, medicine and international fellowship, it was an opportunity of a lifetime and one I will always remember.

*John Davis Cantwell, M.D.*

# 9

## THE FIVE OLYMPIC PASSIONS IN SPORTS AND MEDICINE

Almost since their inception in 776 B.C., the Olympic Games have emphasized a celebration of Plato's version of the total person, a blending of athletics, cultural and spiritual components.

The 1996 Centennial Games in Atlanta continued this tradition. Over 10,000 athletes competed in 26 different sports. Seventeen religious organizations of different denominations worked together to provide spiritual guidance, places to worship, hospitality and faith-related cultural festivals, including concerts, dance, theater, visual arts, poetry readings and interactive art.

More than 80 new works of public art were added to the Atlanta-area scene, spawned by the Olympic movement. Atlanta's High Museum of Art had exhibits featuring five passions of the Olympics including paintings, sculptures and works of decorative art, made in all parts of the world over a 7000 year time span. Illustrated by works such as Rodin's "The Kiss" and "The Dance" by Matisse, the passions featured included awe, joy, anguish, love and triumph.

**AWE**

The athlete can relate to all of these passions. There is awe during the opening ceremonies where over 10,000 athletes from nearly 200 countries march into the Olympic stadium amid splendor, color and pageantry. There is also awe during certain athletic fetes, The latter include Bob Beamon's extraordinary long jump in Mexico City (1968), wherein he advanced the world record by nearly two feet (causing someone to ask, "What happened to 28 feet?"). Several physicians have turned in awesome performances, including orthopedist Eric Heiden's five gold medals in Lake Placid (1980) and medical student Johann Olav Koss's three world records in Lillehammer (1994).

**JOY, ANGUISH**

The passion of joy is commonly seen during the Games, especially at the end of a medal-winning event or while on the victory stand. Anguish is likewise readily visible, as when Mary Decker Slaney sprawled on the infield of the track during the 1500-meter run in Los Angeles, her Olympic dreams erased, her face a blend of pain and anger. Anguish was seen in Barcelona on the face of Derek Redmond, the British 400-meter runner, who tore a hamstring and limped to the finish line aided by his father, who leaped from the stands, ran past the medics, and gathered up his son in his arms. As Sir Roger Bannister once said, "Failure is as exciting to watch as success, provided the effort is absolutely genuine and complete."

**LOVE**

One could see love in the Redmonds' act to be sure. But often times love is a "behind the scenes" passion. The love of Emil Zatopek and

*John Davis Cantwell, M.D.*

his wife, Dana, both gold medalists in track and field, was overt, as was the love (albeit not enduring, unfortunately) between Hal Connelly and Olga Fikotova in the 16th Olympiad in Melbourne. More subtle was the love between Jesse Owens, the black sharecropper's son and Lutz Long, the blond German in the 1936 games. The bond between these two persisted, even when their respective countries were at war, and it was Owens who carried out the last wish of his friend, after Long's death in combat.

**TRIUMPH**

Triumph does not always imply an Olympic medal. It did in the case of Dan Jansen, however, who overcame several disastrous falls in two Olympiads and finally prevailed in a third, bringing tears of joy to my eyes as I watched him take a victory lap with his daughter Jane (named after Dan's sister, who had died of leukemia the day of Dan's first Olympic competition).

One is also triumphant, in my judgment, when learning to deal with obstacles, whatever they might be. Abebe Bikila became a paraplegic due to a car accident after winning consecutive Olympic marathons. Undaunted by the injury, he took up archery and was a lifelong spokesman for the development of sports for youth in his country.

Bill Havens was triumphant, even though he elected not to compete in the 1924 Games. A member of the champion Yale crew (which included Benjamin Spock), Havens gave up his place on the Olympic team so that he could be with his wife when she delivered their first child. Havens admitted to some second thoughts about his decision, after hearing that his crew won the Olympic crown, but such thoughts were erased nearly three decades later when he received a telegram from Helsinki in 1952. It read: "Dear Dad, Thanks for waiting around for me to get born in 1924. I'm coming home with the gold medal you should have won. Your loving son, Frank."

Frank Havens had triumphed in the singles 10,000 meter canoeing event. His father's personal sacrifice on his behalf was no less heroic.

Physicians, of course, are no stranger to the aforementioned five passions. I am still awed when I see a child born, or see someone complete a 10 kilometer road race with a transplanted heart. I see joy in the faces of patients who update me on their children's accomplishments. There is anguish in the expressions of the man who tells me his only son has AIDS, or a wife whose husband has recently been diagnosed as having a malignant brain tumor.

There is love in the tenderness of a middle-aged woman, who holds the hand of her Alzheimer-affected mother in the nursing home, feeding her, helping to change her soiled nightgown, showing her pictures from good times past.

Finally, I see triumph every day, such as in the parents of a severely handicapped child, who accept him for what he is and seek to make his life as pleasant as it can be, while preserving some free moments of their own. I see it in the stroke patient, who struggles to master the walker, or to learn to write with the opposite hand. I see it in the man with terminal cancer, who uses his remaining weeks, days, or hours to let his family know how much

*John Davis Cantwell, M.D.*

he cares about them, making the act of dying a rich, meaningful experience.

Yes, the passions of awe, joy, anguish, love and triumph. We saw then during the 1996 Olympic Games in Atlanta, and see them still in the everyday lives of health care workers, wherever they might be.

# 10

## A LEAGUE OF HIS OWN

Talk of the athletic versatility takes us back to an era more than 50 years ago when athletes weren't allowed to wear gold neck chains, let alone earrings, and were free of tattoos.

It was the fall of 1937. Germany had moved into the Rhineland, swing bands were in vogue, Errol Flynn was swashbuckling across the movie screen, and a sandy-haired high school freshman entered a varsity football game in the small mideastern Wisconsin town of Shawano (population 5000, give or take a few). The young athlete, Bill Reed, was embarking on a career that would cause his name to be etched in his school's athletic hall of fame.

His football debut was dramatic. He entered a scoreless tie in the fourth quarter and promptly threw the winning touchdown pass to his brother, John, to beat a team coached by still another brother, Al.

He was a three-time all-conference halfback and twice led the league in scoring. A proverbial triple-threat, he did most of the running and passing and also handled punts and place-kicks.

Reed wasn't big by today's standards (5' 10", 160 pounds), but he was fast and elusive - as if guided by a sixth sense. In basketball, Reed was one of only two high school players in Wisconsin to use the new one-handed shooting style. As a freshman, he was a star on Shawano's state championship team and was named all-state. He again led the

*John Davis Cantwell, M.D.*

team to the state title as a junior and the championship finals the following year. He made all-state each year.

**Bill Reed as a high school football star**

*Adventures on Seven Continents And Other Essays*

In an era of low-scoring games, (teams seldom got as many as 40 points), Reed's magic produced a conference record 925 points. The record lasted for 16 years.

In Reed's freshman year, the school Latin teacher, who also was a tennis buff, watched the young man play tennis on the town's only court - two concrete slabs behind the school - and saw some promise.

What promise! The teacher talked the school into fielding a tennis team in Reed's sophomore year. Reed won the state singles championship and led his mates to the state team title. He did it again as a junior and senior, never losing a singles match in those three years.

His forte was patience, returning the ball from side to side until his fatigued opponent made an error. Bobby Riggs, the reigning world king of men's tennis at the time, was brought into town by an area business executive and tennis fan to play the young star in an exhibition. Riggs won, of course, but Reed made him work for the victory.

Reed won four varsity letters in track and was the conference 100-yard dash champion. The school didn't even have a track. Reed practiced by running around the block.

He won 15 varsity athletic letters. This was exclusive of baseball (which turned out to be his best sport) because the school did not have a baseball team. Reed played during the summers with the city team and an American Legion team in a nearby town.

Reed went to Notre Dame on an athletic scholarship after graduating from high school. But like so many others, his college career was cut short by World War II. Before going to Europe with an Army Medical Corps unit,

*John Davis Cantwell, M.D.*

though, Reed played football, basketball and baseball for teams at Camp Grant, Illinois. He was a standout in all three sports against many of the nation's top collegiate powers.

**Bill Reed with the Boston Braves, 1952**

*Adventures on Seven Continents And Other Essays*

After the war, Reed embarked on a professional sports career. He played basketball with the Oshkosh All-Stars in a league which evolved into the National Basketball Association. He also signed a baseball contract with the Boston Braves and began his career in the Braves' farm system.

He was a career .312 hitter, mostly in the minors. After working his way up the ladder through Green Bay, Evansville and Hartford, Reed opened the 1952 season as the Braves' second baseman. He got the major league season's first hit in the opener.

Age was a factor, however. He was a 29-year-old rookie and, despite being the Braves' second leading hitter with a .250 average, he was a victim of the club's youth-oriented rebuilding program. He was sent down to Milwaukee - then the Braves' top farm team.

Reed had been attending college in the off-season and, after graduating from St. Norbert College in suburban Green Bay, he became a successful business executive with the American Can Company.

Now retired, Reed lives in Houston, Texas. His wife, Eloise, his high school sweetheart, died recently. He still attends the Astrodome for baseball games, especially when the Braves are in town, and he occasionally visits the Braves' spring training camp in Florida.

Reed's exploits have served as a measuring stick for high school athletics in Wisconsin for a half-century. But he was a tough act to follow. He was, indeed, a young man in a league of his own.

*John Davis Cantwell, M.D.*

# 11

## THE BOYS OF WINTER

The movie, "Hoosiers," was loosely based on a true David versus Goliath scenario. In 1954, tiny Milan High School swept to the Indiana State Basketball Championship, defeating Muncie Central 32-30. The winning shot was made by a boy whose home lacked the facilities of plumbing, electricity and telephones. Nearly 50 years later they still talk about that basket, for such events were big news in small midwestern towns then, and perhaps even now. "Not as important as God," one woman said, "but right up there."

I watched the movie, flooded with waves of nostalgia, for I was there. Not in 1954, but two years later, in the small (pop. 7000) Wisconsin town of Shawano.

Our town had a rich athletic tradition. I grew up hearing tales of the legendary Billy Reed and had the opportunity to observe a cavalcade of high school stars, including two older brothers. One of the brightest stars was Dick Gast, who later became the first 12-letter athlete at Lawrence University. I still vividly recall the high school basketball game in which he outscored Eau Claire's Chuck Mencel (a future college all-American and all-Pro) and led the Shawano Indians to a stunning upset, scoring a school record thirty-three points in the process. My practical education in basketball was on an outdoor court and in YMCA and grade school leagues. Programs in the Catholic, Lutheran, Indian and public schools were good breeding grounds for developing

*Adventures on Seven Continents And Other Essays*

skills. Players who had been fierce rivals in grade school were, seemingly overnight, students in the same high school and learning to play together under the calculating eye of new coach, John Kenney.

Coach Kenney didn't have the checkered past that Gene Hackman portrayed in the movie, but he did share Hackman's sense of absolute authority. In one game, the other guard, (Marty Gharrity) and I each had about twenty-five points early in the third quarter, within range of Gast's school record. Kenney elected to experiment with a new offensive formation, moving Gharrity to forward and stating that the new guard and I weren't to shoot. I finished with twenty-five points while Gharrity went on to smash the record. I never questioned the decision.

The 1956 season was one of peaks and valleys. The former included a ninety-four point team record in the opening game. The low points included two losses to the worst team in our own conference. We began to gel by tournament time and reached the crescendo by edging Appleton in the state finals. We were treated to a rousing reception by the hometown folks, with police escorts and rides through Main Street on the city fire trucks.

The following year we successfully defended the title. In my senior year an overtime loss to Milwaukee North kept us from a possible third championship.

Twenty-five years later the "Boys of Winter" returned to Shawano to celebrate the Silver Anniversary. The reunion was held on a farm located several miles west of town and belonging to the team's former center. The outing for me was like being transported back in a time capsule. Guys who were "on my case"

*John Davis Cantwell, M.D.*

years back were still on it. I revelled in the good-natured locker room-type banter. One of the players addressed our old coach as "John" and was given a stern reminder that it was "Coach Kenney" (in jest, I think, although I'm not sure).

**Members of Wisconsin's 1956 and 1957 state high school basketball championship teams**

During the plane ride back To Atlanta I reflected upon the experience. I realized that my value systems haven't changed much in the ensuing years. I still believe in the importance of discipline - for myself, my children, the medical students and residents I supervise and the patients I deal with. I continue to believe in the value of teamwork, as demonstrated in a recent cardiac case at our hospital where medical and surgical colleagues battled throughout the night in an effort to save a young man's life. I recognize the importance of good leadership and am thankful that in high school and college basketball I was guided by the likes of John Kenney and Vic Bubas.

Basketball isn't a very big deal today in city schools such as the one my youngest son went to. His games were rather poorly attended. The players don't practice on their own a fraction of the time boys did in the 1950s. On the one hand, maybe it's for the better, placing the sport in a better perspective with the many opportunities life has to offer. On the other hand, I view the deemphasis with a certain sadness. The hours I spent, shoveling snow off the driveway, stretching out the frozen net, working on left-handed drives and dreaming of playing in the state championship game before 15,000 screaming fans, those were hours well spent, a sort of metaphor of life. In the process. I learned the kind of commitment it takes to reach the top. The lesson can be applied to anything I pursue today, if I dare to dream, to pay the price and seek excellence for its own sake.

*John Davis Cantwell, M.D.*

# 12

**SEASONS**

Blossoms fall, skin wrinkles, and the child becomes father to the man. According to Ecclesiastes, everything has a season, and I find this particularly true of the life of a man.

As a boy, growing up in Wisconsin, I changed athletic gear as a tree changes the color of its leaves. In spring and summer, I oiled my baseball glove, donned a Philadelphia Phillies cap, and pounded doubles off the chicken-wire fence at the end of our vacant lot.

In the fall, I would slip into a tattered football jersey, with the number 37 stenciled on it (the number worn by Doak Walker, the triple-threat halfback at Southern Methodist), and practice angling punts into the coffin corner and kicking field goals over the clothesline.

The winter months were the longest, and probably explain why basketball was my favorite sport. Embalmed in a heavy coat, stocking cap and mittens, I would shovel the snow off our driveway, stretch the frozen net so the ball wouldn't stick, and pretend that I was Tom Gola, LaSalle's great all-American, or Frank Ramsey, the Boston Celtics' "sixth man," working on twisting jump shots and practicing one-and-one free throws. The scenario: Madison Square Garden, our team trailing by a point, and only one second showing on the clock.

My father, a busy obstetrician, had a fan-shaped basket built out from our garage. When one of my friends insisted that the basket wasn't 10 feet high, Dad got out the stepladder and tape measure to prove him wrong, only to discover that the basket was only 9 feet 8 inches from the ground. The basket was torn down and rebuilt, at some cost, I suspect, for Dad didn't want our team to lose a future state championship on that account. He believed in doing things the right way, whether it was work or sports.

Soon it was 1960. The theme from "A Summer Place" and "Teen Angel" were the big hits. Elvis was discharged from the Army, Gary Powers was shot down over Russia. Kennedy was running for president, blacks were staging a sit-in at the Woolworth counter in Greensboro, N.C., and I was a sophomore guard, fighting for a spot on the Duke Blue Devil team in the Atlantic Coast Conference.

My prep career had been solid, with the two state championships. However, as a 5-foot-8-inch walk-on, my chances seemed slim. The new coach, Vic Bubas, promised that all spots were open even though there were many returning lettermen. My roommate, also a guard, saw that he had virtually no chance to make the varsity and offered to slack off when guarding me so that I could get more shots and show what I could do. I declined his kind sacrifice, told him to play his usual way, and made the squad anyway as Bubas, true to his word, cut the co-captain. I called my parents (the operator thought I was kidding when I told her the home phone number was 4) and they were equally thrilled.

The team was a talented, diverse crew. John Frye, all-state in four sports in West Virginia, was called "Legs" because of redwood-sized lower extremities. He was a pre-divinity student and we fought to sit next to

*John Davis Cantwell, M.D.*

him when our Piedmont Airlines charter hit turbulent weather, figuring that our changes were enhanced. Howard Hurt, with the rugged looks and temperament of Carmen Basilio, the old boxer, was the team leader. Doug Kistler was a top rebounder. Fred Kast, whose spine looked like it had been run through a woodplaner, was dubbed "Flatback." Jay Beal had a crewcut, exposing his odd-shaped head, and we would try to palm it, as one does a basketball, when he least suspected it.

I was "Dachshund," for obvious reasons. During a freshman game at Virginia, Frye and Hurt discovered an old dachshund in the basement of the fieldhouse. Sneaking into my locker, they outfitted the dog in jersey No. 24 and set him loose on the main floor during intermission. The dog must have gotten a little excited, for my uniform had a somewhat pungent odor that kept my opponent at bay during the varsity game.

The turning point for me that season came at Clemson, in their little bandbox gym. Press Maravich was their coach and young son Pete, no doubt, was in the stands. We tried to maintain our sanity as the Clemson brass band blared at us whenever there was a lull in the action. I came off the bench to hit four of five shots and eventually got to start a few games, running out into darkened gyms with a spotlight on me, the announcer blustering that "...and at the other guard, from Shawano, Wisconsin..."

We finished the regular season in the lower half of the standing. Billy Packer and Lennie Chappell of Wake Forest and Doug Moe, York Larese and Lee Shaffer of North Carolina were formidable opponents. We caught fire in the A.C.C. tournament, however, eliminating South

Carolina in the opener and then upsetting North Carolina and Wake Forest on consecutive nights, sending us into the National Collegiate Athletic Association tournament in Madison Square Garden. We trounced Princeton, got by St. Joseph's, and reach the quarter-finals before succumbing to N.Y.U., led by Tom "Satch" Sanders.

Had we won that game it would have meant going to California for the finals, competing against the likes of Oscar Robertson, Jerry Lucas and John Havlicek. It was just as well for me as I was beginning to fall hopelessly behind in my pre-medical studies. During my junior year, Art Heyman pushed me down another notch on the roster. Jeff Mullins was on the horizon, and the handwriting was on the wall. I went to Northwestern Medical School but continued to play basketball there and at the Mayo Clinic were I did my internal medicine residency.

The ensuing years have gone by. The gray hair about my temples is a gentle reminder that I approach the autumn of my life. Vic Bubas was assistant to the president at Duke and later commissioner of the Sun Belt Conference. Howard Hurt has been a coach and later a principal of a high school in North Carolina and a motivational speaker. Jay Beal is a lawyer and Fred Kast an executive. Doug Kistler's season ended prematurely when he was killed in an auto accident. His two sons and the community youth program he started in Charlotte, N.C. carry on.

I practice cardiology in Atlanta. On the wall of my office is a picture of the 1960 Duke team with an inscription from Coach Bubas, reminding me that champions have "discipline, desire, sacrifice and

*John Davis Cantwell, M.D.*

organization." My medical work consists of trying to instill such inspiration into fat, fatigued and flatulent 40 year olds to modify their lifestyles and hopefully reduce their risk of heart attacks. I also work with post-coronary patients, encouraging them to become athletes again, to be self-disciplined and determined to achieve their maximum potential, to attack life and reap its positive features rather than to be attacked by its tensions and demands.

**Duke University's first Atlantic Coast Conference basketball champions, 1960 (The author is on the left in the first row)**

I have tried to teach my children the love of the athletic participation that my parents and older siblings passed on to me. I felt sure that my first-born son would be everything I wasn't - All-American, Rhodes

Scholar, you name it - but a diagnosis of mental retardation changed all that. It gave me a better perspective on life, however, and opened to me the joys of the Special Olympics, which I have served as team doctor. I have discovered that retarded children do surprisingly well in various athletic events, boosting their self image and arousing parental pride as they strive to do the best that they can. Their sports participation and accomplishments are positives in lives too often filled with negatives.

My youngest son, a stocky blond, is a healthy, athletic guy, for which I am grateful. Through him I relived the seasons of my youth, booming spirals to him in the autumn and teaching him to switch hit in the spring and summer. I coached his church league basketball team, and tried not to show favoritism, but did. We practiced together in the back yard, on a basket precisely 10 feet off the ground.

Occasionally my mind would wander, I confess, and the clock turned back to 1950, when I was a youngster. Suddenly I am Gola once again, on the line in the Garden, one-and-one, behind by a point, one second showing on the clock. Before I can shoot, my concentration is broken by a shout from the kitchen. Dinner is getting cold, and we must come in right that instant! I set the ball down, put my arm around my son, and head for the house, confident that there will be other moments, additional challenges, and many more seasons.

*John Davis Cantwell, M.D.*

# 13

## A GATHERING OF LEGENDS

I tore open the letter from Mike Krzyzewski, head basketball coach at Duke University. On the initial reading, it seemed an invitation for me to play in the "Legends of Duke" basketball game, a fund-raising endeavor that would also help rejuvenate the Duke basketball spirit. Grant Hill, Christian Laettner and Bobby Hurley would be there. So would Dick Groat, an All-American in both basketball and baseball in the early 1950s, plus two of my former teammates, Art Heyman and Jeff Mullins.

My heart accelerated. Perhaps I would go belly to belly with Hurley, taking no prisoners, scratching and clawing, getting in his face, messing with his rhythm. Or maybe I would drive on Hill, Number 33, forcing him to commit before I dished the ball off or soared high for a lay-up.

I studied Coach K's letter again. On more careful perusal, I realized he wasn't asking me to play, but rather just to attend the event and the post-game reception for all former players at the posh Washington Duke Hotel. I decided to go anyway. I wanted to see Groat again, to thank him for being the main reason I selected Duke, trying to emulate his success in the two sports. My roommate, from an even smaller town than I, had also come to Duke for that very reason.

We both fell far short of Groat, as most would. I did get to start a few basketball games and to play against the likes of Roger Kaiser, Billy Packer, Larry Brown and Tom

"Satch" Sanders. Most of my contribution was as a reserve, however. Baseball was even less fruitful. I did make the varsity, but reported late from post-season basketball tournaments and never did get to play in a varsity game. Eventually I gave up the sport, electing to spend spring afternoons in the Duke Gardens, pondering the poetry of Emily Dickinson and the sonnets of Shakespeare.

I did get to play against Groat, in a pick-up basketball game when he was passing through Durham en route to spring training with the Pittsburgh Pirates. His quick reflexes and wrong-foot shots off a cross court drive are still memorable.

The Legends game was a showcase of former talent, also including pros such as Danny Ferry and Johnny Dawkins. Dawkins permanently retired the jersey number I once wore - 24 - in 1986. I had unofficially "retired" it in 1961 when I packed it in my suitcase as I headed off to medical school a year early, driven off by the two undergraduate guards, Heyman and Mullins. Between us, Dawkins and I scored over 2600 points for Duke in our careers. If truth be told, 2556 belonged to Dawkins.

My youngest son, Ryan, flew up from Atlanta for the affair taking precious time form his junior medical student duties. He had seen Duke go to the Final Four in each of his four years as an undergraduate. I wanted to be sure he met Groat and especially Mullins and Heyman. The latter was nice and told Ryan that I was a fine outside shooter and a real battler. He added, with a twinkle, that I couldn't jump or penetrate worth a flip, but otherwise gave all I had, a pretty fair retrospective in my own judgment.

*John Davis Cantwell, M.D.*

During half-time, the nine former Blue Devils posed beneath their number banners. There was also a recreation of perhaps the three most famous shots in modern Duke basketball history. Gene Banks missed his 15 footer this time, the shot that buried North Carolina in 1981. Laettner also failed on his "buzzerbeater" that nailed Connecticut in 1991. Then the clock was set at 2.1 seconds. Grant Hill inbounded the ball from under his own basket. Coach K set the stage, telling what he had been thinking as the play evolved in the battle against Kentucky. Laettner broke high above the three-point line, grabbed the ball and squared to shoot. As the ball left his hand, the horn sounded. The shot was buried in the net, and the crowd went nuts.

The players rolled on the floor, exuberantly exchanged high fives, experiencing the joy once again. A chill of excitement swept through the whole stadium.

Laettner requested that all members of the 1991 and 1992 national championship teams come down on the court. He then asked all former players and coaches to join too, in a great show of togetherness. I bounced down the stairs from the upper balcony, greeting former coach Vic Bubas and wandering among giants like Gulliver, in the land of Brobdingnag.

It was a night to remember. Although I made but a small ripple during my playing career, I was there, a tiny part of an evolution of Duke basketball success, trying to push myself to be the best that I could be.

*Adventures on Seven Continents And Other Essays*

That part of me is woven into the fabric of the 1960 championship banner, Duke's first Atlantic Coast Conference title. Look for it the next time you are in Cameron Indoor Stadium. It hangs from the rafters, not far from where the legends numbers are immortalized.

*John Davis Cantwell, M.D.*

# 14

## Maddux

An added privilege of being a team physician is a rare opportunity to have an insider's view of a superstar. As it was regarding Phil Niekro and Dale Murphy, it now applies to Gregory Alan Maddux.

One of my favorite sights at Turner Field occurs at precisely 7:33 p.m., when the bullpen gate in right center field swings open and out comes Maddux, one of the best pitchers in baseball.

Flanked by his personal catcher and his pitching coach, Leo Mazzone, Maddux strides toward the mound like a gunfighter, or perhaps a matador, radiating confidence with every step.

The thing that impressed me most about him is that at first glance he seems rather ordinary. He isn't particularly big, nor is he muscular. As I.J. Rosenberg once wrote: "He will never be mistaken for a decathlete - his mid-section has a small roll and his arms are skinny." He likes to wear his glasses (before laser surgery), rarely combs his hair, and enjoys blending in with the crowd.

Put him on the mound, however, and he is a standout, one of the most graceful pitchers you will ever see. The Sporting News placed him 39th on their list of the 100 greatest baseball players ever. He narrowly missed the All-Century Team, losing out to Walter "Big Train" Johnson. Over a six-year span, his statistics compare favorably to those of Sandy

Koufax, considered one of the best over that time span.

What are the secrets of his success? I would list the following:

1. He is a well-coordinated, all-around athlete. His quick reflexes on balls hit up the middle have made him an 13-time Gold Glove winner.
2. He throws all of his pitches (fastball, change up, curve and slider) well. His compact and controlled mechanics are exceptional ("He throws as if inside a phone booth," wrote Tom Verducci.) He makes each pitch look inviting to hit, writes Thomas Boswell, then has them "sink, cut, or curve" to the outside or inside part of the plate.

    The secret of pitching, as Maddux once said, "is to make your strikes look like balls and your balls look like strikes." In other words, outguess the hitter, mess up his timing, try to fool him.
3. He has a gambler's instincts. Maddux lives in Las Vegas, where his father was a blackjack dealer. A formidable poker player himself, Greg detects when an opponent has a good hand "by the way he strokes his chin or suddenly stops fiddling with his chips."

    He studies hitters the same way, reviewing videotapes of their home runs, noting which pitch they hit. The batter will never see that pitch again from Maddux as long as he lives. If he notices a batter's foot open up slightly, as if trying to hit the ball to the opposite field, Maddux will adjust accordingly.

*John Davis Cantwell, M.D.*

    His adjustments generally occur before the fact, not after.
4. He is a fierce competitor. No matter what the game is, baseball, golf, cards, he comes at you with everything he has.

**Greg Maddux**

*Adventures on Seven Continents And Other Essays*

I like to work Sunday afternoon games when Maddux is on the mound. He works quickly and throws strikes. The game starts at 1:10 p.m. and I am usually home before 4, firing up the grill.

I once wished him "good luck" before a game and he gave me a funny look, and no response. I later realized that he probably doesn't consider luck to be a significant factor, as compared with skill. Another team physician asked him whether he was "throwing" in Chicago the next afternoon. "It isn't throwing, doc" he responded, "it's pitching. There *is* a difference."

A cool "dude" (one of his favorite words) he injured his hand late in the 1999 season diving for a foul ball near the visiting team's dugout. When I walked into the training room to view the x-ray, Maddux casually mentioned, "I think I cracked my pisiform bone, doc, see what you think," and went about his business. He was close: it was the triangular bone.

In listening to post-game interviews, I noticed that Maddux never makes excuses and never speaks in a negative sense about his pitching. In his last regular season appearance, in 1999, his final attempt to win 20 games, the New York Mets chased him with seven runs in the fourth inning. His response was vintage Maddux: "You've got to give them credit…I wasn't too upset with how I pitched in that inning. I was upset with the outcome. You never want to end the way I ended today, but I feel good about the way I've thrown the ball…everyone knows our season starts next week (the playoffs)."

He also never complains. When the umpires were shrinking the strike zone early last

*John Davis Cantwell, M.D.*

season, and teams were hitting .350 against him, he never said a word.

During Mark McGuire's 70-homer season in 1998, I went to the stadium on my off-day to watch Maddux pitch against him. The first pitch was on the low inside corner and McGuire hit it foul, deep into the lower left field seats. The third pitch broke outside at the last moment and McGuire took it for a ball. The fourth pitch seemed outside, but darted in across the edge of the plate, and McGuire was toast. In the division playoffs that same year, against the Cubs, Maddux threw about eight or nine pitches to Sammy Sosa, not one of which was in the strike zone, and struck him out swinging.

Sometimes when watching him pitch, my mind will wander back to my high school and college baseball days and I will wonder how I would bat against him. I'd try to be aggressive, as his first pitch is a strike about two-thirds of the time. I'd also try not to get behind in the count. Al Martin, a Pittsburgh outfielder, has had more success against Maddux than most. He commented: "Once he gets you deep in the count, he can carve you up and when he gets two strikes on you, you're done." Jeff Wetherby had a brief major league career, a "cup of coffee" as they say. He faced Maddux only once, and homered. He had only 12 additional at-bats in the major leagues, never getting another hit. His solution to Maddux: "Protect the plate - and pray a lot."

A baseball scout for the Montreal Expos, Phil Favia, once commented that "Maddux is so good we all should wear tuxedos when he pitches." I especially like what Giant's pitching coach, Dick Pole, said of him: "If

*Adventures on Seven Continents And Other Essays*

you look up the word pitcher in a dictionary, his picture should be there."

*John Davis Cantwell, M.D.*

# 15

## The Ultimate 10K: John Colter's Run For His Life

Several years ago, I stood before a monument in Three Forks, Mont., commemorating an event that had taken place there in 1808. It involved a man, John Colter, who had run roughly 10 kilometers over prickly pear while stripped naked, in an effort to save his life from pursuing Indians.

Colter was not your average guy. He was from an established family in the Shenandoah Valley of Virginia, a family that included judges and physicians. About 5 feet 10 inches in height, Colter "bore an open, ingenious and pleasing countenance of the Daniel Boone stamp," according to a friend. In 1803, he had been chosen by Meriweather Lewis and William Clark to be part of their historic expedition to the Pacific Coast. A skilled hunter, Colter "had been frequently selected by the two captains for special duty on the cross-country journey" leading trapping parties into the wilderness and opening the way for the western fur trade.

After completion of the Lewis and Clark expedition in September 1806, Colter sought and was granted his discharge to pursue private hunting interests. Lewis and Clark were so appreciative of his stellar service that they "gave him his pay and fitted him out with traps, tools for building canoes, powder, lead and enough other necessary supplies to last two years." In 1807, the 31-year-old Colter set off by himself on foot, carrying "a pack of 30 pounds weight, his gun, and some ammunition to penetrate a region (the Grand Tetons and Yellowstone Park area) wholly unknown to white men."

In the fall of 1808, Colter and another former Lewis and Clark expedition member, John Potts, were trapping in the Three Forks area. About 600 Blackfeet Indians suddenly appeared along the shores and signaled the two to land their canoe. Colter saw no alternative and headed the canoe to shore and jumped out. Potts tried to escape, pushing back into the stream, but was riddled with arrows.

The Blackfeet seized Colter and decided to make a sport of his death. The chief asked if he could run fast. Colter (who spoke the Blackfeet tongue) lied and said that he was a "very poor runner." The Indians thereupon stripped him naked, gave him just a 300 to 400-yard head start, and then pursed him with a vengeance across the 10 kilometers or so distance. Looking back after several kilometers, Colter noted that he had outrun all but one of the Blackfeet, who was armed with a spear. About one-half mile from the Jefferson River, Colter observed that the Indian was only 20 yards behind him. Colter stopped suddenly and spun around with outspread arms to face his attacker. The surprised Indian tried to stop abruptly but fell, breaking his weapon. Colter "instantly snatched up the spear head and pinned him to the ground," killing him.

Close to passing out, Colter ran on, reaching the Jefferson River and plunging in. He found "a large mass of driftwood" where he could keep his head above water and still remain unseen. The main Indian party came "screeching and yelling like so many devils"

*John Davis Cantwell, M.D.*

but never could find him. At nightfall, hearing no more sounds from his pursuers, Colter swam silently from the river, "a considerable distance." Still naked, his feet "covered with prickly pear spines," he finally made his way to a fort 200 miles away.

  I thought of this remarkable man (who died of jaundice at age 38) just recently, as I observed Colter Bay and the Teton Range he first spotted. I also think of him when I struggle in 10-kilometer events like the Peachtree Road Race, trying to overcome lumbosacral disc pain, a Morton's neuroma or the heat. After thinking about his toughness and courage, my rather trivial afflictions suddenly seem insignificant, and I persevere, even accelerating a bit toward the finish line.

*Adventures on Seven Continents And Other Essays*

# MEDICINE

*John Davis Cantwell, M.D.*

# 16

## MEMORIES OF MEDICAL SCHOOL

When my youngest son started medical school, it brought back a flood of memories of my similar beginnings, over 30 years ago.

Several months before I was to start, I met a recent medical school graduate who was soon to become an intern. I asked what he would suggest I do over the summer, to prepare myself for the ordeal ahead. Drawing me close, with his arm around me, he whispered his main recommendation in my ear: "Just rest." I did as he suggested, reading the novels of Thomas Hardy and the sonnets of Shakespeare, and also worked on my golf stoke. It was sage advice.

I could take the train to Northwestern back in those days, climbing aboard in the little depot in my home town of 5000 and disembarking in what Carl Sandburg referred to as the "hog butcher for the world." The medical school is on the shore of Lake Michigan, only several blocks from dynamic Michigan Avenue, one of the country's premier shopping areas. It made little difference to me, as we were generally too busy to be distracted.

My dad watched me pack, including my football, baseball glove and hand weights. "Goin' to camp?" he asked, with a mischievous smile on his face. He had started out as an ice-cream salesman, realizing that his true calling was medicine, and had graduated from Northwestern in the early 1930s. I didn't know a lot about what medical practice entailed as I was growing up, but through my father I saw the impact a competent, kind physician could

John Davis Cantwell, M.D.

have on people in need, and decided to join the ranks.

There were about 120 of us who gathered for freshman orientation, including a student who grew up across the street from me and who had attended my first birthday party. There were only four or five women. One was commuting to Chicago from South Bend, Indiana, where her husband was in law school. She tried studying on the train and doing housework in the evening. It didn't work, needless to say. We had one black in our class, a friendly guy from Mississippi. Some irregularities were apparently discovered on his application, and he was dismissed after a few weeks.

The professor who did my application interview turned out to be one of the best teachers that first year. I was a bit uncomfortable, on a senior elective in psychiatry, to do a workup on him after a failed suicide attempt over a break up of his romance with a young laboratory assistant.

I was 10 pages behind the first day of anatomy lab. No one had told me of the advanced reading assignment. My laboratory partner was a bright lad and carried me the first few days. At a nearby dissecting table, one student who obviously *had* read in advance, was telling his lab partners where to make their incisions and what they were looking at. After a while, his dissecting partner handed him the scalpel and asked him to do some of the work while he got a drink of water. The "authority" took an awkward swipe with the scalpel, turned pale, and excused himself, dropping out of school on the spot.

The dropouts had their own style. Late in the year, one excused himself from our group, while walking to class for an exam, to return for his slide rule. He cleaned out his room instead and was never heard from again. One student was only going to medical school to please his pushy parents. Upon graduation he was going to pursue his dream of becoming an English professor. He faded out after two months. One woman made it to the last half of her senior year, only to quit because she didn't want to deliver babies in ghetto homes (a requirement then, and the most fun I had in school). A bright student who usually got the top grade on anatomy exams flunked the course when the professor discovered that he never came to the lab. Exams were returned to the lab, and we grabbed them up in a piranha-like frenzy. His "A" paper was always the only one left, arousing suspicions.

We lived in Abbott Hall, on Lake Shore Drive, in tiny rooms with one bunk bed and two small desks. My first roommate was temporary, as he was getting married in six weeks. We were to learn more than we wanted to know about Hodgkin's disease, which affected his wife several years later. My next roommate, Frank, had been a college wrestler, from a prestigious medical family. His father and brother had been valedictorians of their respective medical school classes, and his uncle was one of Chicago's most prominent physicians.

Frank slept in the nude, and left the windows wide open, a problem to me in subfreezing weather. He studied late, long after midnight it seemed, and I could hear his repeated sniffling, from some kind of sinus congestion, and wonder if I was ever going to sleep peacefully again. He would finally crawl up to the top bunk, only to spring down sometime later and stand under the hall light,

*John Davis Cantwell, M.D.*

reviewing something he had forgotten. We wrestled once after a party. I was doing okay until he suddenly started doing certain maneuvers and I recalled, too late, about his college career. I negotiated a draw and made it a point not to tangle with him again.

My older brother, Art, was an intern at nearby Cook County Hospital. We'd talk by phone on occasion at night, and he'd invariably ask me the innervation and blood supply of obscure muscles.

Art was working on the obstetric ward at Cook County, and invited me out to help him deliver babies. I watched him deliver one or two, and then he said the next one was mine. That birth went well, but the pelvic area seemed more distended than usual when I was trying to get the placenta out. Art concluded that it must be twins and helped me deliver the second baby. I tried one more case, a virtual repeat of the first. "It might be twins, again," I said. "It couldn't be," was Art's response, "they are pretty rare." The second twin appeared shortly thereafter.

I wore my scrub hat like I saw the doctors do on television, with a shock of hair showing, to the chagrin on my surgically-oriented brother.

Dr. Loyal Davis, Chief of Neurosurgery, and Ronald Regan's father-in-law, insisted what we use the reflex hammer he designed. He also made each of us schedule an appointment to see him, whereupon he would chastise any of us who said they wanted to become a general practitioner. Dr. Davis kept us waiting, purposely I would guess, so that his secretary could have us peruse his meticulous case files. He would never tolerate abbreviations on student or housestaff workups, acting bewildered if he came upon "HEENT" in a physical exam report. As I was browsing through one of his files, a check fell out. I picked it up and noticed it was made out to "Dr. Loyal Davis." Under the sum was written "One Brother." A young man had died on the operating table. I guess his brother blamed Dr. Davis, rather than the brain tumor. Fortunately, Dr. Davis didn't quiz me during my interview about what I saw in his files, as he had done to several others.

Abbott Hall, where we roomed, had long and narrow hallways. At one end of the hall was a telephone booth. One of my classmates used to hunch down in the bottom of the booth, below the window, and talk with his girlfriend who was a student on the undergraduate campus in Evanston. One night, an upperclassman decided to do some bow and arrow practice down the hallway. The arrow pierced the wooden door of the telephone booth, flushing out my classmate who narrowly missed a potentially serious wound. I often wondered how the dean would explain that to the young man's parents. ("Dear Mr. and Mrs. Wilson, I regret to inform you that George was stuck by an arrow in the thigh, while sitting in a telephone booth...")

I tried to keep fit by doing pushups after rolling out of bed each morning, using my arm weights, and running on the outdoor cinder track adjacent to the medical school. The track was the scene of my greatest athletic triumph, the place where I broke the world record for the one-mile run.

It happened this way. To keep my mind from unpleasant thoughts of upcoming examinations, I would stage imaginary one-mile races. One day to my surprise (and delight), the only other person on the track was Tom O'Hara, from

*John Davis Cantwell, M.D.*

Loyola University, the recordholder in the indoor mile. Studying him with sidelong glances, I made my move coming around the far turn and edged him at an invisible tape, whereupon I threw up my arms in victory and collapsed in a heap (a la Roger Bannister). O'Hara looked at me with a curious expression and kept going. I did not have the heart to tell him I had just wiped him out with a splendid 3 minutes and 55 seconds.

One day, en route to class, we spotted an attractive group of young coeds, whom we had never seen before. One in particular stood out above all the others with her blond hair, blue eyes and all-American good looks. We learned subsequently that they were speech students from the undergraduate campus, visiting the medical school to look at laryngeal muscles on cadavers. I literally met Marilyn over my cadaver, and began to see her on my one night off each week, ice-skating on a pond in Evanston, going to movies, or attending sorority parties to clear my mind momentarily of the stress of having to learn more that I thought humanly possible.

Along with many of my classmates, I would study week nights and Sundays from 6 p.m. until about midnight in a large room in Abbott Hall, on the second floor. Several of my Duke University teammates and fraternity brothers were in Chicago for job interviews, and paid me a surprise visit. Told I was in the study room, they snuck up behind who they thought was me and shouted in unison "dachshund!" my basketball nickname. The student was startled by the sudden shock, and the perpetrators mumbled their apologies and beat a hasty retreat, with me right behind.

In 1990, we returned to Northwestern for the silver anniversary of our medical school class. My roommate, Frank, is a general surgeon in a small town in Michigan, still with a wrestler's physique, happily married, and the father of a young child. The pipe-smoking, bald-headed guy who always sat on the front row and complained about how ludicrous it was to memorize things is a highly successful urologist at a major medical center and has developed innovative techniques in treating kidney stones. The class valedictorian is an expert in metabolic diseases. My anatomy laboratory partner is an associate dean at the University of Pennsylvania.

We laughed and partied at our reunion, glad that we had done what we did, but not wishing to repeat it. We felt fortunate to be members of a fine profession, and managed to suppress worries about health care changes certain to be thrust upon us in the future.

As my son studied in our basement, until 1 a.m. or so, I wished him well and hope that in 30 years he can look back with the same degree of satisfaction I have and realize that he too is a member of a wonderful profession. My only advice for him was to keep his eyes peeled for a prospective wife as he walked to class and studied his cadaver, and to be alert for steel-tipped arrows if he used the telephone booth on campus.

*John Davis Cantwell, M.D.*

# 17

## TO A SON ENTERING MEDICAL SCHOOL

It is a natural tendency for fathers to pass on advice to their sons.

Harvey Penick was a legendary golf teacher and former coach at the University of Texas. Over sixty years ago he began writing notes and observations in what he came to call his Little Red Book. His intention was to transmit things he had learned to his son, Tinsley. Penick followed in his father's footsteps as a golf professional. Penick felt that "with the knowledge in this little book to use as a reference, it would be easier for Tinsley to make a good living teaching golf no matter what happens when I am gone."

<u>Harvey Penick's Little Red Book</u> has had phenomenal success, such that the author "no longer has to order off the right side of restaurant menus." The same can be said for H. Jackson Brown's <u>Life's Little Instruction Book</u> written for his son, Adam. The first volume of aphorisms has sold over five million copies.

Physicians gain a wealth of experience in their careers. Their children often follow them into the profession. Only a few physicians succeed in writing aphorisms that help pave the way for their offspring. One of the best was William Heberden, (see chapter 41) born in London in 1710, and best known for his original description of angina pectoris and of the distal finger joint nodes seen in degenerative arthritis.

Heberden was educated at Cambridge and soon became one of the most remarkable clinicians of his day. As a physician he was inclined to trust his own clinical observations and experience rather than merely follow the traditional, and often dubious, medical practice of the day. His friends ranged from Ben Franklin to Queen Charlotte. Heberden took notes, in Latin, at the bedside of the sick over a 50-year career in order to hand them over to his son should the latter select a career in medicine. He retired from his practice, "not for a wish to be idle," but rather before he could "no longer do justice to my patients."

William Heberden, Jr., did follow in his father's footsteps. He published the notes one year after the death of his 91-year-old father. <u>The Commentaries on the History and Cure of Disease</u> subsequently became a prominent textbook of medicine, and Heberden, Jr., eventually became the personal physician to King George III.

When my youngest son, Ryan, entered medical school, I gave him some practical advice based on my years of practice.

- Ask patients what name they go by. As you get to know some of them well and call them by their first name, this will avoid referring to George Robert Smith as George when all of his family and friends call him Robert.
- Treat all patients with the same degree of respect. My uncle practiced medicine for 50 years. At his funeral, a farm couple came up and said, "We were nobodies, but he treated us as if we were king and queen."
- Use the medical history as a way of establishing common bonds with a patient.

John Davis Cantwell, M.D.

Ask where they grew up, went to school, what hobbies they have. Once, when working in a prison hospital, I had difficulty relating to a particularly demanding inmate. I discovered that we were both Green Bay Packer fans. That common interest helped our relationship a great deal.
- Always ask patients if they have been under any unusual stress recently. Many won't spontaneously mention this. It might explain their symptoms.
- When inquiring about chest pain, use a variety of adjectives in your questioning. For instance, ask about any tightness, fullness, heaviness or any unusual sensation in the chest, neck or arm. Some patients will deny chest pain, but will tell you on further questioning that it feels like an elephant is standing on their chest when they walk uphill.
- Be especially wary about chest sensations, especially if effort-induced. Better to hospitalize a patient overnight for observation and monitoring than to see a note on your desk the next day indicating that the patient had died suddenly at home.
- Always check blood pressures in both arms and with the patient in the supine and standing position. Because of this oversight, a patient can be overtreated with antihypertensives, have orthostatic syncope, and get confused. Use the bell of your stethoscope when checking the blood pressure, for the Korotkoff sounds are of lower pitch.

- Auscultate over scars, especially in patients with cardiomyopathy (heart muscle disease) or unexplained heart failure. You might hear the to-and-fro murmur of an arteriovenous fistula (an abnormal connection between an artery and a vein), the reason for high-output cardiac failure.
- Auscultate the heart with the patient in the supine, left lateral, sitting and standing positions. The murmur of mitral valve prolapse may only appear when standing, and the murmur of hypertrophic cardiomyopathy will often be accentuated.
- Routinely look between the toes and in the scalp, and feel for epitrochlear lymph nodes near the elbow area. You will rarely find anything significant, but it will be a reminder to both you and the patient that a good physical examination should be thorough.
- At the end of your examination, ask the patient if there is anything else you should discuss. Occasionally the patient will point out a little lump or something you might have missed.
- Buy multiple pairs of the same shade of dark socks. It will save you time in the mornings as you dress for work.

Above all, learn to appreciate the wonderful profession you have chosen. It will take you into the innermost aspects of patients' lives. As William Carlos Williams once put it, "My medicine was the thing which gained me entrance to these secret gardens of the self." Medicine has taken me into the locker room of the Atlanta Braves, to prison hospitals, to the worlds of kings and queens, to Olympic

*John Davis Cantwell, M.D.*

sports medicine clinics and to homeless clinics. I treasure every experience and know that you will do the same, my son.

# 18

## I WAS A YOUNG DOCTOR THEN

It happened nearly 30 years ago, but remains fresh in my mind, as though it occurred yesterday. It had a profound impact on my life.

We were medicine residents in those days, assigned to a three-man rheumatology service at the Mayo Clinic. The patients were both fascinating and challenging, given the myriad of disease they had, such as temporal arteritis and Wegener's granulomatosis. Our teaching attending had worked with Dr. Phil Hench, who had won the Nobel Prize for his clinical studies on corticosteroids, so rounds were a blend of practical clinical advice and historical reminiscences.

Creighton, a Midwesterner with hair the color of a Nebraska wheat field, had been bothered by a chronic sore throat, but in his usual way, didn't mention it to anyone. He did order a complete blood count on himself, as physicians sometimes do, and listed himself as the doctor to whom the results should be sent. To his shock and dismay, the white blood count exceeded 200,000/mm$^3$, with a marked left shift in the differential. He consulted a hematologist, a bone marrow was ordered, and the diagnosis of acute myelogenous leukemia was established. I have occasionally wondered why it happened to him, rather than to Dave (the other rheumatology resident) or to me. Our attending met with Dave and me in a small conference room. He said merely that Creighton was real sick, such that the two of us would

John Davis Cantwell, M.D.

have to divide up his patients and share his night call. Creighton continued to make rounds with us, even bringing in articles for discussion and sharing pearls that we would need when it came time to take our board examinations. We never discussed the specifics of his illness. When he was admitted to the hospital for short stays, to have platelet transfusions, I would stop in for brief visits. We talked only about the present, or the past, and never of the future. He commented about some of his symptoms and the clinical response to his chemotherapeutic agents, with the insights that only the afflicted can have. As Goethe once wrote, "From disease I have learned much which life could never have taught me in any other way."

I would occasionally see him on the streets of Rochester and wonder what he was up to, and what he was thinking. I noticed in the medical library that he had checked out several of the hematology texts. My wife and I invited him for dinner, and Dave gladly joined us, arranging for someone else to take call for several hours. Creighton reciprocated by inviting us to his apartment for dessert and to view his slides from an expedition to East Africa, telling us about the migration of the wildebeests, and of the predators, too.

We said good-bye at the Christmas break, casually, as the head priest did to the students in the movie, "Au Revior de les Enfants." I didn't know if I would ever see him again.

In early January he came back to the service, having fought off an upper respiratory infection most of his vacation time. He soon developed another, which progressed to pneumonia. I visited his room a time or two, but his dyspnea made it about impossible to converse. I felt most uncomfortable anyway, and didn't know what to say. His parents arrived, just about the time he was placed on a respirator.

I didn't go by to see him again - I just couldn't - but did inquire as to his status on a regular basis. I didn't seek out his parents. I should have.

Creighton died a week or so later. I wrote his parents, a nice letter telling them what a fine man he was and how much I had enjoyed working with him. They never replied, nor did I expect them to.

I have never forgotten Creighton, nor will I ever. The experience taught me several valuable lessons. First, I was impressed with how he chose to live out his brief life, after having been given a virtual death sentence back then. He didn't drop out of medicine, travel around the world or settle on a tropical island. Instead, he chose to continue the path he had selected, making ward rounds when he could, studying disease in others and himself, interacting with his peers in a positive way (and never in a maudlin one), and sharing what talents and experiences he had acquired in 30 years.

I learned from him how capricious life can be, and that none of us has a crystal ball in which we can see how long we have on Earth. I decided to squeeze life for all that I could, making use of each day, month and year, and hardly ever procrastinating. I have hiked the Inca Trail, visited Antarctica, seen the world's tallest mountain, and climbed into Hezekiah's tunnel. More importantly, I have tried to make time for my children, as they were growing up, coaching athletic teams and

*John Davis Cantwell, M.D.*

being present at piano recitals. I made up stories to tell them at bedtime, chased them through the house on my hands and knees pretending to be the Grinch, and playing games wherein we hid each other's slippers, sometimes in the cookie jar.

My remembrance of Creighton has also made me a better physician, especially when dealing with the critically ill and dying. Take Frank, for example. I have been his cardiologist, helping to guide his rehabilitation process after his heart attack, to the point where he was able to jog three miles at a time. Unfortunately, he subsequently developed pancreatic cancer, began to lose weight, and eventually was confined to his home.

He lived only several miles from me. On autumn weekends I would bicycle over to his house for a visit, admiring the burnt orange maple leaves and deep red dogwoods along the way. Sometimes we would talk about his disease but often it was about his World War II experiences, our mutual home state of Wisconsin, or the poetry of William Butler Yeats, which we both enjoyed. Occasionally we would just sit, and enjoy the comfort of silence together. I talked with his wife and children, and whomever else came by. They knew I cared - because I was there.

I was a young doctor when confronted with the challenge of dealing with Creighton's disease. I still have a lot to learn, but I am trying, stimulated by his memory, and how I didn't quite measure up to the task back then.

# 19

## GLOBAL ASPECTS OF CORONARY HEART DISEASE AND LONGEVITY

We recently had dinner with a delightful man from Eritrea, said to be 115 years old according to his youngest son. The father had made his first airplane trip to visit his son and felt that he was in paradise amid Atlanta's spring greenery. I asked him through an interpreter about the secrets to his long, healthy life. He had never smoked, drank only a low-alcohol beer, kept physically active in a mountainous terrain, ate low-fat meat, and lived one day at a time, with regular reading of the Bible.

Dr. Alexander Leaf recorded similar case studies during his two-year sabbatical to Soviet Georgia, Hunza, and South America. As others subsequently discovered, the ages of Dr. Leaf's subjects tended to be inflated. Nonetheless, the oldsters were remarkably vigorous and often free of cardiovascular diseases that are so prevalent in younger Americans.

An interest in fitness and longevity, along with global aspects of cardiovascular disease, have taken or will take me to the far corners of the Earth, from a Masai village to a Nepalese hospital, to a hotel in downtown Helsinki and a chateau in Bordeaux, and perhaps to a Tarahumara Indian cave in the Sierra Madre region of Mexico.

John Davis Cantwell, M.D.

## MASAILAND

Clinical coronary heart disease is virtually unknown among the Masai tribesmen of East Africa, despite a diet of meat, milk, occasional blood and sometimes even urine. While in Nairobi we visited the 1000-bed hospital and leafed through the diagnoses listed in the cardiac catheterization lab books. Those identified as Masai had rheumatic vascular heart disease, and cardiomyopathy, but I couldn't find one with coronary atherosclerotic disease.

Some feel that the Masai (see chapter 57) have low coronary risk because of their vigorous exercise habits, but I wasn't overly impressed with these, especially in the "elders" (those over age 26!). The Masai do walk a lot and are trim. Metabolic studies suggest that they suppress their bodies' production of cholesterol with a high-fat diet, unlike Americans. Cholesterol metabolism is complex. On the same high-fat diet, some will absorb less from the gut than others, have an elevated rate of disposal (as bile acids), and a reduced rate of cholesterol biosynthesis. Additional studies on the Masai, using new techniques of metabolic analysis, should help in furthering our understanding of their paucity of clinical atherosclerosis.

## A NEPALESE HOSPITAL

On the way back from Mt. Everest, Dr. John Griffin and I visited the small medical facility Sir Edmund Hillary built in the Himalayan village of Khunde. The physician, a New Zealander, asked my opinion about a middle-aged Sherpa who was complaining of chest pain. As if to read my mind, the physician said he knew one thing it wasn't, namely an acute myocardial infarction, because he had yet to see one in the Nepalese of his region. Sure enough, the patient subsequently produced some blood-streaked sputum, mentioned a recent injury to his leg, with apparent phlebitis, and the most likely diagnosis of pulmonary embolism was rendered.

One of the reasons the Sherpas are usually spared coronary disease is that they succumb to other disorders first. The average life span is probably less than 50. One woman we met was said to be 55, but looked 80. Accidents and trauma are common (one patient we saw had been clawed by a bear) and respiratory disease is prevalent, fostered by poorly ventilated, smoke-filled huts. Like the man from Eritrea, the Sherpas are trim and fit, trudging up and down the hilly terrain to fetch wood, water and food. Trekkers have done them no favors with gifts of cigarettes, however, and as the amenities of western civilization close in on them, coronary disease won't be far behind.

**FINLAND**

The Seven Countries Study identified Finland as the heart attack capitol of the world. I wanted to visit the region to personally observe the lifestyle, to sample the food, and to meet with Dr. Jaakko Tuomilehto, one of their top epidemiologists.

In Helsinki we roamed through the downtown area, observing the statue of Nurmi, the "flying Finn," near the Olympic stadium and the number of drunks sleeping in the parks. The food reminded me of my native state of

*John Davis Cantwell, M.D.*

Wisconsin, with a plentitude of cream, cheeses and rich desserts.

Regional differences occur within Finland as to mortality and morbidity of cardiovascular disease. The highest rates were found in the county of North Karelia. In 1972, comprehensive community programs in coronary risk factor reduction were implemented in North Karelia. The adjacent county of Kuopio served as a control. In a 10-year follow-up study, Tuomilehto and colleagues noted significant reductions in coronary risk factors in the intervention county when compared with the control county. Cardiovascular event rates likewise declined more.

There were no surprises in the risk factors observed in Finland. They mirror those in the United States, only more so. Physical activity levels didn't seem enough to override the impact of diet, cigarettes and hypertension, nor did alcoholism.

**BORDEAUX**

A national television program in July, 1992, and subsequent articles in newspapers and lay magazines suggested that the French may have fewer heart attacks than Americans because of their diet of red wine, cheese and foie gras. Claims were made that the wine might a) decrease blood clotting by altering platelet function, b) increase the good type of cholesterol, HDL, or c) lower the total cholesterol through the action of resveratrol, a chemical produced in the skin of the grapes to combat fungal disease.

The French indeed have lower heart attack rates than in the U.S., the second lowest rate, in fact, among industrialized nations (trailing only Japan). Their death rates from liver cirrhosis, however, more than double ours.

As observed during my hospital ward rounds with Bordeaux cardiologist, Dr. Jean-Paul Broustet, heart disease is certainly not uncommon in France; it is the major cause of death, as in the U.S. A lag factor might be involved in the French data. For example, even though they consume as much fat as Americans do, this has been a relatively recent phenomenon. If this trend continues, perhaps the coronary rates in France will increase as those in the U.S. continue to decline.

There are ample data to suggest that moderate amounts of alcohol (one to two drinks per day) are associated with lower cardiovascular events and with elevated HDL levels. As for resveratrol, one can get it from grape juice and avoid the many problems associated with alcohol abuse.

While awaiting the final word from ongoing research on the "French paradox," my wife and I toasted Dr. and Mrs. Broustet with a 1986 vintage at beautiful Chateau d'Issan, sampled the pate, and hoped for the moment that maybe the combination did indeed have medicinal values.

**THE TARAHUMARAS**

The Tarahunara Indians live in the Copper Canyon area of North Central Mexico. I have made plans on several occasions to visit them but had to defer, once because my mother was ill with a stoke and another because Aeromexico went bankrupt. Living at elevations of up to 7000 feet, Tarahumaras nevertheless

*John Davis Cantwell, M.D.*

run races of over 100 miles, kicking a small wooden ball as they go. One of their hunting techniques is to run after a deer until the latter becomes exhausted. In the Mexico City Olympics, two Indians participated in the marathon: "They lost badly, complaining about the weeniness of the distance and the fact that they were required to wear shoes."

The HDL cholesterol levels of the Tarahumaras are low (mean of 25 mg/dl), rather surprising in view of their running habits and their penchant for spending "an estimated one hundred days a year preparing, drinking and recuperating from the effects of tesgüino (corn beer)." Their diet is varied and includes "wolves, rats, catfish, eels, flies, grasshoppers, worms, toads, lizards, rattlesnakes, juniper berries, wood fungi, cactus fruit, catkins, 39 kinds of wild weeds and 13 varieties of roots."

In a recent study, researchers at the University of Oregon fed 13 Tarahumaras their traditional diet for a week and then a diet typical of affluent societies for five weeks. This caused the blood cholesterol levels to increase by 39 percent and the triglycerides by 18 percent. Since the HDL also rose, the ratio of LDL to HDL changed very little. The authors concluded that if the different diets were to continue, the risk of coronary heart disease in the Tarahumaras might increase. In view of the HDL rise, however, this is only speculative.

Schultheis reminds us that it would be a mistake to romanticize the Tarahumaras:

"Their lives are hard, harder than we can imagine. Their heartland is crumpled and corrugated till there is hardly enough flat space to lie down… Their shanties are full of smoke; their dwarf corn is shot full of worms; their tesgüino gives them dysentery. When they are sober they are gloomy; when they are drunk - which is most of the time - they argue, fight and seduce other men's wives."

"Hard lives, hard deaths. I would not want to be a Tarahumara."

**SUMMARY**

Global aspects of coronary heart disease and longevity are interesting to consider but difficult to study. Birth dates in remote areas of the world, as Dr. Alexander Leaf discovered, are hard to come by. As seen in the Tarahumara Indians, so many factors need to be considered that even multivariate analyses seem inadequate.

In the meantime, common sense, and considerable data, tells us to avoid tobacco, exercise regularly, use alcohol in moderation, keep dietary fat low and fiber high, stay trim, and to work at simplifying our lives rather than making them overly complex. We would do well to emulate the Mediterranean lifestyle, both in diet and an enjoyment of our fellow beings. My friend from Eritrea would agree, I'm sure, that we should take our religion seriously, live life, as Osler said, in 24-hour compartments, and not worry about tomorrow.

*John Davis Cantwell, M.D.*

# 20

## HIPPOCRATES REVISITED

Hippocrates, a contemporary of Socrates, was born around 460 B.C. His father was a physician who most likely practiced at the Asklepieion, the Health Temple of Cos. The latter, excavated in 1904 and located outside the town of Cos, was both a diagnostic and treatment center and also a shrine to Asklepias, the Greek god of healing and the son of Apollo.

Hippocrates is mentioned by both Plato and Aristotle. He traveled widely, in Thrace, Thessaly and Macedonia and other sites, espousing new concepts in medical practice that helped divorce the profession from the "superstitions and vagaries" of the Asklepian cult. He emphasized the importance of learning by direct observation and experience and was opposed to those whose opinions were unsubstantiated.

The plane tree of Hippocrates is on the Greek island of Cos. Forty-five feet in circumference, with limbs at least two feet in diameter, it has endured for over two millennia, as have many of the concepts attributed to the man who taught medical students under the shade of its branches.

Most of the Hippocratic writings were composed between 430 and 330 B.C. It is difficult to know for sure which are genuine works of Hippocrates himself or of his followers. The writings are important for at least three reasons:

1) They provide an ethical ideal of the physician
2) They allow insights as to the "original development of rational medicine in the West"
3) They have had an influence on medical thought that has existed for hundreds of years.

Some of my favorite aphorisms are as follows:

- "Life is short, the art long; opportunity is fleeting, experiment is dangerous, judgement is difficult."
- "In the case of athletes, too good a condition of health is treacherous if it be an extreme state."
- "The undernourished do not bear an illness so well as the well-nourished."
- "Desperate cases need the most desperate remedies."
- "Never prescribe drugs until you have made a thorough examination of the patient."
- "A woman is never ambidextrous." (I question this. A friend of my daughter's was a switch hitter in softball).
- "The art consists in three things - the disease, the patient and the physician. The physician is the servant of the art, and the patient must combat the disease along with the physician."
- "All part of the body that have a function, if used in moderation and exercised in labours in which each is accustomed, become thereby healthy, well-developed and age more slowly, but if unused and left idle they become liable

*John Davis Cantwell, M.D.*

> *to disease, defective in growth and age quickly."*
> - *"Sometimes give your services for nothing, calling to mind a previous benefaction or present satisfaction. And if there be an opportunity of serving one who is a stranger in financial straits, give full assistance to all such. For where there is love of man, there is also love of the art."*
> - *"The physician must have two special objects in view with regard to diseases, namely, to do good or to do no harm."*

I have taken the liberty to modify the Hippocratic Oath, with some trepidation, as one might have in altering aspects of the Ten Commandments. The alterations were made for the following reasons:

1) I don't swear by the Greek god, Apollo.
2) Daughters also might wish to learn the art of medicine.
3) Cutting persons "under the stone" needs amplification. (It applies to any procedure which one isn't qualified to do.)

The only real controversial part of the oath concerns abortion. The "pro life" versus "pro choice" debate is likely to persist.

Hippocrates died about 375 B.C., at the age of 65. He had a profound effect on the practice of medicine, and continues to influence our behavior even today.

## MODERN HIPPOCRATIC OATH

I swear by God, the ultimate healer, that, according to my ability and judgment, I will keep this oath and this stipulation - to hold my medical teachers in high regard, help them if they are in need, and to help their children likewise if in need, to look upon them as my own, teaching them this art, if they shall wish to learn it, without fee of stipulation; and that by precept, lecture and every other mode of instruction, I will impart a knowledge of my art to my own children, and those of my teachers, and to disciples bound by a stipulation and oath according to the law of medicine, but to none others. I will follow that system of regimen which, according to my ability and judgment, I consider for the benefit of my patients, and abstain from whatever is deleterious and mischievous.

I will give no deadly medicine to anyone if asked, nor suggest any such counsel; and in like manner I will not give medicine for abortions, or do abortions, unless the life and/or well being of the mother is at stake.

With purity and with holiness I will pass my life and practice my art.

In dealing with patients who need procedures for medical problems outside my expertise, I will refer them to proper subspecialists.

Into whatever facility I enter I will go into it for the benefit of the sick or in the hopes of preventing or delaying disease, and will abstain from every voluntary act of mischief and corruption or from any sexual liaison with a patient. Whatever, in connection with my professional practice, or not in connection with it, I see or hear, in the life of men and women, which ought not to

*John Davis Cantwell, M.D.*

be spoken of to others, I will not divulge, because all such things should be kept secret.

While I continue to keep this Oath inviolated, may it be granted to me to enjoy life and the practice of the art, respected by all men and women, in all times! But should I trespass and violate this Oath, may the reverse be my lot!

# 21

## AN EXPLOSION IN CENTENNIAL OLYMPIC PARK

**Preface**

Knowing that the Olympic medical experience would be a unique one, I decided to keep a journal during my one-month stay at the Olympic Family Hotel, the Marriott Marquis. Accordingly, I packed an ample supply of note cards, in addition to Montaigne's *Essays*, the *Bible*, and Mark Twain's *Autobiography*.

Some of the journal entries are confidential, a record perhaps for a future generation; other notations are mundane but reflect the scope of issues I was confronted with. The most dramatic entry was on July 27th, when a bomb exploded in the park and changed the whole complexion of the Games.

**July 27, 1996**

Our evening International Olympic Committee Medical Commission (IOC-MC) meeting lasted over three hours. A Russian athlete had been caught taking a non-formulary drug, Bromantan, also used by the Russian army. The Russians claim that the drug is an "immunostimulant" and helps counter the effects of heat. Data we had, from Russian medical abstracts, suggested that the agent might also be a psychostimulant and might mask the detection of certain anabolic steroids, such as epitestosterone. We were to continue the discussion the next evening.

*John Davis Cantwell, M.D.*

I went to bed around 1:15 a.m., exhausted, only to be awakened by numerous ambulance sirens. I turned on my cellular phone so I could be reached if necessary by someone who might not have the Marriott Marquis phone number.

Almost immediately, my phone rang. I was to call Dr. Gwynne Brunt, medical officer on duty in our Command Center, right away.

I reached for a pen and pad of paper, to make notes of Gwynne's comments, but dropped the pen after he said "explosion in Centennial Park."

I threw on some clothes and went dashing out of the hotel, passing Dr. Patrick Schamasch (Medical Director of the IOC-MC) en route and giving him a quick update on what had transpired. He asked me to keep in touch with him throughout the night, as he would be advising IOC President Juan Antonio Samaranch.

My first inclination was to swing by the park on my way to the ACOG Command Center in the Inforum (four blocks from my hotel), to personally survey the damage. My cell phone range again, however, and it was Elizabeth Martin, Director of ACOG's Medical Services, pleading with me to go straight to the Command Center as our protocol directed.

Near the Inforum I identified myself to the police and security officers and told them where I needed to go. They advised me to hop in a van, which was waiting to enter the Inforum parking lot, and I was surprised to see ACOG President Billy Payne in the front seat. We didn't say very much to each other as neither of us knew the extent of the damage. The latter became apparent as we looked down at the park from Payne's private balcony, and saw that the area with injured spectators occupied only a small portion of the park. One body was covered up. A number of ambulances were lined up in a very orderly fashion, to rush the stretcher cases to nearby hospitals.

In the ACOG Command Center, large video screens enabled me to observe the happenings in the park and to follow the commentary of NBC's Tom Brokaw and local television stations. I started making contact with the Olympic Ring hospital emergency rooms, and with an ACOG employee, Scott Mall, who was in the park. Within the next hour it became evident that there were two deaths and about 100 other injuries from shrapnel. I relayed this information at regular intervals to Dr. Schamasch and to ACOG officials. Elizabeth Martin, who arrived at the Command Center shortly after I did, helped me record the names of the victims, as an ACOG secretary was worried about her son who had been in the park that evening. We reassured her that her son was okay, and sent work to President Samaranch, through Dr. Schamasch, that no athlete or IOC members were among the injured.

Richard Babb, R.N. and paramedic, was part of the 11 person (including one physician) medical team on duty at the park during the explosion. In my debriefing with him on July 29th, I asked him to record his impressions. He wrote as follows:

> "At approximately 1:15 a.m. this large explosion, that I can only describe as (like) a cannon going off, occurred. For about 2-3 seconds everyone looked at each other with that confused look and asked 'what was that?' Then it registered that something was wrong. I immediately told Barbara Riggs, the on-duty venue

117

*John Davis Cantwell, M.D.*

> administrator, that I was going to the scene to evaluate the situation.
> Within one minute of the explosion, I got to the scene to find 75 to 100 people lying on the ground, with even more people taking care of them. My mobile teams of EMTs were already on the scene, taking care of the people with injuries.
> After about 30 seconds of surveying the scene and realizing that no one was taking command from a medical point of view, I called into the main medical (command) station to tell them to call for ambulances."

Richard Babb and his team did as they were trained to do in a level 3 disaster, namely to evacuate the walking wounded (in the event of another bomb), identify the deceased, and expedite ambulance removal of the stretcher cases.

About 30 ambulances responded to the call. Within 35 minutes, the park was cleared of all individuals who needed medical care. Area hospitals activated their disaster plans and called in additional man (and woman) power.

One hundred and eleven individuals were eventually seen at 11 area hospitals, Georgia Baptist Medical Center saw the most, 44, and admitted five, including the daughter of Alice Hawthorne, who was killed by the explosion. Grady Memorial Hospital saw 33 cases and admitted 21, so they obviously received more seriously wounded patients. Piedmont Hospital and Crawford W. Long, other hospitals in the Olympic Ring, saw 15 and 5 patients respectively. I stayed at the Command Center until 6:30 a.m., at which time we had a debriefing with A.D. Frazier, ACOGs chief operating officer. I then headed back to the hotel, to eat breakfast, to attend the daily IOC-ACOG coordination committee meeting, and prepare for the day's work.

The Games would go on. Flags were at half-mast for a day. Athletes had moments of silence in memory of the victims. Medical volunteers donned their red polo shirts and headed back to work.

I returned to the park for the reopening ceremony, heard Andrew Young's inspiring words, noted the bouquets of flowers scattered about the base of the AT&T edifice (where the bomb had been placed), and saw the children once again at play in the fountains. I was looking for a short stocky AT&T guard, known only by our medical team as "Richard," to thank him for his good work in evacuating the building, probably saving additional lives and preventing further injuries. Another guard gave me his full name, told me he would not be on duty until 6 p.m. that evening, and had me leave my card, and cell phone number, in case he showed up earlier.

That afternoon I turned on the news, and knew that Richard wouldn't be calling anytime soon.

**Afterward**

Several days after the games, I walked into the Atlanta Braves' clubhouse, as the physician on duty that night. A player rushed up and asked if I'd "had a blast" at the Olympics. Without thinking, I said I did, after which he danced away, shouting to anyone within range, "He did it! He did it! He confessed!"

*John Davis Cantwell, M.D.*

Once again I had been victimized by locker room hijinks.

# 22

## THE HORSE AND BUGGY DOCTOR

It was one of the most unusual memos that has appeared on my desk: "Dr. Cantwell - Call Oliver Koonz at 872-1188. He used to live with your grandfather." Surely there was some mistake. My grandfather died in 1938, at age 80, two years before I was born.

I returned the call and learned that the message was correct. It was from Dr. Koonz, a dentist now in his 80s, who had come to live with my grandparents when he was 14. In exchange for room and board he had driven my grandfather on housecalls in a model T.

Our telephone conversation was too brief. Dr. Koonz was just passing through Atlanta, and I had an appointment I needed to keep. We exchanged addresses and I asked him to please write and tell me some things about a man I greatly admired, but never knew. Several weeks later his letter arrived as promised.

My grandfather was the youngest son of an Irish farmer who had immigrated to America from Tipperary because of the potato famine. Grandfather taught grade school for two years and then became a pharmacist (and the town postmaster). He did the latter for six years, saved some money, and entered Rush Medical School in Chicago, graduating in 1887.

### THE ERA

To my knowledge, Grandfather never wrote about any of his medical experiences. Many of his 50 years of medical practice were in the

*John Davis Cantwell, M.D.*

**My Grandfather, William H. Cantwell, M.D.**

era depicted by Hertzler in his 1938 medical classic, **The Horse and Buggy Doctor**. I got a better feel for what my grandfather must have experienced - indeed, I could almost imagine his voice - by noting a number of Dr. Hertzler's observations, including the following:

- "Expectant treatment...is treatment which one does not ever expect to be efficient. The doctor employing (it) has only the satisfaction of knowing that he is doing nothing injurious - a merit, it may be added, that is today sometimes overlooked."
- "It is not the dying but the living who suffer."
- "At least three-fourths of the knowledge therein asked for (on the National Boards) is useless as far as the practice of the healing art is concerned."
- "By the time a doctor reaches (age 70) his mind is so full of tragic memories that the limit of endurance is just about reached. He forgets his successes, as things normally expected of him; but the tragedies, like Banquo's ghost, will not down (disappear easily)."
- "A speed of seven miles an hour was good time for a team (of horses)" on a housecall. "In muddy roads, when the horse cannot exceed a walk, three miles an hour is average time."
- "As I look over the old casebooks, I wonder now just how much good I did. Certainly the medicines I dispensed were merely symbols of good intentions...Many of these families are still grateful. That close contact made the closest of

## John Davis Cantwell, M.D.

friends. I sometimes think I would like to end my medical career amongst these intimate contacts."
- "With the coming of the automobile, new problems presented themselves to the country doctor. For a number of years they were too expensive and too unreliable to make them practical for the doctor's country driving."
- "It was this silent faithfulness of the old doctor in the hour of grief that endeared him to the families that he served. The old country doctor was a man of few words because there were no words."
- "…the satisfaction one gets out of life is measured by the efforts one exerts in achieving a worthy end, not in the actual achievement…As I battled the elements to reach my patients, I had the greatest personal satisfaction in my achievements."
- "Whiskers indicated maturity and most young doctors attempted to emulate their elders in the hirsute adornment, with the result that they made themselves ridiculous instead of venerable."
- "A case seldom turned out to be as serious as represented by the messenger."
- "My father (a farmer) asked me to promise never to refuse to attend a sick person, whether he could or would pay or not…I have kept the faith; that is, almost. I have always refused to attend a drunk with a headache."

- "Malpractice suits...are dependent on the presence of a lawyer in a state of malnutrition, and have no relation whatever to the acts of the doctor. The doctors of that day were tried at the quilting bees of the community, not in courts of law."
- "Ignorance sometimes saves the doctor from doing foolish things."
- "No one who knows women as well as the family doctor ever calls them the weaker sex."
- The doctor "...is sometimes praised for doing nothing and often condemned for failures that are inevitable, despite the fact that his measures are both correct and timely. There is one consoling thought: it is generally the ignorant who condemn the doctor. Intelligent people give him credit for doing his best."
- "When one is confronted by a five-hundred-dollar necklace encircling a forty-cent face he may know that he is up against a real problem."
- "No one understands so well as the family doctor that a great part of human suffering is not due to organic disease. Really, the sufferings caused by disease are for the most part of short duration...The suffering of grief, whether it be due to circumstances beyond the individual's control, or if it be superimposed, endures throughout the years. In the passing of the old family doctor these patients have lost their best friend, and their chief protector."

*John Davis Cantwell, M.D.*

**THE MAN**

With a better understanding of the era my grandfather lived in, I could now focus on the man. What was he like: How did he manage to cope with the rigors of a half-century of medical practice, in often difficult times?

"He was Irish," wrote Dr. Koonz, "tall and handsome, a dapper dresser. You never had to wonder as to what his thoughts were."

I recall stories about him. He disliked hypocrites almost as much as busybodies. Once, after completing a housecall, he was cornered by a nosy neighbor who demanded to know what was wrong. Drawing her close, as if to whisper a secret diagnosis in her ear, he shouted - "She's sick!" - and abruptly departed. He once kicked a chair over and marched out of a funeral of an old friend when the minister droned on and on ad nauseam.

We shared an enjoyment of poetry, and of athletics. Regarding the former, I treasure books of poems by Owen Meredith, William Cullen Bryant and Henry Wadsworth Longfellow which had belonged to him and were given to me by my grandmother. As for sports, Dr. Koonz emphasized how Grandfather loved football, basketball, and especially baseball, my own favorites. He managed the local baseball team one summer in 1888. I have a picture of that team, along with the gold-headed cane the players gave him after the season. Grandfather never missed the state basketball tournament, according to Dr. Koonz, and undoubtedly would have enjoyed seeing his grandson perform in three such events.

I didn't realize that he had gastric ulcers. Because of these, Dr. Koonz related, my grandfather gave up chewing tobacco, smelly cigars and nipping on a bottle of brandy that he kept in his office: "The can of chewing tobacco, the cigars, and the brandy stayed on the table of his inner office. He said to himself, 'there they are! If you are damn fool enough to use them, go ahead!' He never broke down, and didn't have much sympathy for the person who said he couldn't (do something)."

After 50 years of practice the community wanted to honor him with a surprise party, inviting among other all the "babies" he had delivered through the years. He got wind of the affair, and did not want to attend, for he was a modest man who felt that he had only done his job. Like Doc Pritham (**The Big-Little World of Doc Pritham**) he "accepted a doctor's duty for exactly that, a duty to be performed, without unnecessary emotion or spiritual dedication, certainly without fanfare. It was just a man's job to do the best he knew how." Grandfather's physician-sons reasoned with him and he finally agreed to attend, staying until the last guest had departed and loving every minute of it. A picture of the occasion adorns the wall of my medical office.

I returned from a visit to my hometown in Wisconsin, mainly to visit my mother, then 88 years old, who was in a nursing home; and my two brothers, one a surgeon and the other a pharmacist. I brought back my grandfather's medical bag, which had been in a tackroom on a farm our family owns. The medical bag is durable, as my grandfather was. Inside are a few samples of drugs that I still use today - digitalis, quinidine sulfate, nitroglycerin. The handle is smooth, from years of use. Sometimes I like to slip my own hand in that handle, and think about my grandfather. He was

*John Davis Cantwell, M.D.*

the first of four generations of physicians in our family, the patriarch.

The yellowed newspaper clipping of his 50 years in practice celebration closed with this fitting tribute:

> *"When a man has given the best years of his life to humanity he carves for himself a lasting monument in the heart of the community he has served. The people turn with admiration and respect to 'the doctor,' remembering his sacrifices, his understanding, his genuine sympathy, his kindness and his charities."*

Grandfather died within a year of the community celebration. On his tombstone an appropriate inscription would read "Above all else, the crown of a good name." His grandsons (including two physicians and a pharmacist) and great-grandchildren (including an internist and a nurse) will carry on the tradition he began.

# 23

## CARDIOVASCULAR MILESTONES IN THE 1900s

Sir William H. Broadbent had completed a distinguished career in 1900 when he published (with his son, John) the third edition of *Heart Disease*. A consulting physician to London's St. Mary's Hospital, Broadbent was also "physician extraordinary" to the Queen of England.

In perusing his textbook a century later, one is struck by the tremendous advances that have taken place in the field of cardiovascular disease since.

For example, no mention was made of the ECG. It was not until 1901 before a Dutch physiologist, Willem Einthoven, reported the technique, for which he received the Nobel Prize on 1924.

The terms "blood pressure" and "hypertension" are not listed in the book's index, for the auscultation method of determining systolic and diastolic blood pressure was not reported until 1905, by a Russian surgeon, Nicolai Korotkoff. The latter received so little credit for his accomplishment that when his son subsequently learned the technique in medical school he was unaware that the one who had already discovered this was his father. A vast array of effective drugs are now available to treat this disorder, a marked and gradual change over the past 25 years. The etiology remains elusive even today. "Heart attacks," "myocardial infarction," and "coronary thrombosis" were not mentioned in 1900. The concept of thrombotic occlusion of a coronary artery was reported by James Herrick, M.D., in 1912, and did not become widely known until over two decades later. Even in the 1970s, some respected authorities felt that the clot was a secondary event, until De Wood et al proved otherwise.

The concept of exercise stress testing did not develop until the late 1920s, when Fiel and Siegel checked the ECG after situp activity, and Felberbaum, Finesilver and Master did so in conjunction with step exercise. Bruce and others popularized treadmill testing, which is commonplace today in the U.S. Cycle ergometry testing is prevalent in certain European countries.

Cardiac catheterization as a diagnostic tool was unknown to Broadbent. In 1929, a German surgical resident, Werner Forssmann, performed his self experiment, after duping the operating room nurse, and eventually received the Nobel Prize in 1956 for his discovery.

In 1900, treatment of bacterial endocarditis was futile: "Various drugs have been tried without success. Salicylates were worse than useless…General tonics…do no appreciably affect the course of the disease." Alexander Fleming, Howard Flory and E.B. Chain changed the prognosis with the discovery of penicillin, which impacted other cardiac disorders, mainly rheumatic fever. Physician Fleming and biochemists Flory and Chain shared the Nobel Prize in 1945. In Broadbent's day, the prognosis of cyanotic congenital heart disease was poor. That changed in 1944, when surgeon Alfred Blalock and pediatrician Helen Taussig developed the "blue baby" operation, attaching the subclavian artery to the pulmonary artery to improve suboptimal pulmonary blood flow.

Without electrocardiography, ventricular fibrillation was not know as a common mechanism of sudden death in 1900. Surgeon Claude Beck first deployed open chest defibrillation in 1947 to a young patient. The concept of cardiopulmonary resuscitation was advanced in 1960, thanks to the efforts of William Kouwenhoven et al. Closed chest defibrillation was first used by Dr. Paul Zoll in 1956. Mobile defibrillation (using a converted ambulance) was developed in Belfast, Northern Ireland, by Frank Pantridge et al in 1966. The implantable defibrillator became available in 1980 and its effectiveness demonstrated by Arthur Moss et al. Lown developed cardioversion in 1961.

Mitral stenosis was treated with "mercurial purgatives," "strychnia and iron," digitalis, venesection, nitroglycerin, quinine and "nux vomica" in 1900. Eliot Cutler was unsuccessful with mitral commissurotomy in the 1920s, but Charles Bailey and Dwight Harken independently performed successful operations in 1948.

Syncopal episodes were mentioned by Broadbent, mainly in association with valve rupture and endocarditis and with aortic regurgitation. The first permanent external pacemaker was used in 1958 by inventor Rune Elmqvist and surgeon Ake Senning on a man with Stokes-Adams syncopal attacks. Although the concept of gene therapy for various cardiovascular disorders is new, it dates back to 1953 when James Watson and Francis Crick discovered the structure of DNA, the building block of genes. Working together in a "shabby shack sandwiched between the imposing academic buildings on the flower- bordered lawns of

*John Davis Cantwell, M.D.*

Cambridge," the two uncovered the structure of the substance which carries life's hereditary information, for which they received the Nobel Prize in 1962.

Three major advances occurred a half century after Broadbent's day. In 1953, John H. Gibbons, Jr., developed cardiopulmonary bypass, leading to the rapid development of open heart surgery less than a decade later. Echocardiography became available in 1954, due to the combined talents of Sweden's Helmuth Hertz (a physicist) and Inge Edler (a cardiologist). Four years later, F. Mason Sones, at the Cleveland Clinic, photographed the accidental injection of contrast media into the right coronary artery of a young man with postrheumatic valvular heart disease, leading to the development of coronary angiography.

The first viable prosthetic heart valve in 1960 reflected the combined talents of surgeon Albert Starr and electrical engineer, Lowell Edwards. Early prototypes of the valve were manufactured in the small workshed of Edwards' cabin, near Mt. Hood. The first patient only lived 10 hours postoperatively, but the second recipient survived 15 years, dying after a fall from a ladder. Broadbent recommended exercise therapy for certain types of heart disease, primarily valvular, citing the program of Germany's Oertel. The latter used terrain hiking above an elevation of 2000 feet, wherein "the patient is required to walk a certain distance up a gentle ascent each day, the distance and pace being gradually increased." More formal cardiac rehabilitation programs in the U.S. evolved in the 1960s, promoted by Cleveland's Herman Hellerstein, et al.

Availability of the heart-lung machine and coronary angiography opened the door for aortocoronary bypass surgery. The first successful aortocoronary saphenous vein bypass graft was done by Michael De Bakey's group in Houston in 1964, but not reported until the 1970s. Favaloro et al in Cleveland reported the first case and rapidly advanced the technique in the late 1960s.

James Black, an academic and industrial pharmacologist from London, became aware of alpha and ß-adrenergic receptors through the work of Ray Alquist at the Medical College of Georgia. In 1964, Black developed the first ß-receptor blocker, propranolol, a multipurpose drug that was subsequently used to treat ischemic heart disease, arrhythmias, hypertension, and entities, such as performance anxiety. Black subsequently developed the histamine $H_2$ receptor antagonist, cimetidine HCL (Tagamet[R]) and was rewarded with the Nobel Prize in 1988 with subsequent knighthood.

CCUs were advanced in the early 1960s, reflecting the early work by Hughes Day, who opened the first such unit in Kansas City in 1962.

Broadbent does not mention the midsystolic click or the click-mid to late systolic murmur but others had attributed the click to post pericarditis or to extra cardiac sources. In 1963, John Barlow's group from Johannesburg, South Africa, clearly showed that the click-murmur reflected prolapse of the mitral valve, now known to be the most common cardiac valvular condition in the world, affecting 2% of the population in certain countries.

The first cardiac transplant was performed by another South African, Christiaan Barnard,

John Davis Cantwell, M.D.

in 1967. The first patient, Lewis Washkansky, died of pneumonia 18 days postoperatively but "lived long enough to begin a new life. He opened the way for others." Today over 50,000 such operations have been done worldwide with an 8.7 year survival rate of around 50%.

In the early 1970s, nuclear scans of the heart were reported by H. W. Strauss, Barry Zaret and others, using radio labeled substances, such as thallium and technetium. Dual isotope scans are commonplace for today's cardiologist, as is the combination of echocardiography with exercise testing and the use of adenosine, dobutamine and dipyridamole in subjects unable to undergo the stress of exercise.

Although Sol Sherry had first reported use of streptokinase for patients with acute myocardial infarctions in 1958, progress was delayed because of concerns over adverse immune reactions and drug-associated fever. Russian cardiologist, Evengy Chazov, began using intracoronary streptokinase in 1976. Peter Rentrop promoted its use in Germany in 1979. The concept gained additional credibility after De Wood demonstrated the high prevalence of an occlusive clot in the involved coronary artery early post myocardial infarction.

Building upon earlier work by Dotter and Zeitler, Andreas Gruentzig began making prototypes of a balloon catheter in his kitchen in 1972, and performed the first coronary angioplasty in 1977, in Zurich. The technique spawned the advent of advances such as atherectomy and the use of stents.

The word "cholesterol" is not mentioned in the Broadbent index, yet is a household word today. In 1985, Texans Michael Brown and Joe

Goldstein won the Nobel Prize for their work on low density lipoprotein receptors, leading to the development of potent drugs, the statins, which have markedly improved the prognosis in patients with dyslipidemia.

One of the most dramatic public health achievements in this past century has been the 60% decline in age adjusted death rates from cardiovascular disease since 1950. In addition to the decrease in the mean blood cholesterol and blood pressure levels in the U.S. population, the decline in cigarette smoking, the emphasis in physical training and the overall improvement in cardiovascular medical care have all been contributing factors.

Automatic external defibrillators, products of the 1990s, are now commonplace on airlines and are being positioned in targeted areas ranging from casinos to athletic stadiums and large office buildings.

The external beam computed tomography (EBCT) scan was first used by S. R. Tanenbaum and associates in 1989, to detect calcium deposits in coronary arteries. The first large clinical series was reported by Arthur Agatston in 1992. A very promising noninvasive technique, the EBCT scan has its advocates and detractors. Longitudinal studies should help clarify its clinical usefulness.

As we progress into the new millennium, a variety of new modalities are being assessed, ranging from therapeutic angiogenesis to percutaneous myocardial revascularization. Identification of the vulnerable plaque, repair of genetic defects, application of the techniques, such as magnetic resonance imaging, and searching for the etiology of hypertension are among the gamut of possibilities.

*John Davis Cantwell, M.D.*

Given the dramatic advances in the past century, one can barely imagine what a cardiologist might write in 2100 AD, using Topol's textbook of cardiovascular medicine as the state-of-the- art source in 2000.

As for Dr. Broadbent, Sir William lived seven more years after the third edition of his textbook was published, dying of pneumonia and empyema in 1907. In spite of the great success he achieved, and the many honors bestowed upon him "...he remained always the same cheery, simple unaffected man that some of us first knew more than 40 years ago." His son John became dean of the medical school at St. Mary's Hospital, where "his wealth of clinical experience and his easy accessibility, together with his North Country honesty and loyalty, were appreciated by those in close contact with him."

# 24

## APRIL AND MURRAY

Her name was April Jones. She was 17, with coal black hair, as pretty as she could be. Murray was in his late 40s, a little overweight, brilliant, a bit of a wise guy, a character in other words. The latter made him atypical of attending physicians at the Mayo Clinic, who tended to be pretty conservative, apropos to their Midwestern locale.

April's and Murray's worlds intersected when she was admitted to the Hematology-Oncology service at Rochester, Minnesota's St. Mary's Hospital. I was the resident on duty.

April had acute myelogenous leukemia, a death sentence back then, usually in three to six months. The disease had already claimed one of my fellow residents, presenting as a flu-like illness and then running rampant through his hematopoietic system, wiping out blood platelets and white blood cells and rendering him defenseless to life-threatening infections.

Before I went in to meet April to do her admission history and physical examination, I was called aside and told that her parents didn't want her to know the diagnosis. The Mayo Clinic frowned on this type of subterfuge, preferring an open, truthful approach to medical care, but April's parents had insisted.

On our first attending rounds, Murray stood at the foot of April's bed, listening to my presentation of symptoms and signs without mentioning the "L" word. When I finished, he

John Davis Cantwell, M.D.

looked her in the eye and said, "April, you're beautiful. You look just like Peggy Fleming" (who had just won an Olympic gold medal in figure skating). She smiled, shyly, but didn't say anything.

Her parents were always in the room when our rounding team would come by. They would sometimes ask how their "naughty thing" was coming along and how much longer she would need to be in the hospital. April never asked any questions. We were careful with our choice of words. She knew the truth, I felt sure, but played along with her parents' little charade.

April was still in the hospital when my rotation came to an end, and I moved on to another service at Methodist Hospital. I said goodbye, and wished her well. She thanked me and smiled. She really did look like Peggy Fleming, I thought.

I lost touch with her. Thirty years passed quickly. My son, Ryan, was now a medical resident at Mayo. Murray was still on the teaching staff.

I asked Ryan to introduce himself to Murray. I was sure that he would remember me, or so I hoped. He did, and immediately began teasing Ryan that he was a much better resident than I ever was.

I gave Ryan the name - April Jones - and wanted him to ask Murray about her, to see if he remembered her as vividly as I did, and to get some follow-up. Before Ryan could do so, Murray died suddenly and unexpectedly, the victim of probable ventricular fibrillation in the setting of severe asymptomatic coronary disease. Ryan sent me his obituary. I noticed that he had been voted the Internal Medicine Teacher of the Year Award so many times that they finally inducted him into the Teacher

Hall of Fame, a fitting epitaph for a remarkable man and physician. I thought of Murray and April just the other day, when I was reading a poem in the new book, <u>Blood and Bones</u>, a compilation of poetic works by various physicians, including Atlanta's John Stone, M.D.

One of the poems, "Candor," by John Graham-Pole, deals with a more direct approach to a child with cancer. Joe is eight years old, "his cancer is running rampage." His mother has enjoined the doctor to be "square with him."

After beating around the bush a bit, the physician says, "Joey, you're going to go to heaven." His words were "lost in (the boy's) howl like a wolf's." "Whatever else was right to do, this wasn't it," thinks the doctor. But after a few minutes of tears "on cheeks of mom, dad, nurse and me," Joey:

> "determines he's grieved enough. Time to lighten up, knowing me at other times a joker, a wearer of odd socks, funny noses, he spies memos, charts, photocopies, journals - jetsam of an urgent life - scattering my carpet, and becomes the stand-up comic, offering his own joke, 'didn't your mom tell you to pick up after yourself?'"

A candid approach, or an ostrich approach, which is correct? As difficult as it was for the physician, the family and for Joey, I prefer the former approach. You can tell the truth or as Emily Dickinson wrote, you can also soften the blow by "telling it slant," offering a ray of hope for the patient to cling to.

*John Davis Cantwell, M.D.*

# 25

## Why Cows Walk Backwards: Reflections on J. Willis Hurst, M.D.

After a year of cardiology fellowship under Eugene Braunwald in San Diego, I came to Atlanta in the Public Health Service, assigned to the Atlanta Federal Penitentiary. Desirous of continued academic stimulation, I began attending Dr. J. Willis Hurst's late Wednesday afternoon case conferences at Grady Memorial Hospital.

Dr. Hurst asked the audience what diagnosis was likely if they saw a cow walking backwards. Nobody knew. "Pericarditis," he said. The cow might have swallowed some metallic object or a piece of barbed wire that eroded through the esophagus and was irritating the pericardium. As with a human, who leans forward for pain relief, the cow would walk backwards.

The audience chuckled, apparently in disbelief. The next week a speaker phone was rigged up so that Dr. Hurst could confer with the veterinarian at the University of Georgia, who confirmed the likely diagnosis. Nobody laughed.

In another session Dr. Hurst emphasized the importance of auscultating over scars, especially in patients with unexplained congestive heart failure, looking for arteriovenous fistulae (abnormal connection between the artery and vein) which could be the underlying cause. The very next day I saw a patient on sick call, with symptoms and signs of heart failure, and a surgical scar on his upper leg from an old compound fracture. I listened over the scar and heard the typical, continuous bruit of a fistula. I have only detected one other since, but always search for it.

**With J. Willis Hurst, M.D.**

Dr. Hurst was an intimidating force, demanding excellence in medical care. Sometimes I even dreamed about him, cajoling me to upgrade my medical problem list on a patient or to palpate the thyroid very carefully, to detect a small nodule I had missed. Occasionally I would hide from him, a brief respite from the rigors of wards 6A and

*John Davis Cantwell, M.D.*

B, lurking in the bathroom near the Cardiac Clinic, leafing through a journal or an unread sports page. I almost expected a rap on the door of the toilet, with Dr. Hurst telling me to get back to the ward and work up a new patient with possible ochronosis of the heart.

Like all of his former cardiology fellows, he has had a strong influence on my medical habits and practice ever since. I passed many of his dictums on to the medicine residents under my supervision for many years at Georgia Baptist Medical Center.

## NOW

To get an update on his activities at age 80, we met for lunch at Fishbone's Restaurant (featuring a piranha bar), near Piedmont Hospital. Dr. Hurst was five minutes early for the lunch, as he had taught me to be. I wanted to interview him, to see how he spent a typical day, almost 30 years after I had finished my cardiology fellowship.

His day begins around 4 a.m., seven days a week. He rides a stationary bike for 15 minutes, lifting some arm weights at the same time, has coffee and bran muffins, and then sits in one of two chairs. His "writing chair" is surrounded by books and reference sources. His "thinking chair" is in a separate area.

At 6 a.m., five days a week, he leaves for his office at Emory University Medical Center. He meets with house staff on the cardiology service from 7 to 8 a.m., reviewing their workups. At 8 a.m. he is back at his office, reviewing faxes and e-mails. His long-time secretary, Carol Miller, arrives at 9 a.m. and they discuss his schedule for the day. He works in the library from 9 to 11 a.m.

Twice weekly he has teaching sessions at Emory from 1:15 to 2:15 p.m., with house staff assigned to cardiology, teaching them the basics of interpreting electrocardiograms (ECGs) and uses the computer to enhance the teaching of cardiac auscultation. On Tuesdays, eight months per year, he meets senior medical students at Grady for lunch and then does a patient-oriented teaching session with them from 1 to 2 p.m., followed by an hour-long session on the basic principles of the ECG with the cardiology fellows.

Every other Wednesday, at noon, he meets with all medical house staff at Crawford W. Long Hospital and analyses cases unknown to him, emphasizing the medical history, physical exam, chest x-ray and ECG.

Most days he returns to his office at Emory by mid-afternoon, for more writing and thinking, and goes home by 4 p.m., bringing a bagful of work with him. He may read or write, "depending on what is pressing." He occasionally takes a 10- to 15-minute "cat nap."

Evenings are spent at Emory functions or with additional reading and writing. He believes in the teaching of his mentor, Dr. Paul Dudley White, that to be really good at what you do depends on what you do after your regular workday, the latter involving "other people's work."

He has cut down on his speaking and traveling, finding the latter "too much of a hassle." He does attend the American College of Cardiology and the American Heart Association meetings each year, "except when they are in Anaheim."

He retires around 10 or 10:30 p.m. His nonmedical reading preferences are

*John Davis Cantwell, M.D.*

biographies. He read two to three novels per year.

His eldest son, John, is a cardiologist and one of the founding members of the group I am a part of, and has three children. Dr. Hurst's middle son, Steve, is in the insurance business and also has three children. His youngest son, Phil, is a clinical psychologist, with two children. Dr. Hurst recently wrote a children's book about heart disease with one grandson and has published a novel, *Prescription For Greed*, with his youngest son. His goal is to write one to two books per year and four to five scientific articles. He also co-edits the journal, *Clinical Cardiology*.

In May 2000, he received the Best Teacher Award, given by Emory Medical House Staff. He also gave the commencement address at the Emory Medical School graduation ceremonies.

A house officer recently asked him how long he was going to keep teaching. Dr. Hurst looked him in the eye and answered, "As long as my memory is better than yours."

## 26

**A DIFFICULT PATIENT?**

The referring physician was moving his office to a northern suburb. The patient needed a cardiologist nearer to his home. He had prior lung surgery for lung cancer and had congestive heart failure due to valvular disease. He was rumored to fuss a bit at the staff if he were kept waiting.

Would I take on this case? Was he, as one might say, a "difficult patient?"

I was running a little behind schedule at his first appointment. He didn't look overly happy when I entered the exam room to introduce myself, but didn't say anything.

I began with general conversation, to help break the ice. Had he done anything special the past summer, I inquired? "I went to Holland." Why did you do that? "Oh, it was a reunion." Of what, I asked. "My Air Force buddies," he replied. His generations wasn't known to be overly verbose, certainly about their war experiences.

I persisted. "What was the special occasion?" He told me that he had made 23 bombing missions, mainly over Germany, during World War II. I later saw a picture of his B-17 plane, the tail shot to pieces during an outing He fared better than one of his colleagues, whose plane exploded in mid-air after a direct hit from German ground fire. In his book, *My War*, Andy Rooney, speaks of the remarkable B-17: "The B-17 did more than any other airplane to win the war…It was not statistically exceptional. It wasn't fast, it

John Davis Cantwell, M.D.

wasn't maneuverable. It didn't carry the heaviest bomb load. What it was, was almost indestructible… with three engines gone, with hydraulic systems drained of fluid, with wounded crewmen on board, the aircraft time after time hauled everyone back home to safety. If airplanes had human qualities, the B-17s would be called valiant."

Later in the war, my patient was given a new assignment. Instead of dropping bombs and killing people, his unit was asked to make three food drops over Holland, missions of mercy (called Manna/Chowhound) for the hungry citizens whose country was still occupied by Germans. Over 20,000 had already died of starvation.

The Germans agreed to hold their fire, but it wasn't really clear if they would indeed do so. The American pilots flew in at an altitude of only 300 feet, dropping their packages of food to the groups of Dutch citizens gathered around little towns throughout the country. One plane went down in the icy North Sea, due to German anti-aircraft fire.

After one food drop, the young pilot looked in his side mirror and could see the Dutch people had pulled tulips out of a large flower bed, to spell "Thanks, Yanks."

**The Reunion**

The American pilots were all invited to attend the 50th Year Commemoration of the Allied Food Drops, the latter having taken place from April 28th to May 5th, 1945.

They were told upon arrival that "during the coming days we intend to show you that the citizens of this county have never forgotten what you did. They have told the story of

*Adventures on Seven Continents And Other Essays*

Manna/Chowhound to their children and grandchildren. You will encounter friendship, gratitude, emotion and memories of half a century ago."

*John Davis Cantwell, M.D.*

**John Powers during World War II**

*Adventures on Seven Continents And Other Essays*

The B-17, with the damage to the tail

The airdrop of food to starving Dutch citizens

*John Davis Cantwell, M.D.*

The week was filled with tears, songs, laughter and toasts with Jeneven (a Dutch gin), wine and beer. Children gave the aging pilots drawings, flowers and various mementos. An elderly lady cried, telling of how her father had been giving his children his own food ration and was close to death when the food drop occurred. One of the invitees was a woman, Noreen Sceurman Nale, who was just a high school student in 1943. Her brother, Lionel, wasn't able to attend, for he was a pilot of the plane that disappeared into the North Sea when the Germans didn't honor the cease fire.

**Follow up**

I have seen my pilot-patient several times since. His remaining lung tissue have been helped a little by bronchodilators. He had an exacerbation of heart failure and was hospitalized recently, but fortunately responded to intravenous diuretics.

When I look at him, I don't seen an elderly man, dyspneic from his residual heart and lung disease, his gait stiffened by degenerative arthritis. No, I picture him at 27, bringing his crippled plane in safely, after braving the anti-aircraft fire. I especially picture the joy he must have experienced dropping food to save the lives of the Dutch citizens.

I try to be on time for his appointments. A difficult patient? I think not. I owe him, and his generation of war heroes, a ton of gratitude.

*Adventures on Seven Continents And Other Essays*

**John Powers 60 years later**

*John Davis Cantwell, M.D.*

# 27

## Searching for Calcutta

"You can find Calcutta all over the world," Mother Teresa once said, "if you only have eyes to see." Trevor Ferrel found his Calcutta on the streets of Philadelphia, the city of "Brotherly Love." I found mine on Peachtree Street, directly across from the new NationsBank building, in the Hippocrates Clinic.

Trevor was age 11, living in the Main Line socialite suburbs, an indifferent student due to his dyslexia, when he saw a news story on television one December evening that would change his life, and the lives of his family. The program was on homelessness in Philadelphia. Trevor thought people "lived like that in India, but not here, I mean in America." He asked his parents if they could go downtown and take a blanket and a pillow to whomever needed it. His parents tried to dissuade him, but finally acquiesced due to his persistence. The smile on the face of the first recipient caused the family to return the next night, with more blankets and, eventually, on a regular basis. The homeless were no longer faceless as Trevor began to call them by name, creating "some kind of personal link," and brought them into focus "as distinct personalities - members of a forgotten community."

The news media picked up on Trevor's activities. Contributions flowed in. Someone donated a van. A foundation was organized. Trevor's father eventually gave up his electronics repair business to work full-time in helping the homeless. In *Trevor's Place*, the father writes:

"*These times (trips to bring food and clothing to the homeless) brought a sense of accomplishment that no other task duplicated. I began to realize that the first trip downtown and its aftermath were shifting my life's direction and priorities. These ragged people, smelly and alien, were affecting my business, without ever crossing the threshold into my shop.*
*...I was hooked on the simple giving that, when received, is given back in the matchless human reward of knowing a person would make it through one more day. To know we were needed and were supplying someone with affection - letting them know that Trevor cared, our family cared, and that I cared, exhilarated me.*"

I experienced similar feelings when working at several of the Medical Association of Atlanta's homeless clinics. Stimulated by Trevor's example, Allen McDonald and I decided to start a weekly clinic through North Avenue Presbyterian Church, locating it in an abandoned building the church owns on Peachtree Street. We chose the name, "The Hippocrates Clinic," in tribute to the Father of Medicine.

The clinic is open each Sunday morning, right after the religious service and meal provided next door at "The Cup." The latter was started by Mamoru Shoji, M.D., a research hematologist at Emory, and also provides addiction control programs and clothing for the homeless.

*John Davis Cantwell, M.D.*

Dr. McDonald provides orthopedic and surgical expertise to the clinic on a regular basis.

About 175 people attend The Cup, and up to 10-15 or so come to the clinic afterwards. The patients are mainly young black men in their 20s to 40s. Many try to find work on the daily labor pools. Perhaps one-third "camp out," as one man put it, as space in formal shelters is limited. Some even live under the church, like the "Phantom of the Opera." Alcoholism and drug abuse have been major contributions to their homelessness. Mental illness is also a problem in some. Bad luck often plays a role - a job layoff, an auto accident, a theft.

I always ask each patient where he (or infrequently she) slept the night before. When one man told me he slept on the street, I asked him why he didn't get into one of the shelters. His response was that it would interfere with his schooling. He was studying to be a nurse assistant (I noticed a Littman stethoscope on the inside of his jacket, and some notes he had made from a lecture). Regulations at the shelter would keep him from getting to his classes on time. I asked where he studied: "In the library," he said, "until they kick me out. Then I read somewhere on the street, until it gets dark."

A week after this encounter I parked at North Avenue Presbyterian Church and walked to the Georgia Tech football game. As I was getting into the car after the game, a young man suddenly appeared at the window, motioning my wife and me. Frightened, I quickly locked the car and drove away. It was then that I realized that the man was probably the nurse-assistant student who was excited to see me and merely wanted to say hello.

Supplies for the Hippocrates Clinic come from gracious colleagues who kindly empty their drug cabinets when I come around. We use a lot of decongestants, cold remedies, extra-strength Tylenol, antifungals, and broad-spectrum antibiotics. We do try to keep stocked in a wide variety of medications, from hemorrhoidal creams to eye drops. The medications are grouped alphabetically, by subspecialty, so we can locate them readily. Pertinent notes on patients are recorded on five-by-seven inch file cards. We don't fill out governmental forms.

One learns to be resourceful. Maids in hotels where I travel are most generous in supplying small tubes of toothpaste, mouthwash and hand lotion. Fragrant soaps from the Lillehammer Hotel, the Homestead, the Opryland Hotel and the Harvard Club of New York have been greatly appreciated by the recipients. Checkout clerks at grocery stores contribute small plastic grocery bags for patients to put drug samples in. Dr. Diana Lacky and Atlanta Medical Associates located a used exam table for us when our patient load necessitated another one. We ask people to donate sweaters, coats and stocking caps in winter months and short sleeve shirts and t-shirts from road races in the summer. I am always tickled to see "Westminster" or "Duke University" jackets in the office waiting room and am still on the lookout for the red Antarctica parkas my wife and I parted with. The men favor baseball-style caps. I tease them if they have a logo other than the Atlanta Braves. One laughed with me as I read the saying on his cap, "I'M AS BAD AS I LOOK."

I have learned a lot from Dr. Shoji. He instills pride in the clientele by expecting

*John Davis Cantwell, M.D.*

them to tithe, to be orderly, and to clean up their plates and cups after the meal. The patients, in return, expect a few things from us. They complain, and rightly so, if we give them outdated drug samples, or put a cold stethoscope on their chest.

Why do physicians volunteer to work in homeless clinics? For me, I suspect it's to get out of going to Sunday School, and so I can wear old clothes to church and go without a necktie. For others, it's probably because man has an innate desire to reach out to those less fortunate, with no other ulterior motive than the self-satisfaction that comes from the encounter.

Can just one person make a difference? Ask Trevor. He didn't even have to travel to India to do so.

# 28

## To A Son Entering Medical Practice

Dear Ryan:

You will soon be entering the private practice of Internal Medicine. The three years of residency have gone fast. I am happy that you could train at an institution like the Mayo Clinic, a center noted for academic excellence, a caring attitude and an emphasis on thoroughness.

Based on my experience in 30 years as an internist-cardiologist, I would emphasize a few things that might be of help to you in your outpatient practice:

1. Jot down the sex and birth dates of patients' children on their main registration sheet. They always enjoy talking about their children, and will appreciate your interest in them.
2. Try to return patients' calls throughout the day. Don't keep them waiting too long, especially if they are anxious about a symptom or a condition.
3. Mail results of all laboratory test, x-rays and the like to patients, adding a personal note.
4. Be careful about chest pain of indeterminate cause (not fleeting or chronic and not anginal in nature). Better to err on the side of being overly cautious than to miss something that could cause a serious problem. Remember that patients with certain

*John Davis Cantwell, M.D.*

conditions like diabetes or hypertension are more likely to have silent ischemia (insufficient blood flow to the heart muscle) and that shortness of breath on effort can sometimes be an angina pectoris equivalent.
5. Don't make new referrals wait weeks to see you. Alert your secretary that you will try to work them in, coming in a little earlier or doing so over the noon hour.
6. Tell patients to have you interrupted if they really need to speak with you. Some get very frustrated by voice mail and by excessive roadblocks at the main desk. Very few will abuse this.
7. You will work more efficiently if the top four sheets on one side of a patient's chart have the following information:

   A. Problem list.
   B. List of current medications.
   C. Flow sheet of pertinent laboratory data.
   D. Dates when next studies like mammograms, PSAs, colonoscopy, blood lipids, exercise tests, etc., are due.

8. Spot-check the serum potassium levels on patients taking steroids as well as those on diuretics, especially if they are also on digoxin.
9. Recall that exercise or pharmacologic stress scans aren't prefect. If a patient has anginal pain despite a normal scan, consider ordering an

outpatient cardiac catheterization study.
10. Have copies of common items in your office files, including things like the Surgeon General's Exercise Guidelines, exercises for low-back pain, non-drug ways to facilitate sleep. Patients will appreciate receiving these.
11. Rakel's **Current Therapy** is the single most useful reference I have found for common medical problems. It is user-friendly, gives brand names of drugs as well as generic ones, and is updated annually.
12. Have your secretary or nurse tell patients if you are running behind. Stick your head in the room and apologize, telling the patient you will be with them as soon as possible. If they see that you are aware and concerned, few will be disgruntled.
13. Ask your nurse to record the patient's last weight next to the current one. Some will have lost weight and will be a little chagrined if you haven't noticed.
14. Leave little notes to yourself by your telephone regarding when important tests you have ordered (such as Holter monitor studies, chest x-rays) are due. Your staff won't always be aware of the importance of such tests and it might be days (or sometimes weeks) before you get the final result. Rarely, the result will be placed in a chart without you ever seeing it.
15. See patients with uncontrolled hypertension at frequent intervals, up to every two weeks if need be, adjusting their drug dose each time until the

blood pressure has been normalized. Have the patient obtain a digital home blood pressure kit and record pressures on graph paper so you can compare home reading with office ones.
16. Work hard at your profession, as I know you will, but take time out for special family events. Accompany your son to school on that first day, and help coach his Little League baseball team.

Despite some managed care headaches, I have found office medical practice to be so enjoyable that I plan to forego retirement, unless forced to do so by medical or other reasons. I can't think of another profession that exceeds the intellectual challenges and the joy of working with patients, trying to prevent disease and to cure it whenever possible. I hope that after nearly three decades of practice, you will feel as I do.

With love,
Dad

# BOOKS AND WRITING

*John Davis Cantwell, M.D.*

# 29

## BOOKS I'LL NEVER PART WITH

I recently catalogued 1500 of my books in the process of becoming an antiquarian bookseller. My colleague, Dr. John Griffin, warns me that it might be a mistake. He sold several of his books once and missed them so much that he bought them back.

One must overcome this personal attachment to books to become a dealer in them, realizing that there is joy in delivering a treasured book into the hands of a client who will enjoy it and treat it well. The best example of this was Frank Doel, of **84 Charing Cross Road** fame. His correspondence with Helene Hanff is precious, both in the written medium and on video. One can imagine the shock when Ms. Hanff's letter of September 30, 1968, to Mr. Doel drew the following response four months later:

> "Dear Miss,
> I have just come across the letter you wrote to Mr. Doel…and it is with great regret that I have to tell you that he passed away on Sunday, the 22nd of December; the funeral took place last week on Wednesday, the 1st of January.
> He was rushed to hospital on the 15th of December and operated on at once for a ruptured appendix; unfortunately peritonitis set in and he died seven days later.

*John Davis Cantwell, M.D.*

He had been with the firm for over 40 years…Do you still want us to try to obtain the Austens for you?"

I thought of Frank Doel when I visited a used book store in the Cotswolds, in the charming town of Chipping Campden. I asked the proprietor if his books were "on line," available through the Internet, as seems fashionable these days.

They were not, he replied, and he doubted if they ever would be. "These books are special to me," he said. "Part of the joy in this business is seeing who they are going to, and visiting with them about themselves and about books in general. You lose this personal aspect with modern technology." I couldn't argue with that.

**Going Into Business**

I divided my books into 16 categories (Table I). I tried to price them fairly. After all, it is a business, and one needs to make at least a small profit from each transaction. On the other hand, I didn't want to gouge clients, as I feel one local bookstore does. I tried to bear in mind how much the book was worth to me, how much I would pay for it.

I plan to mail out brochures upon request and also work out a consignment relationship with Atlanta Vintage Books. They do subscribe to the Internet and, I must confess, it works pretty well from the buyer's standpoint. Before our recent trip to the Cotswolds, I searched multiple used bookstores in vain for Susan Hill's, **Shakespeare Country**. At Atlanta Vintage Books, they found two copies within minutes via the computer, one in Scotland and another in the United States. I requested the latter copy, gave my Visa card number, and asked that the book be sent by UPS to my home. Three days later it was resting on my front porch.

I plan to join the Georgia Antiquarian Book Sellers Association (GABA), to give my **Heart to the Himalayas Books** greater exposure. To join, one needs to have two members as sponsors and obtain a business license from the state. The GABA sponsors a superb book fair at Gwinnett Civic Center each October, drawing dealers from all over the country and from abroad.

**Classification of Books**

1.  Art and Architecture
2.  Biography/autobiography (literary)
3.  Biography/autobiography (general)
4.  Fiction
5.  Humor
6.  Margaret Mitchell
7.  Medicine
8.  Mountains and Mountaineering
9.  Nonfiction
10. Poetry
11. Polar
12. Presidential
13. Religion
14. Sports
15. Travel and Adventure Travel
16. War

**Books I Won't Sell**

Twelve of my books are not for sale. They aren't necessarily classics, nor extremely valuable, but they have special meaning to me.

*John Davis Cantwell, M.D.*

**Sports**

I can't part with **Doak Walker: 3-time All-American**. I checked this book out of our little public library when I was 10 years old and later found a copy of my own, which I had Doak sign. I modeled my high school football career after him, wore his number - 37 - and tried in vain to emulate his talents as a left halfback, punter, place kicker and defensive back.

On short notice, I had the opportunity to meet Doak, on January 20, 1998. I cancelled my office appointments and flew to Dallas to see him present the Doak Walker Award (the best college running back award) to Ricky Williams, from Texas. It was a thrill to visit with Doak and to tell him what an impact he had on me, as a small boy in Wisconsin.

Ten days after our visit, Doak Walker was in a skiing accident and became a quadriplegic, facing his toughest opponent to date. Along with thousands of other fans, I sent him letters and faxes, hoping it would help in some small way. He died a few months later.

**Murph** is also very precious to me. My first year as one of the Braves' team doctors was Dale Murphy's rookie year. He is the epitome of how a person should conduct himself, not just on the athletic field but in the act of living. He signed his autobiography, thanking me for all that I do with the team.

With Ricky Williams and my boyhood football hero, Doak Walker, Heisman Trophy winners 50 years apart

   In truth, it was worth whatever time the job required to get to know this member of the human race's Hall of Fame.

   I have also gotten to know Hank Aaron in a special way in recent years, and vividly recall him from my childhood, when he joined the Milwaukee Braves in the mid-1950s and began hitting line shots with those thick wrists. Aaron's ***I Had A Hammer*** tells about his early days, including the hardships of segregation, of his rise to fame, and of the tremendous pressure of chasing down the Bambino's record. It also says a lot about the character of Aaron's parents. When he became

*John Davis Cantwell, M.D.*

very successful, he offered to buy his folks a much nicer home than the one in Mobile in which he had grown up. His mother thanked him but declined, telling him that the only thing she wanted was to have God in her heart. Her little home suited her and her husband (who died recently) just fine.

I'll also keep the **First Four Minutes**, because it reflects one of those rare moments in your past where you can recall exactly where you were when an event occurred. I was walking through Lauerman's Department Store in my home town on May 6, 1954. Suddenly there came an announcement: "We interrupt this program to give you a news bulletin. Roger Bannister, an Oxford medical student, has just broken the four-minute mile barrier!" Bannister's feat is considered the single most important achievement in track and field in the past 50 years.

*Adventures on Seven Continents And Other Essays*

**With Sir Roger Bannister**

A modest man, Sir Roger deflected all talk about his great achievement when we met several years ago in Atlanta. A probing intellect, he seemed more interested in learning all about the person he was talking to rather than to reflect upon his fame.

His book is one of the best written sports accounts I have ever read. In telling about the self-discovery of his running talents, he writes:

*John Davis Cantwell, M.D.*

"I remember a moment when I stood barefoot on firm, dry sand by the sea. The air had a special quality as if it had a life of its own. The sound of the breakers on the shore shut out all others…I was startled, and freighted, by the tremendous excitement that so few steps could create…

I was running now, and a fresh rhythm entered my body. No longer conscious of my movement, I discovered a new entity with nature. I had found a new source of power and beauty, a source I never dreamt existed."

When in Oxford recently, I stopped by the Iffley Road Track, the scene of his epic-making event. The track is synthetic now. Only a small marker tells of the historic occurrence. I visited with the groundskeeper, who sensed that I appreciated athletic history. "Just a minute," he said, "I have something for you." He returned from an area behind the adjacent sports field, cradling a plastic cup. "Here. Take this home with you," he commented. The cup was filled with cinders from the finish line of the original track. He had scooped some up when the track was being replaced 20 years before for a moment such as this.

## Novels

I'll keep at least three novels, including **Gone With the Wind**. This masterpiece is a rare signed first printing. Margaret Mitchell became annoyed by the intrusions in her routine and stopped signing copies only six months after the book was released. Her brother, Stephens, subsequently tried to get her to sign his copy, only to be refused. My copy should be passed down through succeeding generations. Maybe it will have a special place, near the old family **Bible**, like it did in Pat Conroy's home. As Conroy reflected:

"For the most part, I was raised in a home without books, but the ones displayed and laid out flat for the inspection of visitors were the **Bible** and **Gone With the Wind**, in no particular order of importance...
  To Southerners like my mother, **Gone With the Wind** was not just a book, it was an answer, a clenched fist raised to the North, an anthem of defiance...
  I owe a personal debt to this novel that I find almost beyond reckoning. I became a novelist because of **Gone With the Wind**..."

I have previously written about my contact with Olive Ann Burns, who wrote the classic **Cold Sassy Tree**. The signed copy she gave me will always have a special place in my home library. The same applies to Wallace Stegner and his masterpiece, **The Big Rock Candy Mountain**. Stegner directed the creative writing program at Stanford for many years. His powerful account of his early years and of his parents merits a reserved spot on my bookshelf.

## Medical Works

**Paul Dudley White: A Portrait**, a tribute to one of America's greatest cardiologists, is a book that had a strong impact on me as I was beginning the practice of medicine. Dr. White seemed to really enjoy all facets of medicine.

*John Davis Cantwell, M.D.*

He combined a private practice with teaching and clinical research. He traveled widely and shared views with physicians world-wide. His main interest, as is mine, was preventive cardiology. He loved to exercise and kept physically active, chopping wood and bicycling, until shortly before his death at age 87. His sense of adventure was such that he once tried to put a small harpoon into a whale to record his heart rate, only to have his boat nearly sunk by a companion whale which apparently preferred non-invasive studies.

Dr. Jeremiah Stamler wrote **Your Heart Has Nine Lives** for lay people, back in the 1960s, emphasizing the prevention of coronary atherosclerotic heart disease. Dr. Stamler was a professor of mine at Northwestern Medical School. He further influenced me to become a preventive cardiologist at an international teaching seminar in Sweden in 1971, and through his subsequent writing and lecturing. The book, which is still highly applicable, is a reminder to me of the importance of a mentor, and of the impact a well-written book or article can have.

During my 11-year tenure as Program Director of Internal Medicine at Georgia Baptist Medical Center, Sir William Osler was my role model. In dealing with difficult situations, I would invariable ask myself, "What would Osler have done?" and try to respond accordingly.

His **Practice of Medicine** was first published in 1892 and was the major textbook for practicing physicians for many years. When I stepped down to take the Olympic medical job, my former chief residents presented me with a first edition of Osler. That I will always keep, and the same for a third edition that belonged to a man I was named for, David John Davis, M.D., Ph.D., who was Dean of the Illinois Medical School for 19 years.

**Family Books**

The family **Bible** was given to me after my grandmother died, at age 97, in remembrance of her. In it are recorded births, marriages and deaths in the family, dating back over 150 years. There is also a handwritten note from my great-grandfather, who had been a Civil War veteran, blacksmith and logger. The inscription is not original to him, but a message he wanted to pass along to future generations:

"I expect to pass through this life but once. If there is any kindness to show, or any good thing I can do to my fellow beings, let me do it now. Let me not defer nor neglect it. I will pass this way but once."

One day perhaps I'll add a paragraph that might be of help to my great-grandson.

The final book I intend to keep is **From Wales to America: 1848-1948**, written by David John Davis, my mother's uncle. In the book, Dr. Davis tells of a farmhouse in northeastern Wales where the family lived for 400 years. In 1845, the youngest child, John Davis, immigrated to America. Three years later, he convinced his parents and siblings to leave their home and to join him in New York, which they did. His father became quite ill on the arduous trans-Atlantic voyage on the ship, "Gertrude," and died near Utica, New York.

*John Davis Cantwell, M.D.*

Not long ago, we traveled to Wales, searching for the old Davis farmhouse. I had three bits of information to go on:

1. The farm was seven miles west of the small town of Llanfyllin.
2. The farm had been called Rhiwlas (meaning "verdant slope"), and,
3. A cousin had sent me two pictures of the stone house, made 71 years ago.

We took the road west from Llanfyllin, towards Bala. The farmhouse seven miles out looked a little like the pictures I had. The owner's wife studied the photos and shook her head, "No, this isn't the place." She did recall a farm named "Rhiwlas," on another road west of town, toward Lake Vyrnwy.

We located the sign for Rhiwlas, followed a winding dirt road up one-fourth of a mile, and saw the house, little changed through the centuries. The present owner had lived there for 41 years. They had a copy of the same book I have, and knew all about the Davis family.

I carefully studied the farmhouse, which for centuries had passed to the oldest son, generation after generation, until an 18-year-old boy uprooted his family to come to America, and eventually to Wisconsin, where I was born. The experience helped put my life into perspective, part of the ongoing continuum of humanity. As Tennyson once wrote, the great world spins forever "down the ringing grooves of change."

**Summary**

My idea of a home is like Carl Sandburg's "Connemarra," near Hendersonville, N.C., with book shelves in very room, even the bathrooms and the basement.

Books are treasured companions. Osler was even buried with one of his favorites, **Religio et Medico**, by Thomas Browne.

Books are also meant to be shared. In the process, one can either lend them or turn a hobby into a side business. The ideal for a book seller was Frank Doel, a man who obviously cherished people as well as literature.

I will be parting with many of my books, mainly to make room for others, (as my wife, unlike Sandburg's, sets certain limits on the amount of space in our home that is devoted to books). Some I simply can't part with. I have tried to explain why.

*John Davis Cantwell, M.D.*

# 30

**Tales of a "Best-Selling" Author**

He was an orphan, and grew up "in a nest of foster children," exposing him to "some of the more tragic situations that confront helpless people." He learned to work hard as a young boy, arising at 4:00 a.m. to deliver newspapers from grades 7-12. Material possessions were few but, at an early age, he learned to appreciate music, art and literature.

*"My life...could be rather bleak, for I had none of the clothes and games and equipment that boys my age would normally have had. All I really had was that music, the art I remember so well and the endless books from the library; the essential elements of those three I could take with me intellectually and without burdening my knapsack. These riches never fade. The great songs echo still, the colors of the paintings do not fade. They accompanied me as a I trudged the lower heights of Nanga Parbat in the Himalayas and comforted me as I stood lashed to the wheel while our small boat wallowed through the tail end of a Pacific typhoon. They have echoed in my mind when I needed consolation and been at hand when I required dedication to some old task or inspiration in a new."*

His first novel, written when he was 40 years old, was only mildly successful initially, but stimulated him to write another - **The Fires of Spring**. He sent the latter to an agent, who not only rejected it, but advised him that he had no great future as a writer. His disappointment was short-lived, for later the same day he received word that the first novel - **Tales of the South Pacific** - had just won the Pulitzer prize.

In his autobiography **The World Is My Home**, James Michener recounts the details of his fascinating life. Of the 14 chapters, I enjoyed those on travel, people, writing and "meanings" the most.

Regarding travel, the most delightful place Michener has ever visited is Bora Bora. Rome and London tied as the most rewarding city. Karnak and the temples along the Nile rated the "best ancient ruin," Angkor Wat (in Cambodia) the "most romantic," and Kyoto the "most spiritual." The one place he chooses never to return to is Calcutta ("The poverty there, the death in the streets, the incredible living conditions were too much for even me to take...") One of the few places he hasn't seen is the South Pole... "I have known the world, have loved it and would happily visit once more its farthest corners, but sooner or later the sands in the mariner's glass will run through and even Ulysses' ship must come to dock."

One of the people he most admired also happened to be a boyhood hero of mine, Robin Roberts, the Philadelphia Phillies' Hall of Fame pitcher ("A big, uncomplicated chunk of all-American boy, witty, handsome, valiant through the last out in the final inning.") He also had high regard for Domingo Ortega, the Spanish bullfighter:

John Davis Cantwell, M.D.

*"...I would like to resemble him, a man who sticks to his job, who conducts himself with a certain sobriety and serenity, and who stays at the task until he acquires a reputation for being a serious worker with a serious purpose."*

Not all of his favorite people were heroic athletes. Consider a Scottish woman named Morag, who lived on the small island of Barra, in the Outer Hebrides:

*"...an extraordinary woman. She had been born in an era before rural doctors knew how to correct clubfeet, but this deformity did not keep her from enjoying life, although it had prevented her from finding a husband. Somewhat overweight, decidedly blowsy and without any teeth, natural or false, she did not look prepossessing, but her warm heart, her desire to participate in whatever was happening on her island, and her love of both storytelling and singing made her a special person whose memory I cherish."*

In the chapter on writing, Michener provides insights on his phenomenal success. Most serious authors, he adds, write their first novel at 4:00 a.m. or 11:00 p.m., while holding down full-time jobs. Three aspects of his upbringing that shaped his writing included, 1) voracious reading as a boy and as a young man, 2) "wide and vivid experiences" (ranging from travels in the South Pacific to operating behind Russian lines in the 1956 Hungarian Revolution), and 3) his apprenticeship as a New York editor. He considers books to be "one of the finest

*Adventures on Seven Continents And Other Essays*

symbols of our civilization," and wants his own to look right, be well-printed and properly bound, to feel good to the hand and to be inviting to the eye. His aim as a writer is "to use ordinary words to achieve extraordinary results" (indeed, I only had to look up the meaning of two words in the autobiography: <u>sententiously</u> and <u>coruscating</u>).

Michener dislikes the term, "best-selling author." To him, this implies that the author is interested only in making money and that the books he writes are junk. In his historical novels, he tries never to "abuse fact or invent situations contrary to known conditions" (unlike Oliver Stone in the movie, *JFK*). He is a strong believer in publishing his work for…" writing is never complete until it's published…Any honorable and legal device whereby the writer can communicate his work to others is just as much publishing as having it brought out in a fine hardcover form by Knopf."

How had he kept his writing career viable into his ninth decade? He listed four suggestions:

1) Stay in contact with young people;
2) Keep physically active;
3) Remain alert to all that happens about you, and;
4) Have a "burning desire to maintain a productive creative life, always looking ahead to new challenges, never back to old victories."

He also advises young people to study the works of Plato and Socrates, the behavior of "the three Thomases" (Aquinas, More and Jefferson), the austere analysis of Kant, the

John Davis Cantwell, M.D.

political leadership of Lincoln and Franklin Roosevelt, the educational theories of John Dewey, and the pragmatism of William James.

In the final chapter on meanings, we learn how the author overcame a number of personal affronts, including letters from some of the "real Micheners" accusing him of being a fraud and of trying to be better than he really was. At least one of the countries that initially banned his books later presented him with the highest award a civilian can achieve. He lived long enough to see Poland and Hungary emerge from Soviet domination, but wasn't sure the Afghanistan freedom fighters he helped support were much of an improvement over their predecessors.

Throughout his long and productive life, James Michener has focused on engaging in tasks "that had some significance" and "to associate with people who were trying to accomplish worthy ends." He wanted to be remembered for helping convert a jail in his hometown into an art museum, for financial contributions to multiple graduate writing schools, and mainly for "that row of solid books that rest on library shelves throughout the world." His most favorite book? - "Always the next one."

## 31

## The Lost Diary of Agnes Von Kurowsky

He was 19, a native of Oak Park, Illinois, wounded in battle while serving food to the troops in the front lines. She was 26, a Red Cross nurse from Washington, D.C. When she appeared on the wards, "the entire placed seemed to brighten because of her presence. Besides having what the boys called 'it,' she was kind, quick, intelligent, and sensitive to the moods of a patient; what's more, she was blessed with a sense of humor that verged on the mischievous. She was firm without being too strict, light-hearted yet professionally serious. Altogether the perfect temperament for a nurse."

He had dated little, if at all, in high school. It was easy to see why he should fall for her, for "...she had a sparkle that others didn't possess. Fresh and pert and lovely in her long-skirted white uniform, moving lithely as she went about her tasks, wasting no time yet never seeming to hurry, she radiated zest and energy."

He also stood out: "a good-looking son-of-a-gun and good natured too...he had a strong jaw and a wide boyish grin that revealed an even row of dazzling white teeth, and his jet-black hair and dark eyes contrasted starkly with the snowy pillow... there was no question about his magnetism or his mental alertness." She kept a diary during the year in which they met. It was known to no one, "perhaps not even her husband," until after her death. It was a "cloth-bound volume purchased in Italy,

*John Davis Cantwell, M.D.*

labeled AGENDA 1918. Frayed and stained, it showed the ravages of time" when it came into the hands of Henry S. Villard, in 1984. The diary was later published, together with the 52 letters she wrote to him. Unfortunately his letters to her were burned by one of her subsequent suitors, who was extremely jealous. The diary entries "…show her weighing romantic options and exploring the new identity she was developing for herself. The letters suggested that (she) knew what he wanted to hear." For example, nowhere in the diary does she indicate that she loves him, Yet, in the letters, she tells him that she loves him, that she misses him so much, and that she sometimes wished they could marry "over here" (in Italy).

Her name was Agnes von Kurowsky, the daughter of a naturalized citizen of Polish-German extraction, the granddaughter of a Polish general. The family had moved to Washington when she was 13. She went on to Bellevue Hospital's School of Nursing, after which she applied for a Red Cross assignment abroad. She left a physician-suitor behind.

The wounded soldier's name was Ernest Hemingway, the son of an Illinois surgeon. He too had volunteered with the American Red Cross, serving initially as an ambulance driver and briefly as the head of a rolling canteen service, bringing food to the Italian troops in the front line. After only six days of the latter he was hit by the explosion of a trench mortar (called an "ash can"), which had been hurled from the Austrian lines. It was designed to explode on impact, shooting pieces of steel in all directions. They counted at least 227 shrapnel wounds in his legs. An Italian near him was killed, another lost both legs, and a third soldier was badly wounded. Hemingway, despite his own injuries, apparently lifted the latter onto his back and was attempting to carry him to the rear, when hit in the knees with machine gun fire. He was subsequently taken to a recently opened hospital in Milan, where he met Agnes. In his novel, **A Farewell to Arms,** written 11 years after the experience, Hemingway describes the nurse (named "Catherine Barkley"):

"*She looked fresh and young and very beautiful. I thought I had never seen anyone so beautiful.*"

In the book, the two have a torrid relationship, culminating in a pregnancy. In real life, it was more of a flirtation. Her diary makes first mention of him on July 20th, 1918. Within the next five weeks she is aware that Hemingway "…has a case on me, or thinks he has." She goes on to write that "he was talking last night of what might be if he was 26 or 28. In some ways - at some times, - I wish very much that he was. He is adorable and we are very congenial in every way. I'm getting so confused in my heart and mind I don't know how I'll end up. Still, I came over here to work and until the war is over I won't be able to do anything foolish…". Agnes was assigned to other hospitals, including ones in Florence and Treviso. Hemingway returned to the front, for only one day, before being sent back to the hospital in Milan with acute hepatitis. Agnes wrote 52 letters to him between September 25th, 1918, and March 7th, 1919. She was obviously aware of their age difference, addressing him as "Kid, My Kid," "My Dear Boy," "Ernest, My Boy" and "Bambino

*John Davis Cantwell, M.D.*

Mio." He obviously had a talent for expressing himself in words, based on her response to his letters: "I guess every girl likes to have some man tell her how nice she is, and how he can't do without her. Anyway - I am but human, and when you say these things I love it, and can't help but believe you."

Her letters are encouraging to him:

> *"I love you, Ernie, and I miss my boy."*
> *"...I'm always comparing you with him (her doctor friend in New York) in my mind's eye, and the comparison always comes out beneficial for you, and he is left in the dust."*
> *"I miss you so, dear, and I love you so much."*
> *"I sometimes wish we could marry over here but since that is so foolish I must try and not think about it."*
> *"I wrote to my mother that I was planning to marry a man younger than I - and it wasn't the doctor..."*

On January 1st, 1919, she seems to put him down a bit:

> *"...you are to me a wonderful boy, and when you add on a few years and some dignity and calm, you'll be very much worthwhile..."*

Perhaps his visit to her, in Treviso, on December 9th, 1918, triggered a downturn in her emotional attachment. As she later recalled: "the men laughed their heads off at him...They thought he was the biggest joke. He came in with a cane, you know, and all his medals, and those American doughboys, they just roared."

Hemingway was shipped back to the States on January 4th, 1919. A reporter from the **New York Sun** greeted him, as he walked down the gangplank, and wrote of his heroic deeds. Hemingway subsequently gave lectures in his hometown, outside Chicago, apparently embellishing some of the episodes.

Agnes's "Dear John" letter to him was dated March 7th, 1919:

> *"Ernie, dear boy,*
> *...can you forgive me some day for unwittingly deceiving you?...I am now and always will be too old, and that's the truth, and I can't get away from the fact that you're just a boy - a kid. ...I expect to be married soon"* (to an Italian officer).

Agnes never married the Italian officer, as his mother objected. She never saw Hemingway again, which is surprising since they both had homes in Key West, Florida. She visited Cuba several times, when he was there, but didn't bother to seek him out as she was told "he drank so heavily." Three years after her "Dear John" letter to him she received a note from him, the contents of which aren't known. He was married at the time to his first wife, Hadley (who was even older than Agnes). Excerpts of her response are as follows:

John Davis Cantwell, M.D.

*"Dear Kid,*
*...you know there has always been a little bitterness over the way our comradeship ended, especially since I got back and Mac (a mutual friend) read me the very biting letters you wrote her about me. ...I always knew that it would turn out right in the end...now that you have Hadley. ...Is there any chance of knowing when your book will be out? (His first book,* **Three Stories and 10 Poems** *was published in Paris is 1923). How proud I will be some day in the not-very-distant future to say - Oh yes, Ernest Hemingway. Used to know him quite well during the war."*

Henry Villard had taken time off from Harvard College in 1918, also to serve in Italy as an ambulance driver for the Red Cross. He occupied the hospital room next to Hemingway. He too was infatuated with Agnes:

"I kept thinking how sympathetic and lovely she was, doubly attractive so far from home. All right, she was a few years older than I, but then older girls are quite likely to appeal to young men who have lately turned 18."

Villard was living in Switzerland in 1962, when contacted by Carlos Baker, who was writing a biography on Hemingway. Baker was aware that Agnes was the nurse immortalized by Hemingway in *A Farewell to Arms*, and gave Villard her address in Key West. Villard happened to be in the area, in 1976, and asked to see her. He found that she had married a man from Georgia, in 1928, whom she had met on a steamboat from Haiti. She was divorced after a short time, and remarried a hotel manager

(William Stanfield, Jr.) who had three children from his own prior marriage. Villard found that at 84, Agnes "was no longer the blithe spirit her patients had known. Not in the best of health, she was nonetheless tall and straight as ever, and the old charm came through."

She recalled Hemingway as "interesting" but "impulsive, hasty, not to say impetuous. He didn't really know what he wanted. He hadn't thought out anything clearly." She was afraid he might turn into an aimless wanderer after the war ended. She added that he "thrived on adulation" and that he "learned to play on the sympathy he received." His medal of valor had been won at an outpost "where he had no business to be," a place "where he had been expressly told not to go."

Agnes resented being taken for "the alter ego of the complaisant Catherine Barkley" in the novel. She even moved from Key West, after the Hemingway Museum opened, when a tourist guide referred to her as "Hemingway's girl." She considered Catherine an "arrant fantasy" of Hemingway's: "He invented the myth years later - built out of his frustration in love." Of his suicide, she said, "It was a messy way to die, but what he did was understandable, considering that his mind was impaired, that his powers as a man and a writer were failing."

Agnes von Kurowsky lived to age 92. She contacted Henry Villard, when the end was near, to see if he could help arrange her burial at the Soldiers Home National Cemetery in Arlington, Virginia. He did as she requested, and the "lost" diary and letters to Hemingway were her posthumous gift to him. (The collection can now be seen in the John F.

*John Davis Cantwell, M.D.*

Kennedy Library in Boston.) At her funeral ceremony, Agnes was cited for "gallant and commendable services" with the American Red Cross in Italy during World War I. A young boy of 19 would have agreed. In *A Farewell to Arms*, Hemingway certainly did embellish his romance, as is a novelist's prerogative. But true to life, he considered "Catherine" a lovely woman and a devoted nurse, Perhaps the pain Frederic Henry felt, when she dies during childbirth, is symbolic of the author's own sense of loss, when she rejected him because he was too young and immature – and just a kid.

# 32

## Olive Ann Burns: A Fond Remembrance

It was not the best of times, as Dickens would say, when I first met Olive Ann Burns. She was in the intensive care unit at Georgia Baptist Medical Center, in heart failure, and post-chemotherapy for a lymphoma. "He's an author too," my nurse told her, much to my embarrassment. She was kind and suggested that we exchange books, which was a far better deal for me than for her.

I had heard of *Cold Sassy Tree* and took it along on a trip to Washington, D.C., that next weekend. I don't remember much about the meeting as I spent most of the time engrossed in the world of Grandpa Blakeslee and his grandson, Will Tweedy.

I could hardly wait to tell Mrs. Burns how much I had enjoyed the book and to hear what she had planned for the sequel. I told her what I predicted would become of Will, Love Simpson, Lorna, Hosie and Lightfoot, and then listened intently as she briefly outlined her plans.

Olive Ann Burns finished only 15 chapters of the sequel, which she entitled *Time, Dirt and Money*. It is a miracle that she got that far, given the extent of her illness. She wanted the chapters published as, "a gift to her readers...one way of saying goodbye, both to her and to the unforgettable characters she created." It is a wonderful last gift, even moreso with the stirring reminiscence by her editor and friend, Katrina Kenison.

John Davis Cantwell, M.D.

**The Book**

The title, *Time, Dirt and Money*, reflects Sanna's tendencies to anxiety and perfectionism. These are three entities that such a person worries about most. I do think that the publishers were wise to select "Leaving Cold Sassy" as the title on the book jacket, for it has more widespread appeal and calls to mind the extremely successful first novel (which has sold over one million copies to date).

The book is a portrait of Will's and Sanna's marriage, based heavily on that of Burns' own parents, Ruby and Arnold. It could serve as required reading by any couple seeking the services of a marriage counselor. In her notes, Burns states that the marriage was "nearly destroyed by poverty, disillusionment, and disappointment, but that it survived and flourished again, years after both husband and wife had all but given up on finding happiness together." True love eventually came to them "once they learned to accept each other just as they were, for better or worse, and for all time."

**The Characters**

In 1972, Burns began to record the stories of her parents' lives "as a keepsake for herself and her family" after she learned that her mother was dying from stomach cancer. Taking notes as her mother spoke, the two were drawn close together, "diverting their attention from pain and illness." Burns reviewed love letters her parents had written during World War II, grocery bills dating from the depression era, and even report cards, telegrams, and a floor plan of their family home. After her mother's death, Burns interviewed her father, who "painted a vivid picture of Commerce, Georgia, at the turn of the century, a picture that later served as a model for Cold Sassy." And one of his favorite stories was about his Grandpa Power, a store owner in Commerce, the model for Grandpa Blakeslee.

From her notes, Burns tells us that "the theme of Sanna is disillusionment - her life is the pursuit of happiness and perfection, but she finds (these) impossible to obtain. Her idea of happiness is constant joy, no changes. "A lot of her anxieties probably related to the absence of a strong mother figure in her life, during the formative years."

Will was the opposite. He likes challenges and changes, trying new things. To him, living "is a matter of making things work, if you can." The harder things got, "the more excited and challenged he felt."

Sanna, like Burns' own mother, had four children in four years (Olive Ann was the baby). To Will, "the children made me nervous as heck, Sanna was a witch, and the dog was whining and limping." In addition, the depression caused them to lose their farm and their new house, breaking Sanna's heart and Will's pride.

Had she lived to complete the sequel, Burns would have told the "amazing power of love," which she had observed in her own parents' lives. Like Will and Sanna, "there were times, of course, in their life together when he had failed her, and she had failed him, but no woman ever felt more loved and secure and supported than she did <u>when it mattered most.</u>"

*John Davis Cantwell, M.D.*

**The Author**

Olive Ann Burns had "smoky-dark" eyes, like Sanna. The thing that impressed me most about her was her serenity. She seemed to be at peace with herself, even under the most trying conditions. She had realized early during her illness that the worse outcome was not death, but living in fear, so she had prayed for the courage to deal with her lymphoma, and the effects of chemotherapy. That prayer was answered. Instead of always asking God for things in her prayers, she began to submit "appreciation prayers." Rather than to consider her lymphoma a burden, she instead thought of it as a challenge. One year she was able to leave her home only twice, once to vote and the other to view the autumn foliage; yet, she considered the year to have been a happy one. Work on the sequel gave structure to her days, and her many friends "keep me integrated with the outside world." She noted:

> *"I'm convinced true fulfillment is living in God's world one day at a time, savoring it, leaving today's disappointment behind and borrowing no troubles from tomorrow. It's done not only by accepting life, fear, and things that go bump in the night, but also by cultivating love and new and old friendships, and especially by finding a new work or project that makes it exciting just to get up in the morning."*

It wasn't easy. Her husband was seriously ill, also with a lymphoma. They alternated chemotherapy so that "one would be well enough to cook and keep house" while the other was sick from the treatment. Together they turned cancer "into an adventure in living." Andy's outlet was his garden. He surprised his wife by planting a sassafras tree in their front yard on 191 Bolling Road, a tree that now survives them both.

Mrs. Burns honed her skills as a staff writer for the *Atlanta Journal Sunday Magazine,* under the tough demanding editor, Angus Perkerson. He taught her to be obsessive about accuracy and to make her writing interesting. Her gift for capturing dialect (chi'ren, id'n, inner-rest, yore'n, pneumony, Saraday) came from careful listening and jotting down notes, as she also did with the wonderful stories woven into her novels. She wrote and rewrote, and then revised, again and again. The final product was like her recollection view of life in the country:

*"Red dirt roads, dilapidated unpainted houses and barns, porch flowers growing in old coffee cans, mules in the pastures, shy, scrawny children with white rags tied around impetigo sores playing in swept dirt yards, and on hot Sunday afternoons, tenant families sitting on the porch watching cars go by and yearning for the fast lane."*

It was her attitude that I remember most. "Sick as she was," writes Katrina Kenison, "she never seemed to despair. Her brother came to see her in the ICU. As he was leaving, she whispered at him to wait a minute. 'What is it?' he asked, turning back. 'I just wanted you to see me smile,' she said. And she did." Gracious living to her consisted of acceptance and forgiveness.

*John Davis Cantwell, M.D.*

She also had a very practical side. When she lost her hair from the chemotherapy she covered her head in the cool weather with "a blue cut-off pajama leg which she had pulled out of the dishrag bag." Her friends and neighbors had a wig party for her and she stored the wigs around their bedroom until her husband complained that it resembled a "headhunter's trophy room."

After her death the family had an estate sale. My wife attended and bought several plastic ice cube trays. They are much better than our other ones as they don't crack or break when getting the cubes out. Every time I get ice from them I think of this amazing woman, who wrote her first novel at age 60. She would be amused, I think, and delighted too.

# 33

## Six Physicians And Their Common Mistress

"Medicine is my lawful wife," said Anton Chekhov, "and literature is my mistress. When I get fed up with one, I spend the night with the other." And so it has been with a handful of physician-authors through the years. Not ignoring the great physician-authors of ancient times, such as Hippocrates and St. Luke, I would like to focus on six who have been of special interest to me.

### John Keats

John Keats was born in 1795. He was orphaned at a young age; his father was thrown from a horse and died when the lad was 10 years old, and his mother died of tuberculosis five years later. Keats nursed his dying mother and probably contracted the disease from her.

In early school years, Keats was recognized, not as a budding poet, but as an athletic sort who, in spite of his small size, enjoyed games and physical combat. "He would fight anyone, morning, noon and night," said a classmate.

Scarcely a year after his mother's death, Keats was apprenticed to Thomas Hammond, an apothecary who was also a surgeon in a northern suburb of London. Hammond apparently was a drinker and the two did not get along very well. During one encounter, Keats' hand "clenched itself against Hammond" and it wasn't long before Keats moved to separate lodging, putting himself under financial strain.

*John Davis Cantwell, M.D.*

By the time Keats tuned 20 in 1815, he had been trying to write poetry for two years and, supposedly, was almost suicidal over his self-suspected failure. He entered service at Guy's Hospital, a hospital complete with paupers' wards and a madhouse. Most of the patients were drawn from the nearby slums. It was a baptism in reality for Keats. The horrors of hospital life once led him to say that worldly honors were meaningless when one considers young women with cancer. At the same time, he discovered the great books and was to be influence by the likes of Shakespeare and Wordsworth for years to come.

Hints that he was a little different from his fellow students were forthcoming. He described the stomach as "like a brood of callow nestlings, opening their capacious mouths, yearning and gaping for sustenance." He began to dress like a poet, turning his collar down and wearing a ribbon tied around his neck instead of a neckerchief, and let his moustache grow. In the lecture room, according to a fellow student, he "seemed to sit apart and to be absorbed in something else, as if the subject suggested thoughts to him which were not practically connected with it. He was often in the subject and out of it in a dreamy way." Keats himself said, "the other day during a lecture there came a sunbeam into the room and with it a whole troop of creatures floating in the ray; and I was off with them to fairyland."

In March 1816, he was assigned under the notorious Dr. William Lucas, Jr., known as "the butcher of the hospital" who would "cut amongst the most important parts as though they were only skin, making us all shudder from apprehension of his opening arteries or committing some other error." Perhaps this is why Keats himself lacked confidence and was apprehensive. "My last operation was the opening of a man's temporal artery. I did it with the utmost nicety, but reflecting on what passed through my mind at the time, my dexterity seemed a miracle, and I never took up the lancet again."

His first poem was published in May 1816. Despite passing his License of the Society of Apothecaries two months later which would have permitted him to take up a country practice, he began to drift in a circle of poets. His fate was sealed when publisher Leigh Hunt spoke of him and Shelley as "a new school of poetry." Keats, fearful of "every possible chance of doing evil in the wrong direction of the instrument," gave up surgery with no regrets.

In 1818, his brother died of tuberculosis. The same year Keats met Fanny Brawne, the love of his life. In February 1820, Keats himself coughed up blood for the first time. He called for a candle, carefully examined the bed sheets, and said: "This is very unfortunate. I know the color of that blood. It's arterial blood. There's no mistaking that color. That blood is my death warrant. I must die." The ensuing medical treatment was almost worse than the disease; the more blood he coughed up, the more he was bled; the disease-related cachexia was unfortunately treated with a semi-starvation diet. At least one consulting physician thought that the problem was psychosomatic.

In perhaps the biggest therapeutic blunder, he was sent to southern Italy, separating him from Fanny Brawne during the terminal two months of his disease. An autopsy revealed

*John Davis Cantwell, M.D.*

that his lungs were almost entirely destroyed by the disease. He died at age 25 having chosen his own epitaph – "Here lies one whose name was writ on water" and requested that no name be placed on his tomb. His life as a poet had lasted only five years. He had been relatively unsuccessful when he lived (his last volume of poetry sold merely 500 copies) and little regarded for 20 years after his death. Yet his popularity has endured the test of time and his poems such as *Endymion* ("A thing of beauty is a joy forever") and *Ode to a Grecian Urn* ("Beauty is truth, truth beauty") will no doubt remain popular for years to come.

## Oliver Wendell Holmes

Born the son of a minister in 1809, Oliver Wendell Holmes was probably soured on religion when his father was dismissed from the pulpit during a squabble among rivaling factions in his congregation. During Holmes' Harvard years, he showed enough literary talent to be elected class poet. He first tried law, but switched to medicine in 1832 with more success. Holmes became a skilled dissector and was an effective chemist in the Massachusetts General Hospital pharmacy. He spent two years studying medicine in Paris and, upon his return to Boston, won the Boylston Prize for medicine with his essay, *Direct Exploration*, which dealt with a new diagnostic tool – the stethoscope. (Holmes would later poke fun at himself in a poem entitled *The Stethoscope* about a Paris-trained hotshot who made multiple erroneous diagnostic blunders when several flies got into his new stethoscope and created sounds which simulated certain disease conditions.) His most important medical essay was *The Contagiousness of Puerperal Fever*, published in the New England Journal of Medicine and his most famous poem, *Old Ironsides*, was sent to the *Boston Daily Advertiser* as a protest against the destruction of the ship, Constitution.

By 1847, Holmes was appointed Professor of Anatomy at Harvard. In all his years of teaching at Harvard Medical School, he was assigned the one o'clock lecture hour because he had the ability to keep the "hungry and weary" alert. He lived to age 85, contributing numerous poems written for a variety of occasions. His son (and namesake) would become a Supreme Court Justice.

## Arthur Conan Doyle

Arthur Conan Doyle was born in 1859, the son of a poor artist and a civil servant and of a strong-willed mother who pushed him toward a career in medicine. He was an all-around athlete at Stonyhurst School starring in swimming, cricket, football, hockey and ice skating. He also excelled in mischief, causing the master of Stonyhurst to once say to him: "Doyle, you will never come to any good." Doyle particularly liked cricket, saying of it: "It is a jolly game and does more to make a fellow student strong and healthy than all the doctors in the world." He also found time to edit the school magazine, much to the surprise of his teachers who felt he had little talent.

Doyle was a big man - six feet tall, 225 pounds. Upon entering Edinburgh Medical School he added boxing and rugby to his sporting repertoire. When his father's health failed,

*John Davis Cantwell, M.D.*

Doyle was forced to drop out of school temporarily, taking a job as a doctor's assistant. It was not a particularly rewarding experience as he was forced to do primarily scut work and was given little, if any, pay. He began to write short stories at night after a full day of "listening to the throb of the charwoman's heart or the rustle of the greengrocer's lungs." When he did return to medical school, he was greatly influenced by Dr. Joseph Bell, a man who prided himself on the medical deductions that could be made through the technique of keen observation.

Doyle received a medical degree in 1881 and decided to accept a partnership with a fellow physician-athlete, George Budd. The arrangement didn't work. Budd was an assembly-line type of money-oriented physician with poor moral standards. Instead Doyle set up his own practice and whiled away the many empty hours doing life insurance physicals, engaging in sports and pursuing his writing interests. His first year of practice netted a grand income of $300. In 1885, at the age of 26, he decided to marry the sister of one of his patients. He created the character of Sherlock Holmes the following year, based partly upon the physician, Joseph Bell, and named after Oliver Wendell Holmes, whom he admired. It took him two months to write *A Study in Scarlet*, but considerably longer to get it published. His medical knowledge surfaced in the novel as the hero-murderer, Jefferson Hope, dies of a leaking thoracic aneurysm before he can be brought to trial. Doyle initially sold the rights to the story for $125; he was later to buy it back for $125,000.

In 1890, Doyle went to Vienna for specialty training in ophthalmology. He set up practice in fashionable Devonshire Place but few rang his doorbell. Fortunately his fame as an author was spreading. He decided to give up medicine and live entirely by his writing.

He tired of Sherlock Holmes after seven years and decided to eliminate him in *The Final Problem*, having him disappear over the chasm's edge with his rival, Professor Moriarty. Little did he realize the impact this would have on his many fans, who proceeded to wear crepe bands around their hats in mourning. So great was the public demand that Doyle brought Sherlock back in *The Adventure of the Empty Room*.

Doyle's wife developed tuberculosis in 1893. Four years later, he fell in love with Jean Leckie, 13 years his junior but, following his code of honor, limited it to a platonic relationship until the death of his wife in 1906. The middle years saw him knighted and experience the pleasure of being perhaps the most popular writer in the world. He also involved himself in several real-life whodunits and helped to free innocent men on two counts.

He became deeply committed to spiritualism in later years and, in 1923, traveled over 50,000 miles and addressed a quarter of a million people on the subject.

Doyle developed angina pectoris and congestive heart failure at age 70 and died the following year. He remained a sportsman to the end and, shortly before his death, drove a race car around a track at 100 mph. His barbells and boxing gloves were in the corner of his bedroom at the time of his death. On

*John Davis Cantwell, M.D.*

his grave reads his name, date of birth, and four words - STEEL TRUE, BLADE STRAIGHT.

**Anton Chekhov (See Chapter 34)**

**Somerset Maugham**

Somerset Maugham was born in Paris in 1874. Orphaned as a young boy, like Keats, he returned to England as the ward of his rather narrow-minded uncle. He arrived in London in 1892 to study medicine at St. Thomas Hospital Medical School and wrote his first novel, *Lisa of Lambeth*, during his senior year in medical school based on his experience there. "I exercised little invention," he said. "I put down what I had seen and heard as plainly as possible. I was forced to stick to the facts by the miserable poverty of my imagination." He earned around $50 in royalties and apparently decided shortly thereafter to give up his medical career.

His ability to be touched by human pain and suffering, "largely the product of his own unhappy childhood," is nowhere more evident than in is famous novel, *Of Human Bondage*, written when he was in his late 30s. While his Philip Carey had to learn to cope with a clubfoot, Maugham's own affliction was a case of severe stuttering which developed soon after his mother's death. He tried marriage in his early 40s but failed, probably because of his homosexuality. He once told his nephews: "I tried to persuade myself that I was three-quarters normal and that only one-quarter of me was queer - whereas it was the other way around."

He followed a rigid schedule in his writing, from 9 a.m. to 1 p.m. every day. If ideas didn't come to him right away, he would "prime" the pump by typing his name over and over until they finally did. He lived to be 91, and developed the public image of a cynical old man who collected French impressionist paintings and lived the good life on the French Riviera.

## William Carlos Williams

William Carlos Williams, a native of Rutherford, New Jersey, was born in 1883. He grew up in an atmosphere created by an overpowering grandmother and mother and an often absent, weak-willed father. When as a schoolboy athlete, he once collapsed while training for the 300-yard dash, his physician diagnosed adolescent heart strain and suggested that he give up athletics. Williams refused, continuing to play tennis and soccer and to perform as a varsity fencer at the University of Pennsylvania.

He was pushed into medicine by his mother, whose brother was a successful surgeon. At the University of Pennsylvania Medical School he was constantly scribbling in "black and tawny" notebooks while trying, the same time, to learn anatomy and neurology. It was at this time that he befriended fellow Penn. student, Ezra Pound. Williams focused his medical practice on obstetrics and pediatrics. Meanwhile his initial success as a poet was unspectacular: his first book sold only four copies at Garrison's Stationery Store.

With the busy life of a physician, he would steal moments in which to write at night, in the early morning or in-between patients. Often he would pull his car off the road to scribble words on prescription blanks.

*John Davis Cantwell, M.D.*

Reportedly he also stole moments with the ladies, leading to early marital turbulence. He paid multiple visits to an aging nymphomaniac, in Greenwich Village, who wrote him obscene letters, sent nude pictures of herself to him and even came up to Rutherford for a confrontation. She gave up when Williams' wife threatened to call the police. Even late in his life, according to Brendan Gill of the New Yorker, "despite his age and damaged heart he was lacerated by sexual excitement; every young mother encountered seemed to strike him as a Venus." Some of this shows through in several of his poems and plays, such as "A Dream of Love" in which the doctor-hero dies of a heart seizure while making love to a certain Dottie in a New York hotel room. (This was certainly tragic for the doctor and likewise for the play as it left the latter without a hero in the middle of Act II). Williams wrote "The Cure" while partially paralyzed and blinded from his first stroke. The piece concerns a poet, disabled in a motorcycle accident, who nonetheless tries to seduce his nurse.

He continued to write in spite of multiple strokes and heart attacks, cancer of the sigmoid colon and very poor eyesight. Soon after his death in 1963, he was awarded both the Pulitzer Prize and the Gold Medal for Poetry. His physician-son continued to practice medicine in the family home at 9 Ridge Road where his father had lived and worked for a half century.

**Summary**

In looking back upon these six physician-authors, one is struck by their differences and by their similarities. Several died very young, others lived to old age. Tuberculosis was a threat to three; cardiovascular disease claimed several others. Most were ill-suited to medicine, having been pushed into the profession by parents or by fate.

In Keats, we can appreciate man's romantic side - and his courage when facing a devastating disease. Holmes had the ability to create for the occasion, as evidenced by "Old Ironsides." Doyle was a gallant sportsman, if not a successful physician. Chekhov was warm and compassionate, the Hippocratic Oath at its best. Maugham could convey sensitivity and frustration, both of which he knew so well in real life. Williams was so very human - and one of the few physician-authors to actually carry out a busy medical career.

There have been many other talented physician-authors through the years. Francois Rabelais wrote tales of the "outrageous giants," Pantagrual and Gargantua. Sir William Osler was a wonderful writer, fueled by his vast experience and knowledge of classical literature. Walker Percy was dubbed the "moralist of the South" for his thought-provoking messages in novels, ranging from *The Moviegoer* (winner of the National Book Award) to *The Thanatos Syndrome*.

One of Oliver Sacks' books, *Awakenings*, was made into a highly successful movie. Robin Cook and Michael Crichton have had phenomenal success with their novels, some of which have also been adapted to the movie theater. Richard Selzer is a flashy writer, providing great entertainment in works such as *Letters to a Young Doctor* and *Mortal Lessons*. The late Lewis Thomas achieved a following with books

*John Davis Cantwell, M.D.*

including the *Lives of a Cell* and *The Medusa and the Snail*.

On the Georgia scene, John Ransom Lewis served as Georgia's Poet Laureate. Mel Konner combines anthropology with medical essays and books. John Stone has written books of poetry and crisp essays (including *In the Country of Hearts*, one of my favorites). Ferrol Sams' trilogy (*Run with the Horsemen, The Whisper of the River, When all the World Was Young*) has a special place in my medical library, as do works by Neil Schulman (*Doc Hollywood*), and J. Willis Hurst.

When I encounter young physicians who aspire to combine medicine and literary creativity, I encourage them wholeheartedly. As William Carlos Williams has written, "…I have never felt that medicine interfered with me but rather that it was my very food and drink, the very thing which made it possible for me to write."

# 34

## Chekhov's Journey

In 1890, 29-year-old physician-author, Anton Chekhov made a 5,000 mile journey across Siberia to visit the penal colony on Sakhalin Island. He had already developed a cough and hemoptysis, which he must have known were probable indicators of beginning tuberculosis, having lost a brother to this disease just months previously.

On April 21st, he took a train from Moscow to Yaroslavl, and then took a boat down the Volga River and another up the Karma River. From Ekaterinburg, he switched to a four-wheeled springless carriage, following the "Great Siberian Highway," which was "...little more than a dirt track for much of its length, subject to floods, bandits, and wild animals."

Why did he do it?

**The Man**

Chekhov was already a well-known author and playwright. He had grown up in the small town of Taganorg, in southern Russia, the grandson of peasants and the son of a bankrupt grocer. The third of six children, Chekhov stayed in his hometown to finish his preliminary schooling while his family moved up to Moscow in hopes of better fortune. His mother encouraged him to become a physician. He had already been exposed to the profession, during his bout of peritonitis at age 15. Chekhov enrolled in medical school at Moscow University at age 19, living with his parents and eight others in a four-room tenement house. He had received a state scholarship for the school but most of the money was usurped by his parents for household debts. Realizing that he had a talent for writing, young Anton attempted to enhance the family income by selling short stories to magazines such as "Splinters" and "Light and Shadow."

A shy student, he wasn't impressive at first glance, but his work was solid. A professor observed:

> "He collected the elements of the case history together with surprising ease and accuracy … But it was when he had to touch on the ordinary life of the patient, uncovering its intimate details about how the illness developed into its present state that Chekhov seemed to bowl along effortlessly without forcing himself, in contrast to many students and even doctors who find it difficult to relate to the vivid statements emerging from the unique circumstances of patients' lives."

Like most students, Chekhov was influenced by the best teachers. Even after graduation, he returned to hear lectures by Grigory Zakharin, professor of medicine and an advocate of preventive medicine. Another role model might have been Eric Erismann, professor of public health, who in 1875 had surveyed factory conditions in Moscow. Dr. Aleksei Ostroumov was very popular with the students, and Chekhov later chose his ward when he needed hospital admission for tuberculosis.

During summer vacations, Chekhov worked in the Chikinl Hospital, south of Moscow. His attending physician, Dr. Pavel Archangelsky, recalled:

> "Anton Chekhov worked unhurriedly. Sometimes a kind of hesitancy appeared in his manner but he did everything with attention and a manifest love of what he was doing, especially toward the patients who passed through his hands. He listened quietly to them, never raising his voice however tired he was and even if the patient was talking about things quite irrelevant to his illness. The mental state of the patient interested him particularly."

Chekhov took his final exams in May, 1884, and then affixed his doctor's plate on the front door of his family's house. His first medical fees were for treating a woman with a toothache, a monk with dysentery, and an actress with an upset stomach. His practice was slow to develop. He mainly treated family and friends, gratis of course.

He continued to write, publishing his first play, "Ivanov," at age 27. The themes included a wife with tuberculosis and an insensitive physician, fresh out of medical school. He wrote "Ward No. 6" five years later, depicting the depths to which psychiatric care could sink in his time.

**The Journey**

Shaken by his brother's death from tuberculosis (and with hints of his own similar fate), besieged by women he didn't feel strongly about, and bored with the social scene in Moscow, Chekhov startled both family

*John Davis Cantwell, M.D.*

and friends with his decision to visit the penal colony on Sakhalin Island. He felt that the experience might help pay off some of his debt to medicine. "From the books I have read," he wrote, "it is clear that we have left millions of people to rot in prison." He wanted to see for himself, to write a 100-200 page paper that might stir up his fellow countrymen, hoping that he could also submit it for a doctoral thesis at Moscow University. He also wanted to test himself with something sterner than the superficialities of the "cultivated life and social circle" he was wallowing in. He wrote:

> "This journey will be perpetual toil, physical and mental, for six months and it is what I need to shake off my depression and laziness. One must keep in training."

The trip was indeed difficult. He was nearly killed in a carriage crash. Encountering massive floods, he had to unhitch the horses from his carriage and lead them one at a time through the raging waters. His first view of Sakhalin Island was ominous. Forest fires raged out of control, billowing clouds of black-gray smoke: "It seemed that all of Sakhalin was in flames," he wrote.

Drawing on what he had learned about public health matters in medical school, Chekhov went right to work. He had data cards made up in the printing shop of the police station and then set out to interview virtually all of the 10,000 "criminals" imprisoned on the island, except for some sensitive political prisoners who were off limits. In one prison, he found "20 men to a cell, all shackled, emaciated and half naked, and sleeping on the bare floor. They shared a common chamber pot in the corner." The prison lacked any medications for ill prisoners. Chekhov felt that he had seen "...the extreme limits of man's degradation." Common causes of death, besides freezing while chained to logs in sub-zero weather or suffocating in coal mines, included tuberculosis, pneumonia and scurvy.

Chekhov's findings were serialized in the journal, "Russian Thought," and compiled in a book, **The Island of Sakhalin**. He struggled for three years to complete the latter. He asked the dean of the medical school to accept it as a doctoral thesis, but the dean merely smiled and walked away, apparently unwilling to be caught up in a political embroglio.

Chekhov was "haunted by the thought of the children he had met on the island." He collected several thousand books and had them transported to the schools on Sakhalin, hoping to help in some small way.

The trip was anything but a total waste. Chekhov's writings seemed to stir the attitudes of his fellow countrymen (and perhaps the political leaders as well) to the plight of the convicts. In 1896, a governmental commission was sent to Sakhalin to investigate the situation and to make recommendations. Whatever progress was made in the soviet gulag was short-lived, for the murderous Joseph Stalin was on the horizon.

**Afterward.**

Chekhov purchased a home in Melikhova, 50 miles south of Moscow, and lived there for the next seven years, providing medical care for a district encompassing 26 villages, 7 factories and a monastery. He somehow found time to write 27 stories as well. He didn't overemphasize medicine or doctors in the latter:

> "I write about sickness only when it forms part of the characters or adds color to them. I avoid terrifying my readers with illnesses."

Battling plague and cholera, and a multitude of other maladies that claimed 40% of the children before age five, Chekhov did what he could, sometimes lacking even a thermometer. During one five-month period, he made 576 house calls, often at night. His sister, Marya, helped him, and said of her brother:

> "(He) sometimes frowned when they (the patients) called for him when he was ill or very tired. But once we helped our brother to dress, his frown disappeared and the man waiting in the porch could not see any sign of discontentment on his face."

Chekhov relished work, both literary and medical, writing that "In order to live well as a human being one must work, work with love, believe in one's work..." Knowing that he dealt with life and death situations, and that errors in judgement couldn't always be avoided, he felt it necessary for a doctor to learn to live with his conscience. Even so, he was so troubled by the death of the Yanov's daughter that he threatened to give up medicine.

## The Final Illness

A typical physician-patient, Anton rationalized about his illness, used denial and tried to avoid doctors: "I am afraid of being auscultated by my colleagues. What if they find prolonged expiratory sounds or bronchial breathing?" As his illness progressed, he said: "I shall drink mineral waters and quinine, but I shall not allow myself to be examined."

Even some of the doctors tried to rationalize, telling him that his bloody sputum was likely due to a gastric hemorrhage. Chekhov would have none of this: "I listen to them but don't take any notice; I know I have TB."

Well-meaning visitors fatigued him. Tolstoy overstayed his allotted time by a half-hour, discussing immortality. Chekhov mused that "An ill-natured wife might perhaps be able to reduce my visitors by half."

Chekhov rallied some: "I so much want to live, to write more." He traveled to Nice, purchased 319 volumes of French Classics for the library in his hometown of Taganorg, and lived for a while in Yalta, a resort that attracted individuals with tuberculosis. Ever civic-minded, Chekhov "immediately started a fund to finance the building of a sanitorium."

His plays, "The Three Sisters" and "The Cherry Orchard," were being performed at the Moscow Arts Theater. Chekhov met one of the main actresses, Olga Knipper, promptly fell in love, and was married on May 25, 1901.

He tried various remedies for his disease, most likely to satisfy the desires of his new wife and his relatives. One was to take a "kumis cure," a traditional drink of the

*John Davis Cantwell, M.D.*

Tartars, made by fermenting a mare's milk in an old leather sack. It didn't help, nor did he expect it to.

On January 17, 1904, a public ceremony was held at the Moscow Arts Theater to celebrate the 25th anniversary of Chekhov's literary debut. He was too ill to relish the occasion.

Olga took him to the German spa in Badenweiler, where he rapidly deteriorated. She described his last hours:

> "At the beginning of the night Anton woke up and, for the first time in his life, asked himself for the doctor to be fetched. The doctor came and asked for some champagne to be given to the patient. Anton sat up and with great deliberation said to the doctor 'Ich sterbe' (I am dying). Then he took the glass, turned his face towards me, smiled his extraordinary smile and said, 'It's a long time since I drank champagne,' quietly drunk up the drakes, lay down silently on his left side and was soon still forever."

His body was brought back to Moscow in a refrigerated railroad car with "for oysters" stamped on the outside. By the time the funeral procession reached the Novodevichy Monastery, "The crowd was so vast that it blocked the gates, and the pallbearers, immediate family, and close friends had to jostle their way through." The traditional song, "Eternal Memory," was sung. The only funeral oration was by Chekhov's mother, who said simply "What a calamity has struck us. Antosha is no more." As Henri Troyat concluded, given "his dread of bombast"

Chekhov would have appreciated the simple service.

John Davis Cantwell, M.D.

# 35

## Wallace Stegner: A Life Remembered

> I bequeath myself to the dirt,
> to grow from the grass I love.
> If you want me again,
> Look for me under your boot soles
> - Walt Whitman

Authors aren't always the best role models. Hemingway was a boozer, a bully, and a womanizer. Fitzgerald was an alcoholic, as were a number of others. Even Robert Frost, a kindly appearing soul, had his "desert places." As a friend once said to him, "Robert, you're a great poet. You're just a bad person."

Wallace Stegner (1909-1993) was perhaps an exception. A biography by J.J. Benson delves into the life and works of this multi-talented man, possessed of a mind that "burned like a blowtorch in the dark." As Benson states, Stegner

> "...was a remarkable man, not the least remarkable in the making his life and work one piece. His integrity shone forth equally in both. He was not stern, self-righteous, or judgmental, but was a person who could be the life of the party, someone who knew how to have fun and who had a ready sense of humor. Yet he was unbending in his belief in right conduct. He was kind, thoughtful, and generous, a person who was easy to talk to, yet he was held almost in awe by many

who knew him as being somewhat larger than life, in the expectations he had for himself and in his superhuman capacity for hard work."

Stegner was born on his grandfather's farm in Lake Mills, Iowa. His early childhood, depicted in *Wolf Willow*, was on a homestead in Saskatchewan. The latter was "the richest page in my memory, for it was there…for a half dozen years, we had…a house of our own, a united family, and a living, however hard." The youngest of two boys, Wallace had to deal with what sounded like Raynaud's disease, an overshadowing athletic older brother, and an abusive father.

From ages 12-21, Stegner lived in Salt Lake City, entering the University of Utah at age 16, where be became an avid reader and a varsity tennis player. After graduation, he accepted a teaching assistantship at the University of Iowa, where he met a teacher, Norman Foerster "…who would lead him into the studies that would become the basis for his life's work." While at Iowa, he lost all of his savings in the Depression, met his wife (whose love would "sustain and nourish him" for nearly 60 years), suffered through the death of his brother (who had contracted pneumonia "while helping to rescue a motorist in the snow") and the onset of breast cancer in his mother.

In *The Big Rock Candy Mountain* (1943), a powerful autobiographic "novel," Stegner recalled the experience of seeing his brother, "Chet" in the coffin:

"Suddenly he was flooded by memories of terrifying clarity, he and Chet trapping

*John Davis Cantwell, M.D.*

muskrats in the river in Canada, playing soldier down in the burnouts on the homestead, singing together in school cantatas, getting into fights over the Erector set, swimming in the bare-naked hole down by where Doctor O'Malley's tent used to be pitched…

The pride he had felt, the tremendous exuberant exultation when Chet caught the pass in the last quarter to beat Provo, and himself running out to the field hysterical with school spirit, passing through players slimed with black mud from head to foot, only their eyes unmuddied, to grab Chet's hand and pounded him on the back, and the way Chet had grinned almost in embarrassment behind his mask of mud, still holding the ball in his big muddy hands."

Stegner had a brief stay on the faculty at the University of Wisconsin, where he and his wife befriended Phil and Peg Gray (a friendship which became the basis for his wonderful final novel, *Crossing To Safety*). He moved on to Harvard, teaching the likes of Norman Mailer. His advice to the Harvard students was "the best way to learn about writing was to write," especially on something they knew about. He cautioned them that one doesn't know much before age 30, so they shouldn't expect to write well until after that age.

Summer sessions at the Bread Loaf Writer's Conference in Vermont helped Stegner polish his teaching techniques, and enabled him to develop lifelong friendships with the likes of Robert Frost, from whose poems Stegner took the titles for two of his novels.

*Adventures on Seven Continents And Other Essays*

Stegner settled at Stanford in 1946, starting their Creative Writing Program. Over the next 25 years his pupils included Ernest Gaines, Wendell Berry, Robert Stone, Edward Abby, Larry McMurtry, and Ken Kesey. He was on a different wave length with the latter, whom he considered "ineducable."

Stegner won the Pulitzer Prize in 1971 for *Angle of Repose*, based on family letters belonging to Mary Hallock Foote, a 19th century artist and writer whose marriage to a civil engineer "took her out of her genteel life in the East, into the raw West." The narrator is the couple's grandson, wheelchair-bound Lyman Ward, who says of their marriage:

> "What really interests me is how two such unlikely particles clung together, and under what strains, rolling downhill into their future until they reached the angle of repose where I knew them."

The conflict between the grandparents, Susan and Oliver, is that "between the boomer man and the nester woman…the ruggedly individualistic man, strong, silent, and practical, and the woman to whom cultured society is all important." Susan's main flaw was that she never really appreciated her husband "until it was too late." Oliver lacked the ability to forgive, and his life "became a separate line that did not intersect with hers."

Stegner's tribute to his mother, in *Where the Blue Bird Sings to the Lemonade Springs*, was deeply moving to me, for my mother, Montana-bred, had similar unselfish qualities and had great hopes for me, more than I probably merited. At her bedside near the end,

John Davis Cantwell, M.D.

Stegner recalls that his name was the last word she ever spoke ("You're a good boy, Wallace."). For the rest of his life he would "never get over trying, however badly or sadly or confusingly to be what (she) thought I was." Upon facing some "crisis of feeling or sympathy or consideration for others," it was her voice that spoke through him, and inspired him to do the right thing.

His last novel, *Crossing To Safety*, delves into the friendship that Stegner shared with Phil and Peg Gray. Peg is Charity in the novel, a woman "continuously planning, forever making lists - and yet, she becomes irrational in her overplanning and scheduling of every activity, even relaxation." A powerful woman, a "castrator" of her husband, Charity is also the type of person "who empowers others through her love and generosity." Riddled with cancer, Charity's spirit still "gushed and overflowed and swept us up, making us forget pity, caution, concern, everything but the pleasure of her presence." The novel deals with a common theme of Stegner's, namely that "life is hard and unpredictable, and in order to survive, people need the support, physically and emotionally, of others."

Having endured the hippie era at Stanford, Stegner quit teaching there in 1971, stating that he'd had a "belly full." Of the hippies, he wrote, "to a puzzled elder, they often seem to throb rather than think." He was sympathetic to protesters against the Vietnam War, but "couldn't quite go for the notion that breaking all the windows at Stanford helped very much." The turbulent times did stimulate one of his books, *The Spectator Bird*, which won the National Book Award. Issues in the novel included commitment versus impulses, character as opposed to emotions and pleasure.

In March 1993, while visiting in Santa Fe, Stegner was seriously injured in an auto accident. His hospital course was complicated by a heart attack and possible stroke. His last words to his physician were calm and deliberate as always, "do what you have to do." It wasn't enough, and he died 16 days after the accident.

And so ended the life of a great novelist, short story writer, historian, teacher, and environmentalist. Still vigorous and productive at age 84, a list of 10 projects to complete was found by his wife, above his desk, after his funeral.

His ashes were scattered on a hillside near his summer cottage in Greensboro, Vermont. As Benson writes, Stegner "became more joined to the land as he grew older: now he will become that land. Look for him under the soles of your boots."

One beautiful autumn day, in the not-too-distant-future, I will venture to Vermont and do just that.

*John Davis Cantwell, M.D.*

# 36

## Encounters with James Dickey

> "and you and I and all
> There is, all born and dying,
> Forever, at once."

James Dickey was dead.

I knew it was coming. The last photo I had seen of him showed a once macho man who had lost at least 75 pounds, had only tufts of hair and was clad in white socks and sandals. The picture also showed a man looking at the camera with that night fighter-pilot's gaze, surrounded by piles of books and pictures of loved ones.

I suspect it was his hob-nailed liver that did him in, along with chronic lung disease, so severe that he required portable oxygen to teach his English classes at the University of South Carolina. Maybe he had diabetes, too, for in *the Eye-beaters, Blood, Victory, Madness, Buckhead and Mercy,* he tells of thirsting "like a prince, then like a king, then like an empire..." and of seeing a nice young doctor who told him he needed "needles, moderation, and exercise" so he wouldn't look forward to "gangrene and kidney failure, boils, blindness, infection, skin trouble, falling teeth, coma, and death."

Dickey taught students until a week before his death, combining the heroic commitment of a gifted teacher - like Mr. Mangham, his North Fulton High School math teacher - with the survival instincts of Lewis Medlock in

*Deliverance*, and of the downed tail-gunner, Muldrow, in *To the White Sea*.

Dickey was a native of Atlanta, growing up on West Wesley Road and attending North Fulton High School, where my children also went. He was one of the "Buckhead Boys" and had written lovingly of his childhood friends in "Looking for the Buckhead Boys:"

"The Buckhead Boys. If I can find them, even one, I'm home. And if I can find him, catch him in or around Buckhead, I'll never die: it's likely my youth will walk inside me like a king."

Dickey participated in football and track, both in high school and in college. He quit Clemson after his freshman football season to enlist in the Army Air Corps. He was a navigator with a night fighter squadron, and embellished his wartime experiences, claiming that he had been a pilot in the Pacific. Like Alex Haley, he discovered his talent for writing while in the service, composing erotic letters to a girlfriend.

**Early Years**

Between the wars, he enrolled in Vanderbilt, majoring in English. His early career included a year of teaching freshman English at Rice University, a fellowship in England, and a five- and-a-half year stint in advertising, for McCann-Erickson.

I discovered his *Poems 1957-1967* in the late 1960s. By then he had won the National Book Award in Poetry for *Buckdancer's Choice*, was the consultant on poetry to the Library of Congress, and was soon to become world-famous for his novel, *Deliverance*, published in 1970 and made into a movie.

*John Davis Cantwell, M.D.*

Dickey had a cameo role in the film, the sheriff who tells Burt Reynolds, Jon Voigt, and colleagues: "Don't you all come back up here again,. Don't you all do nothing like this again." (I know for sure that Ned Beaty won't go back.)

Dickey was a prolific writer, who often had separate works on four different typewriters. He produced 17 books of poetry, three novels, three other books of prose, and various other works of literature. His topics were varied. His athletic and military experiences were themes in a number of works. He could also write about Jane MacNaughton, his little seventh grade classmate, who caught his eye at a school dance by leaping up and touching "the end of one of the paper-ring decorations." He puzzles as to why the same person, as a mother of four, would "leap to her death from a window of a downtown hotel."

One of my favorites was "The Celebration," when Dickey was surprised at a carnival on the Lakewood Midway by seeing his parents at a distance, "He, leaning, on a dog-chewed cane, she wrapped to the nose in the fur of exhausted weasels." He watches them climb aboard the ferris wheel, "their gold teeth flashing," the "wheel in the middle of the air, where old age rises and laughs."

A brief piece of prose I enjoyed was "Night Hurdling," an account of Dickey's high hurdles final at North Fulton against a boy from Canton. At the fifth hurdle they were dead even:

"The finish-line crowd was coming almost like a hurricane. I concentrated on staying low over the hurdles and made really good moves on the next three. I began to edge him by inches, and by the next two hurdles I thought if I didn't hit the next two I'd make it. I also said to myself, as I remember, don't play it safe. Go low over the last stick, and then give it everything you've got up the final straight."

He winds up hitting the last hurdle, tearing the flesh to the bone, "but his frenzied momentum was such that I won by a yard, careening wildly into the crowd." He crashes into a little boy who lay in the smoky grass crying, his nose bloody, "and I came back, blowing like a wounded plow-horse, everybody congratulating me on a new N.G.I.C. record. But, unlike myself, I went to the boy, raised him up in my arms, wiped the blood from his nose, tried to comfort him and kissed him. In memory, now, that was the best moment I ever had out of sports."

## My Encounters

I had three encounters with James Dickey, at different points in his career. Each was special. Each was memorable.

The first occurred at one of the Delta check-in gates in Atlanta. I was heading for Columbia, South Carolina, to give a lecture. Among the sparse crowd was a man bedecked in a safari outfit, complete with one brim of his hat snapped up to the crown. My initial thought was that maybe I was at the wrong gate, perhaps the flight to Nairobi, to the Masai Mara Game Reserve. On closer observation, I recognized Mr. Dickey and remembered that he was poet-in-residence at the University of South Carolina.

*John Davis Cantwell, M.D.*

I usually don't bother so-called celebrity types in public, knowing how most prefer their private space. I couldn't resist, however, asking Mr. Dickey about Punchy Henderson, one of the Buckhead Boys, "the last of the wind sprinters, and now for no reason, the first of the heart attacks," dying while watching a high school football game. I told Mr. Dickey that Punchy was probably like a lot of former athletes, who stopped being active after their playing days, continued bad eating habits, and got fat and atheromatous. He thought that sounded reasonable.

I wanted to ask him more - about his night fighter days, about North Fulton High School, about Jane MacNaughton, about the high hurdles race with the boy from Canton - but the poet-author was obviously inebriated and in no shape for in-depth conversation. Our boarding call was given. Dickey was turned back by the gate attendant as he didn't have a boarding pass. I started to intervene, to tell the stewardess who he was, but thought better of it. Maybe it would teach him not to drink so much.

I don't recall if he ever made it on the plane.

My second encounter with Mr. Dickey was at North Fulton High School. My children had casually commented that he was returning to his alma mater to give a reading. I blocked out my morning schedule and settled in on the hard gymnasium seats for his performance. It was remarkable! He began by reading a section of *Deliverance*. He told of Lewis, "the kind of man who tries by any means - weight-lifting, diet, exercise, self-help manuals for taxidermy to modern art - to hold on to his body and mind and improve them, to rise above time," one of the best tournament archers in the state, "one of the strongest men I have ever shaken hands with." Unfortunately Lewis breaks his leg as their canoe capsized in the Chatooga maelstrom, and it is up to the mild-mannered Ed to rise to the occasion, to send an arrow into the mountain man who threatens him with a rifle, and then has to track the wounded man into the woods, like one does an animal.

Dickey then shifted to two poems, both perfect for the occasion. One is entitled "The Bee," and is dedicated to the football coaches of Clemson College 1952. The poem concerns Dickey's youngest son, who is stung by a bee and who subsequently runs blindly onto a busy California highway. His father, the "old wingback," comes to life. With the voices of his old coaches ringing in his ears ("G____ damn you, Dickey, Dig! This is your last time to cut and run.") Dickey races to save his son:

"Dead coaches live in the air, son, live in the ear, like fathers and urge, and urge. They want you better than you are. When needed, they rise and curse you. They scream when something must be saved."

Dickey's last poem that day was about Mr. Mangham, his math teacher at North Fulton. Throughout one particular class, Mr. Mangham struggled at the blackboard. He would pause, press "the middle of his brow with a handkerchief, looking at all of us as he stepped quickly out of the room." He "raided the lunchroom icebox, and held a knotted cloth full of soupy cubes dripping down his gray face." The students in that class were

*John Davis Cantwell, M.D.*

apparently amused by their teacher's antics. Only later would they learn that he had suffered a stroke. The impending event "did not stop Mangham for one freezing minute of his death from explaining for my own good, from the good side of his face, while the other mixed unfelt sweat and ice water, what I never could get to save my soul."

The same commitment to teaching would be exemplified to Dickey's own students years later as he struggled right up until his own death to teach them the beauty of the English language. "Every time I put down one word next to another word," he once said, "it's a moment of potential discovery." Marill was probably right when she wrote that he seemed to be striving "to escape mortality through the immortality of poetry."

I last saw James Dickey at Manuel's Tavern one weekend afternoon, late in his career. His head had been shaved, for recent brain surgery to remove a blood clot. He appeared gaunt, unlike the "size XL" virile image he once projected.

Like some of his characters, "ordinary men pitted against an implacable foe that makes no distinctions between good and evil and cares nothing for their survival," Dickey radiated a sort of heroism that comes from "the instinct to survive in the face of extinction." As we learned from his son's memoir, *Summer of Deliverance*, a lot of Dickey's heroic posturing was a facade.

After some of the poems he read that day he smiled, reflecting what Reynolds Price said was "his shamelessly explicit delight in the brilliance of his own poetry." I didn't blame him.

*Adventures on Seven Continents And Other Essays*

One poem to me reflected Dickey's attitude of battling back, of going hard over the last hurdle, no matter what. It seemed that he was in New York City, late at night, hailing a cab. He finally succeeds in getting one, but the driver, clad in a cowboy hat, takes him past old warehouses, then stops in a dark alley:

"And a voice at last, still out of Oklahoma, said, 'I want your money.'
We were present in silence. A brought-on up-backward thock took place, and on the fresh blade a light alive in the hand, new-born with spring-shock. It was mine. At 60. 'I want your car,' I said."

He smiled. And in that smile I could see Lewis, Ed, or Muldrow, switchblade in hand, taking on all comers, looking even death right in the eye.

*John Davis Cantwell, M.D.*

# 37

## Byron Herbert Reece: The Mountain Poet

Several years ago, my wife and I were hiking in Vogel State Park in North Georgia. We came upon a trail dedicated to the memory of Byron Herbert Reece. I recalled the name, but didn't know much about him. I subsequently learned a lot about this remarkable man.

Reece was born in Choestoe ("the land of the dancing rabbits"), in the Brasstown Valley, September 14, 1917. His family lived in a one-room log cabin by Wolf Creek. They had been in that area since the Cherokee Indians had been driven out in 1838. He was named Byron, after a man who bought hogs from his father, and Herbert, after an insurance salesman. He was the fourth of five children.

Ralph McGill thought he looked like a young Abe Lincoln:

> "There was the same lanky thinness; the lean, craggy face, the unruly hair, the deep-set eyes with pain and brooding sorrow in them which laughter temporarily would remove."

The Reeces' nearest neighbors were ten miles away. Byron was eight before he saw his first automobile, and in his 20s before electric lights arrived. He helped his parents and siblings till their 25 acres. The Bible was read daily by the family. Byron was influenced by the Psalms, and by old mountain folk ballads. He enjoyed listening to the poems his aunt had written and would read to him.

Books were scarce, but devoured when available. Favorite authors of his included A.E. Housman, William Butler Yeats, and William Blake. He also loved music, especially Beethoven, "much of Mozart, a lot of Haydn, and a little of Brahms."

Reece entered Young Harris College in 1936. A teacher recalled aspects of the young student:

> "Cynical, truthful, dependable, determined. Has few contacts with folks, and wants but few. Except in mathematics he is about the best pupil…
>
> Widely read. Tastes are literary and artistic. Writes unusually good poetry and short stories, but is like Thoreau about his work. Knows he has ability, but doesn't give a straw whether you know it or not."

He could only spend two years at Young Harris, for his parents were ill with tuberculosis and he was needed on the farm.

His mother encouraged him to write, so he would work all day in the fields and write in the evenings, in front of the fireplace. His ear was trained on the cadences of the Psalms.

*John Davis Cantwell, M.D.*

Byron Herbert Reece at work in the field

*Adventures on Seven Continents And Other Essays*

Byron Herbert Reece writing by the fireplace

*John Davis Cantwell, M.D.*

His first poem was published outside his local area in 1937. In the early 1940s his work began to appear in poetry magazines. A Kentucky writer, Jessie Stuart, was impressed by his work and took some of Reece's poems to his publisher, E.P. Dutton. *The Ballad of the Bones and Other Poems* was published in 1945 and dedicated to his parents, Juan and Emma. The 28-year-old Reece was mowing hay in his fields when the postman brought a package with the first copies. The title of the book was inspired by Ezekiel 37.

Invitations poured in for poetry readings. An enthusiastic woman admirer asked him if he had been named after the famous poets, Lord Byron and George Herbert. "No, ma'am," came the reply, "I was named after a butcher and an insurance salesman."

Reece was told that he should focus more on his writing, "that anyone can plow potatoes." His response: "Anybody can plow potatoes, but nobody is willing to plow mine but me." He went on to say:

> "I'm always torn between two loyalties, one to go on making bread on the farm and the other to get out of my system these things I want to comment on through writing."

In his ballad, "I go by Ways of Rust and Flame," he described "the lonely life experienced by the dedicated writer."

He was poor and frustrated by the difficulties of keeping up with the farm and his writing. In 1947 he seemed "on the verge of cracking up."

Some bright spots were to follow. In 1950, he built a new house, next to the century-old family home. That same year he was featured in *Newsweek* magazine. He was invited to teach the summer term at UCLA, and flew for the first time, not telling his mother because she feared airplane travel. The next year he received the first of two Guggenheim fellowships, and taught at Young Harris College. Reece spent three months at Battey State Hospital. There he wrote four poems, "In Absence," "Underground," "The Seven Days of the Week," and "Always the Wind." There was "a brooding soliloquy of disturbed thought" in his work. He discouraged visitors, fearful that they might contract the disease, and left against medical advice, fearing that he would become too dependent upon others. Three months later, his mother died, his major source of inspiration. He became depressed and first thought of using a gun on himself, as one of his "beloved mentors," Dr. Lufkin Dance, had done in 1946. He saw a physician in Atlanta, who changed his medication. He was also told that his problems probably were related to the fact that he had never married. Reece never returned for a followup visit. His weight dropped from 150 pounds to 125 pounds, too little for his 6-foot frame.

In 1955, he published his fourth and last book of poems, *The Season of Flesh*, and his second novel, *The Hawk and the Sun*. He received favorable reviews. He taught a quarter at Emory University, and again at Young Harris. He spoke of how he carried fragments (of the poems) in his mind "as he hoed or plowed, of how these fragments gradually coalesced, maybe over a period of months, until the ideas ripened." Margaret Mitchell once exuded that "we have a feeling

*John Davis Cantwell, M.D.*

of pride that a fellow Georgian has accomplished such wonderful things."

Reece had a premonition that he "hadn't got much time left." In 1957, his behavior became more erratic. He began to drive aimlessly in his car for hours, at high speed, and was drinking too much alcohol, appearing under the influence even in some classes he taught at Young Harris. He was also a chain smoker and a heavy coffee drinker.

On June 3, 1958, Reece put Mozart's "Piano Sonata in D" on the record player and neatly piled the students' papers he had graded. He thereupon put a .32 caliber bullet through his tubercular lungs, ending his "loneliness." He chose the same room that Dr. Dance had used for that very purpose, 12 years previously.

At his death, Ralph McGill cited one of Reece's poems, "I give my love to earth, where I a longer, deeper sleep will take."

He was only 40 years old, survived by his father, three sisters, and a brother. He is buried in the Old Union Cemetery, in Young Harris. Visitors leave pennies around the base of his tombstone.

To me his life demonstrates several points:

1) That creative genius may become manifest in any setting, even one of poverty and illness.
2) The tuberculosis that ravaged his family is much better treated today, but still a disease to be considered in certain clinical settings.
3) A solitary existence and a tendency to depression is a bad combination.

An editorial after his death summed up his life,

"A poet was among us in the early years of youth. Some of us hardly have realized the caliber of the poet. He was unpretentious, so gently human and plain. Maybe his being so like the rest of us in many ways kept us from knowing how greatly different he was in others.

...he seemed to belong to the ageless hills and mountains. He loved to walk beside the splashing water of Wolf Creek under the shadow of big Blood Mountain. He felt kinship with nature's own creative force as the rich soil burgeoning with new life sprouted the seeds of his fields. For the poet was a farmer."

Ralph McGill added:

"The skies, the clouds, the cold lakes, the tumbling rivers, the forests, the cold, keen nights when the stars looked green as ice, the winds of summer and winter, the wildflowers, the corn and cattle - all these were in his poems as were the prophets and peoples of the Old and New Testaments."

Cook concluded:

"But whenever men retreat to quiet vales of the mind to seek a lifting of the heart in a friendship, a warm joy in simple things, and a catching in of breath at supernatural beauty, there the lonely, questioning spirit of Byron Herbert Reece will have found a haven,

*John Davis Cantwell, M.D.*

and his haunting flute-like music will be heard."

# 38

## The Six Flagraisers on Iwo Jima

**THE EVENT**

It happened in February, 1945. After the United States Marines secured Mt. Suribachi on the south end of Iwo Jima, a small American flag was raised. A colonel wanted the original flag as a souvenir, and requested that a larger replacement flag be put up. Six men helped raise the flagpole. A photographer for the Associated Press captured the moment, in what has become one of the most famous military photographs ever taken.

Three of the flagraisers were killed in battle shortly thereafter. Two others were traumatized by the war experience and died young. The last survivor put the war behind him, stored his medals and letters in several cardboard boxes, and moved on to live a full, productive life. After the latter's death from a stroke in 1994, the cardboard boxes were discovered by his son, James, who was so moved by his discovery that he decided to retrace the lives of the other five men. The end result is the book, *Flags of Our Fathers*.

**THE SIX MEN**

Harlon Bloch grew up in a farm in Texas, getting up at 3:00 a.m. to help milk the cows. A neighbor recalled him fifty years later, "I see him doing farm chores, hay and corn and tobacco, vegetable gardens, mowing lawns, always busy." In high school, he was a football star, the punter, pass-catcher, and

*John Davis Cantwell, M.D.*

blocking back, leading his team to an unbeaten season. He and his teammates volunteered for military duty en masse, shortly after graduation.

Franklin Sausley, from Hilltop, Kentucky, lost his father at age nine and became the man of the house for his mother and younger brother. The freckle-faced youth's last words to his girlfriend, when he left for war in the Pacific, were "when I come back I'll be a hero."

Mike Strank was born in Czechoslovakia and grew up in a two-room rental apartment in Franklin Borough, Pennsylvania. He could have avoided military duty, given his Czech citizenship, but wanted to become a Marine, volunteering at age 19. A born leader, referred to as a "Marine's Marine," he led by example and told the younger colleagues under him that "I want to bring as many of you back home to your mothers as possible."

Ira Hayes was a Pima Indian from Arizona. The oldest of six children, he grew up in a one-room adobe hut. Quiet and shy, he joined the Marines nine months after Pearl Harbor. Two drunk and disorderly arrests were apparently overlooked.

Rene Gagnon was the only child of French-Canadian mill workers in New Hampshire. His parents divorced when he was young and he spent most of his time with a doting mother, acquiring "little experience in the art of mingling with men."

John "Doc" Bradley was born in Antigo, Wisconsin, and grew up in Appleton, both cities near my hometown. He wanted to join the Navy, to avoid fighting with the Army, but was transferred to the Marines and became a combat corpsman.

## IWO JIMA

Iwo Jima was "an ugly little scab of rock…six hundred miles south of the Japanese islands…a dry wasteland of black volcanic ash that stinks of sulfur," one-third the size of Manhattan. A Japanese soldier described it as "a place where no sparrow sings."

It was vital for the United States to eradicate the twenty-two thousand Japanese troops who had tunneled under the surface, for the guns and planes on the island were shooting down too many B-29 bombers flying missions to Japan. The Japanese planned to fight to a glorious death for their emperor, each killing ten Marines before they were vanquished. They underestimated the motives of the Marines, who were also willing to fight to the death, only because of their bond for each other, and their love of their country.

## THE BATTLE

The battle lasted 36 days. Half of the nearly 100,000 men who fought there were killed or maimed. The six flagraisers were part of E Company's 250 force who hit the beach on "D-Day." "Not getting hit," one man said, "was like running through rain and not getting wet." Only 50 of the E Company members escaped being killed or wounded.

The United States fought in World War II for 43 months. One-third of the total deaths occurred in this 36-day period alone, on Iwo Jima. The flag was raised after the Marines captured Mt. Suribachi. It was the "first invaders flag ever planted in four millennia on the territorial soil of Japan." When the flag went up "the entire island erupted in cheers."

The picture, by Joe Rosenthal, was on the cover of newspapers and magazines. The 1/400th second exposure "signaled victory and hope."

The Marines fought valiantly. Bradley "stood up into the merciless fire storm and pulled a wounded Marine back across the 30 yards to safety by himself." He was awarded the Navy Cross for this, second only to the Medal of Honor, for his heroic effort. He never mentioned this to his family. Twenty-seven Medals of Honor were given to others in this battle alone, including one to John Lucas, a high school freshman, who had lied about his age.

Strank, like Hayes and Bloch, had been in battle before, and it showed with his cool leadership. He was drawing some plans in the sand, six days after the flag was raised, when he was killed by "friendly fire" (a shell "tore a hole in his chest and ripped out his heart."). Harlon Bloch, the Texas high school football star, was killed the same day. Franklin Sausley was shot from behind: He "swatted absently at his back, as though brushing away a blue-tail fly. Then he fell. Someone shouted to him, 'How you doing?' And Franklin answered back, 'Not bad. I don't feel anything.' And then he died."

**AFTERWARD**

The three surviving flagraisers were returned to the United States after the battle, as the photo became a symbol for the Seventh Bond Tour. Rene Gagnon hoped to benefit "from his hero cachet - to become a state police officer." He did not qualify and eventually returned to working in the mill, and eventually to janitorial duties. Ira Hayes bounced in and out of jail, with over 50 drunk and disorderly arrests.

John Bradley returned to small town Wisconsin. He married his third grade sweetheart, opened a funeral home, fathered eight children, and became a community leader.

The man with his back to the camera, putting the flagpole into the ground, was misidentified as a Marine other than Harlon Bloch, a man also killed in battle. Bloch's mother was convinced that it was her son: "I changed so many diapers on that boy's butt. I know it's my boy." Ira Hayes knew too, but was told by his superior to keep quiet, as both men were deceased. Unable to live with this, he hitch-hiked 1300 miles in three days after the war, to visit Bloch's father and to tell him the truth.

The Iwo Jima monument was unveiled in Washington, D.C. in November, 1954. Gagnon, Bradley and Hayes were there, the last time they would see each other. Hayes was found dead at age 32, after a night of card playing, boozing, and fighting. Gagnon died of a probable heart attack at age 54, while doing janitorial work.

**THE LAST SURVIVOR**

John Bradley only mentioned the war once to his wife, on their first date. Memories of the torture-death of his best friend, and the loss of other colleagues, some of whom he had treated in the field, were probably the reason he cried most nights during his sleep in the first four years of his marriage.

*John Davis Cantwell, M.D.*

He "lived by simple values, values his children could understand and emulate. He had no hidden agendas; he expressed himself directly. He had a knack for breaking things down into quiet, irreducible truths."

His son, James (the book's author), lived for awhile in Japan as a young adult. One Thanksgiving, while his father was carving the turkey, the son confronted him with his understanding of why the Japanese were forced to bomb Pearl Harbor ("American insensitivity to Japanese culture and FDR's severing of their oil lines"). The father did not say anything. He just kept serving his son turkey.

"He was secure in himself, his marriage, his family. He was a successful man. He owned a large home in Antigo, a small cottage at Bass Lake several miles to the north, and a thriving funeral business.

He possessed the things that mattered most to him: not fame or adulation, but a large, secure family, and the respect of his fellow townspeople, respect that evolved from years of hard work, his attitude of service, and his contributions to his community.

He could afford to nod in silent understanding and hand me another slice of turkey, in return for the slice of bologna I had just handed him."

Bradley had a stroke in January, 1994, and held on long enough until his son could reach his bedside:

"I tried to talk to him. But my words could not compete with his loud breathing. And I was crying, besides.

*Adventures on Seven Continents And Other Essays*

   I silently thanked him for being a good man, a good father, someone whom I could admire. I told him all the reasons I loved him."

*John Davis Cantwell, M.D.*

# 39

## AN "AFFAIR" WITH EMILY DICKINSON

> I dwell in possibility
> A fairer House than Prose
> More numerous of Windows
> Superior - for Doors

Some say that opposites attract, which may explain my fondness for Emily Dickinson. I like gregarious friends, colorful ties and international travel. She preferred solitude, wore white, and stayed home, "behind the latch of a single garden gate."

I first encountered her in college English classes at Duke University. She wasn't much of a looker, as they say. Only one picture of her exists, taken when she was 17. By her own description she was "small, like the wren; and my hair is bold like the chestnut bur; and my eyes, like the sherry in the glass, that the guest leaves."

Thomas Wentworth Higginson, one of her mentors, depicted her as "a plain, shy person, the face without a single good feature … She had a quaint and nun-like look."

But how the little wren could sing. She wrote at least 1,775 poems, only seven of which were published during her lifetime (and all anonymously, and somewhat adulterated). Shortly after her death from glomerulonephritis, at age 55, her sister Lavinia found 60 little packets of folded sheets of poems, "loosely sewn together." Other poems had been jotted down on scraps of paper, or the backs of envelopes.

Emily's grandfather was a founder (along with Noah Webster and others) of Amherst College. Her father was an attorney, statesman, civic leader, seemingly cold and aloof. As Emily wrote, "his heart was pure and terrible," he read "lonely and rigorous books," and "I am not very well acquainted with father." To his credit, he used to ring the church bells, alerting the townsfolk to the presence of the northern lights. Emily's mother was frail, probably afflicted with psychosomatic problems and was later an invalid, dutifully attended to by her children.

Emily, her older brother, Austin, and her younger sister, Lavinia, lived for a time in the home her grandfather had built, the first brick house in Amherst. When her grandfather's savings were depleted, trying to start a college, the family was forced to move to a smaller place (during Emily's 10th - 24th years). The family fortunes improved and her father eventually repurchased the original home, where Emily lived the rest of her life.

Her early friends included Susan Gilbert, an attractive, intelligent, critical orphan who married Austin in 1856. The marriage was not a happy one (either because of or contributing to Austin's affair with Mabel Loomis Todd, the young wife of an Amherst professor). Another childhood friend was Helen Fiske (later Helen Hunt Jackson), who became a successful poet and novelist and who encouraged Emily to publish some of her poems.

The young principal of Amherst Academy, Leonard Humphrey, stimulated Emily's interest in books. A law student in her father's firm, Benjamin Franklin Newton, praised her early poetic works. Both were to die young, as so

*John Davis Cantwell, M.D.*

many did in those pre-antibiotic days, and are referred to in some of Emily's poems.

Emily was attracted to several scholarly men, including Rev. Charles Wadsworth, 16 years her senior and a pastor in Philadelphia, and to Samuel Bowles, editor of the *Springfield Republican*, a family friend, handsome and worldly, four years older than Emily. Found among Emily's personal belongings after her death were three passionate letters, addressed to "Master," probably to one of the two men. It isn't clear whether any of the letters had been sent.

Her formal education was limited to two years at Amherst Academy and one at what is now Mount Holyoke College.

In 1862 Emily was devastated when Rev. Wadsworth accepted a call to a church in San Francisco and Samuel Bowles left for Europe. She busied herself in her creative work, averaging a poem per day for the year. She was intrigued by an article in the *Atlantic Monthly*, written by Thomas Wentworth Higginson, encouraging aspiring writers. Higginson was an editor, author, and minister, soon to be a Union soldier. Emily sent him four of her poems, along with a letter asking him "Are you too deeply occupied to say if my verse is alive?" Higginson later wrote that her first letter "was in a handwriting so peculiar that it seemed the writer might have taken her first lesson by studying the famous fossil bird-tracks in the museum of that college town." Of punctuation "there was little; she used chiefly dashes." Her name was signed in pencil, barely legible.

They corresponded over the years. When asked about her favorite books, Emily replied: "For poets, I have Keats, and Mr. and Mrs.

Browning. For prose, Mr. Ruskin, Sir Thomas Browne and the Revelations." In response to questions about her schooling, "I went to school, but in your manner of the phrase had no education." As for her family, "I have a brother and sister; my mother does not care for thought, and father, too busy with his briefs to notice what we do."

She asked him to be her preceptor: "I would like to learn. Could you tell me how to grow, or is it unconveyed, like melody or witchcraft?" She goes on, "Will you tell me my fault? ... for I would rather wince than die."

Higginson didn't appreciate her writing style, "... with her curious indifference to all conventional rules of verse." He did sense some talent, however, noting that "when a thought takes one's breath away, a lesson on grammar seems an impertinence." He did offer critical comments, which Emily referred to as "surgery" and generally chose to ignore ("I shall observe your precept, though I don't understand it, always.")

They finally met in 1870, eight years after her initial letter to him. As Higginson recalled:

> "After a little delay, I heard an extremely faint and pattering footstep like that of a child, in the hall, and in glided, almost noiselessly...a plain shy person. She came toward me with two day lilies, which she put in a childlike way into my hand, saying softly, also under her breath, 'these are my introduction.'"

Higginson found her "much too enigmatical a being for me to solve in an hour's interview and an instinct told me that the slightest

*John Davis Cantwell, M.D.*

attempt at direct cross-examination would make her withdraw into her shell…". He added, "I never was with anyone who drained my nerve power so much. Without touching her, she drew from me. I am glad not to live near her."

In the last half of her life Emily became increasingly reclusive, living a life of seclusion, not crossing "my Father's ground to any house or town." Her postmaster knew her "by faith," having never set eyes upon her. She did see Ralph Waldo Emerson once, when he stayed at Austin's house next door, and noted that "he looked as if he had come from where dreams are born." Her life was consumed with her correspondence, poetry, and household duties.

She appeared only in white, some speculate as a reflection of her virginity or a sign of "an unconsummated marriage" to one of her fantasy lovers. She might have done it just to be more enigmatic:

> "A solemn thing it was, I said
> A woman white to be,
> And wear, if God should count me fit
> Her hallowed mystery."

Her poetry is often about nature, life, death, faith (and struggles with it), her art, suffering, growth, friendship and love. She seemed resigned to her lack of notoriety, writing for the ages instead of for instant and transient success. She was beginning to enjoy being a "nobody":

"I'm nobody! Who are you?
Are you nobody, too?…
How dreary to be somebody!
How public, like a Frog
To tell your name the lifelong day
To an admiring bog!"

She felt that failure to succeed, in the conventional definition of success, can often result in personal growth. To her way of thinking:

"Success is counted sweetest
By those who ne'er succeed.
To comprehend a nectar
Requires sorest need."

As for personal hurts and illnesses, she writes:

"I can wade grief,
Whole pools of it I'm used to that.
But the least push of joy
Breaks up my feet,
And I tip-drunken…"

Several of her poems refer to the practice of medicine:

"Surgeons must be very careful
When they take the knife!
Underneath their fine incisions
Stirs the culprit,-Life!"

And:

"Faith is a fine invention
When Gentlemen can *see*
But *microscopes* are prudent
In an Emergency."

*John Davis Cantwell, M.D.*

(This is sort of a "praise the Lord and pass the ammunition" philosophy.)

She struggled with the hypocrisies she often saw in conventional religion, and in shallow people with "dimity convictions" (dimity being a dainty white cotton cloth). She was the only family member who did not officially join the church, preferring to "select her own society," to find God in the world:

> "Some keep the Sabbath going to church
> I keep it staying at home,
> With a bobolink for a chorister
> And an orchard for a dome."

Her poetry was her "letter to the world," a world that never paid much attention to her. She measured success by internal feelings, not by acceptance from others:

> "Exhilaration-is within
> There can no Outer Wine
> So royally intoxicate
> As that diviner Brand."

No beauty herself, she saw it all around her:

> "The fact that Earth is Heaven
> Whether Heaven is Heaven or not."

One can picture her, dying of renal failure, looking out her bedroom window:

> "Beauty crowds me till I die
> Beauty mercy have on me
> But if I expire today
> Let it be in sight of thee."

The last of her more than 1,000 letters was to her cousins, and said simply:

> "Little Cousins, Called back.
> Emily."

It became her epitaph.

She had left instructions for her own funeral. Six Irishmen (caretakers of the Dickinson property) were to carry her coffin "out the back door, around through the garden, through the opened barn from front to back and then through the grassy fields to the family plot, always in sight of the house."

Lavinia found the locked box among her things. She unlocked it, lifted the lid, and "discovered a collection of hundreds of poems. Beneath her hands lay her sister's life work, in unexpected profusion."

Lavinia thought that Susan, Austin's wife, might help in getting the poems published. When Susan procrastinated, Lavinia turned to Austin's mistress, Mabel Loomis Todd, who in collaboration with Thomas Wentworth Higginson arranged for publication of 115 of the poems, with more to follow. Emily had written that her poetic talent "was given to me by the Gods when I was a little girl:

> "I kept it in my Hand-
> I never put it down-
> I did not dare to eat - or sleep-
> For fear it would be gone."

*John Davis Cantwell, M.D.*

It had been said that Emily wrote as Thoreau wished to live: "...close to the bone, concentrating the very essence of what she saw in phrases that strike and penetrate like bullets, and with an originality of thought unsurpassed in American poetry."

# 40

## Margaret Mitchell: Her Life and Works

My interest in Margaret Mitchell began after a trip to France in 1974. I was visiting with Monique Broustet, the wife of a Bordeaux cardiologist. Her face lit up when she heard I was from Atlanta, the home town of Margaret Mitchell, and the setting for the marvelous book about Rhett and Scarlett. Monique had read *Gone With the Wind* seven times. Having grown up in the France of post-World War II, she could relate to the central themes of survival and reconstruction. I was embarrassed to tell her that I had never read the book. I was determined to do so upon returning to Atlanta and to learn as much as I could about the remarkable author.

After finishing the book, I also read Mitchell's letters, edited by Richard Harwell. I then devoured several biographies on her and even arranged an interview with her brother, Stephens, over lunch one day at the Commerce Club. I shared what I had learned in a lecture to the Atlanta Clinical Society, at one of the group's spring outings and at a Medical Association of Atlanta dinner-lecture series.

### Early Life

Margaret Mitchell was as unconventional as her father was predictable. Until she started school, she dressed in boy's pants and shirt and tucked her blond hair into a tweed cap. Neighbors called her "Jimmy" after a newspaper cartoon character, probably like today's

*John Davis Cantwell, M.D.*

Calvin. She delighted in competitive play and was good at baseball (a catcher), tennis, and horseback riding. Her riding partners included some grizzled Civil War veterans (Margaret was born only 36 years after the end of the war), who told her many stories and taught her how to swear, something she enjoyed throughout her lifetime. Of the Civil War she once said, "I heard so much when I was little about the fighting and the hard times after the war that I firmly believed mother and father had been through it all…"

Margaret was a voracious reader at a very young age, encouraged especially with monetary perks from her mother. By 12, she had read most of the English classics. She then rebelled and read romances, adventure stories and dime-store novels. She also wrote hundreds of stories and wrote, directed, produced and performed in a wide variety of plays, pageants and skits.

Her family moved from what is now the Atlanta Medical Center area to 1401 Peachtree Street in 1912. Margaret entered Washington Seminary, a finishing school for girls in Atlanta. However, she wasn't a social success, ill-at-ease among the typical seminary girls. She eventually overcame some of these obstacles and became the editor of the annual in her senior year.

At Smith College, she impressed her roommates with her cigarette smoking, collection of soldiers' pictures and daily letters from young men off fighting in World War I. Like most college freshman, Margaret felt very average: "There are so many clever and more talented girls than I. If I can't be first, I'd rather be nothing." In college she clowned and strutted, pulled practical jokes and snuck out to the movies after hours. She was one of the most colorful of girls, self-assured and lacking in pretense.

While in college, Margaret adapted a new name - Peggy (no one had ever called her that before) - gave up the religious Catholic code and abandoned the church. She "remained as faithful to her skepticism as her mother had been to Catholicism." In midlife, her brother appealed to her to return to the Catholic church. She declined, citing the Faustian idea that "when you have made a bargain with the devil, you had better stick to your bargain."

She later claimed to have been a premed major, verified by her brother Stephens. In his book, *Southern Daughter*, D.A. Pyron questions this, however, noting that when she dropped out of Smith (due to the death of her mother), Margaret complained about having to give up "dreams of a journalistic career."

In her early 20s and back at home, Margaret was caught up in Atlanta social events. She would dance all evening, rise early the next day to swim or camp, and then stay up the next night to hunt possum. She had "a pretty wit, a sparkling manner and a most engaging fearlessness. Men adored her. She was infinitely curious, intelligent and forthright. While extremely funny, she could also be implacable and unforgiving, and most of all, capable of purple rage and anger." All was not pleasant at home, however; Margaret "fought constantly and challenged the servants, disputed her father and brother, (and) battled her grandmother (Annie)."

Margaret had an appendectomy in 1919. From then on "sickness, disease, accidents and physical disabilities…became the hallmark of her life." In June, 1920, she injured her foot in a swimming accident. Later that year, she fell off a horse and re-injured the foot and her leg. She was in an out of Saint Joseph's Hospital the summer of 1921 with apparent intestional adhesions. She also had "black circumstances," like depression: "Just let me get upset or mad or cry or be happy - and bingo! Every muscle seems to go slack and the jolly old pep goes...Nothing seems to matter," she said. She felt that something was missing in her life. Episodic insomnia enabled her to write letters and stories during the night. Men were seen as a way out of these black spells.

In 1920, Margaret took part in a charity ball at the Georgian Terrace and did an Apache dance. "The wild shenanigans and manic high-jinx of the rebel Deb soon had all Atlanta jabbering." Even 73 years later, her friend, Helen Turman Markey, still had vivid recollections of that evening and fond memories of Margaret.

In her lifestyle, Margaret "chalked her mark on Peachtree, then dared anyone to cross it." Little wonder that she didn't make the Junior League, which had been organized in 1916. They didn't even care for her year of charity work at Grady Hospital, since she did it mainly on the "social disease" ward.

**Marriage And Work As A Journalist**

Margaret's first husband, Red Upshaw, had much in common with Rhett Butler. Both enjoyed alcohol (Red became a bootlegger) and flunked out of service academies. Unlike Rhett, Red Upshaw was physically abusive; after their separation, Margaret kept a loaded pistol by her bedside. The marriage was unusual right from the wedding day. Margaret carried "a great big bunch of red-stemmed roses (Atlanta had never seen anything like it, before or since)." Except for Margaret's brother, all of the groomsmen, including best man, John Marsh, had been her suitors.

Margaret began work as a reporter for the *Atlanta Journal Sunday Magazine*, amid some skepticism. Debs tended to sleep late and "didn't go for jobs." She was an exception, the first to arrive at work and the last to leave, six days a week. She had "a wide-ranging and intensely curious mind" and could envelop the most minor incident with a real charm in the retelling of it." The 1920s was the golden age of journalism in the U.S., with the likes of H.L. Mencken, Ernest Hemingway, Grantland Rice, Ring Lardner and Damon Runyan. She was in their league, much more than just a good reporter. She had that "extra something" that could give "life and color to the simplest story."

Her short legs dangling from an old kitchen chair, she typed out 120 byline pieces and many unsigned articles in three and one-half years. It helped that she genuinely liked people, was never condescending and was just a great story teller. She was also an abysmal speller and punctuator, and according to her friend, Willie Ethridge, "was the vulgarist thing I ever saw."

In 1925, she married John Marsh, a loyal friend and a good conversationalist, though he drawled out everything. A colorless character, John was very proper and effective as Assistant Director of Publicity at Georgia Power. Rather sickly, he developed hiccups shortly after proposing to her and was bedridden for almost two months. Nine months after their marriage, an arthritic condition developed in Margaret's ankle, which didn't respond to several therapies used at that time. Their combined aches and illnesses united John and Margaret "in the most extraordinary way. It helped define the very nature of their marriage."

Marianne Walker emphasizes how important John Marsh was to his wife's success as an author. A talented writer himself, Marsh was also an editor. He offered her "…ideas, and advice, and at night and on weekends he patiently read and edited every line of her manuscript as she produced it." He "nurtured her imagination by providing a constant environment of creative stimulus." John was self-confident and quiet, while Margaret was effervescent and lacking in confidence. Each supplied what the other lacked.

The Marshs moved into an apartment, affectionately known as "the Dump" and lived there for seven years. On the door were their two business cards, John R. Marsh and Margaret Munnerlyn Mitchell, a source of amusement to Margaret until a visitor called, thinking it a home of ill-repute. The two cards were promptly removed and replaced by one which said "Mr. and Mrs. John Marsh."

Margaret always fretted about money, as had her father. She was determined to pay every cent that she owed and to collect every cent due her. While confined at home with her arthritic condition, Margaret began work on her novel. She was secretive about it, and according to her brother, "always fiercely resented being asked what she was doing, had done, or was about to do." Her housekeeper thought she was just writing letters to friends.

*Adventures on Seven Continents And Other Essays*

Margaret Mitchell (Photo courtesy of Durwood McAlister and the Atlanta Journal

**The Book**

Margaret Mitchell wrote the bulk of *Gone With the Wind* over a three-year period, from 1926-1929. The theme was survival - "a story of land, love of land, and a woman who was determined not to part with it." It was also a story to which anyone who had gone through war, or a depression as in 1929 could relate. As in her newspaper work, Margaret wrote the

*John Davis Cantwell, M.D.*

last section first and the first chapter last. Chapter 24, which contains the title phrase, was the hardest to conceptualize in her mind, yet the easiest to write and the only chapter she didn't have to rewrite at least 20 times. Themes in this chapter included the "tangled relationships between birth and death, being and nothingness, success and failure, autonomy and dependence, girls and women, mothers and children." This chapter came together for her while staying at the Ritz in Atlantic City, "It was cold, wet winter when we were in Atlantic City, and yet I could see clearly how dusty and stifling a red clay road in Georgia looks and feels in September, how the leaves on the trees are dry and there isn't any wind to move them and how utterly still the deep country woods are. And there is the queerest smell in the swampy bottom lands at twilight. And I suddenly saw how very haunted such a section would look like the day after a big battle, after two armies had moved on. So, I came home and wrote it."

The main characters in the book were developed in skillful detail. Margaret tried to put nothing of herself in the story. "I am sure I am not Scarlett," she wrote, "and I could not hope to be Melanie. I thought it would be obvious to anyone that Scarlett was a frigid woman, loving attention and adulation for their own self but having little or no comprehension of actual deep feeling and no reactions to the love and attention of others."

Scarlett was a survivor. She had the courage to persevere "in the face of defeat." She has some sense of responsibility for the weak and the helpless, and could appreciate what was beautiful in her mother, even if she couldn't emulate it. Descriptive terms about her include willful, egocentric, trivial, ruthless, indomitable, coarse, vulgar, vengeful and mean-spirited. "Starved for affection, she couldn't recognize love when it was offered."

Rhett was a scalawag, to be sure, but was also sympathetic, intuitive, compassionate and capable of loving deeply. Mammy was "as uncompromising about right and wrong as possible." On the other hand, Ashley was a waffler.

The title, *Gone With the Wind*, "had movement," according to the author. "It could either refer to times that are gone with the snows of yesteryear, to the things that passed with the wind of the war, or to a person who went with the wind rather than standing against it."

Margaret anticipated sales of only 5000 or so, "because the heroine was in love with another woman's husband for years and they never did anything about it." Considering her own proclivity for swearing, the book is devoid of this. Margaret overruled the proof writers who tried to standardize all her colloquialisms. She was amendable to proposed changes in the manuscript, but refused to consider a happy ending.

Instead, the book was an instant best seller. Within a year, it sold over one million hardback copies and, even today, continues to sell 40,000 hardback copies and 250,000 paperback versions each year. In 1986, on the 50th anniversary of its publication, the book appeared on the New York Times best seller list. This was repeated when the sequel, *Scarlett*, written by Alexander Ripley, came out in 1991.

*John Davis Cantwell, M.D.*

For Margaret Mitchell, her life was changed forever. To her, fame was represented as "The cook is off, the secretary isn't here, the phone is going every minute, the door bell ringing and the door belching strangers who want autographs and want to see what I look like…"

Margaret tried to slip into a local department store to buy a dress. In the changing room, about to try it on, "the curtains…both parted like the Red Sea to reveal a group of bug-eyed gawkers, who, upon viewing Margaret in her petticoat said: 'look how tiny she is. I don't believe she wrote it - she's too little.'"

A heavy-set white woman appeared at her door, with burned cork in her purse, wanting to audition for the movie part of Mammy. Magazine writers would spend a whole afternoon interviewing her and then ask her to write a 5000-word autobiographical piece for them. Tired of all this, Margaret refused to autograph copies of her book after six months, even for family members.

In May 1937, the book won the Pulitzer Prize. In August, Margaret awoke with blindness and was placed at bed rest for three weeks. I wonder about migraine headaches, in retrospect, given her description that "lights of any kind give me a headache. Words run together and a hand grenade explodes inside my skull and I see Roman candles going off for hours."

## The Movie And Other Activities

Under-represented by her own legal counsel, Margaret sold the movie rights for $50,000. Candidates proposed for Scarlett included

*Adventures on Seven Continents And Other Essays*

Katherine Hepburn, Bette Davis, Joan Crawford and Tallulah Bankhead. The part went to India-born British actress, Vivian Leigh. The only part Margaret jokingly said she'd like to play was that of Prissy. The Tara of Margaret's imagination did not have columns, but the movie producers prevailed on this item. Seventeen different people, including F. Scott Fitzgerald, worked on the script at one time or another. Fitzgerald, one of Margaret's favorite authors, read the book and commented "A good novel, no new characters, new techniques, new observations - none of the elements that make literature - especially no new examination into human emotions. But on the other hand it is interesting, surprisingly honest, consistent and workman-like throughout." He added that he pitied those "who consider it the supreme achievement of the human mind."

The movie premiered on December 15, 1939, at the Lowes Theater and went on to win seven Academy Awards in 1940, including best picture and best actress. Hattie McDaniel became the first black to win an award for her portrayal of Mammy.

Margaret Mitchell wrote over 10,000 letters after her book was published. During the World War II years, she christened the Navy cruiser, Atlanta (sunk by the Japanese on November 13, 1942, at Guadalcanal). She insisted on chatting with every sailor on board at the time of the christening.

She wrote to and entertained many of Atlanta's soldiers and played nurse to her ill father, crew of sickly servants and "perpetually frail" husband. She spent time visiting inmates at the Atlanta Federal prison and sponsored their writing contests. A great deal of her time was spent in protecting her book from unauthorized foreign publications. The Japanese quickly sold 150,000 copies before Pearl Harbor and merely sent her a doll as a token of thanks. Margaret's response: "A nation with so much gall certainly should go far."

Medical problems continued to plague her. Her abdominal symptoms were generally attributed to "adhesions," possibly from her prior appendectomy, but I'd also wonder about inflammatory bowel disease, given her history of diarrhea, fever and skin eruptions. Usually no organic condition could be found for her symptoms, yet she vehemently rejected psychosomatic possibilities. She particularly disliked a famous neurosurgeon she had seen at Johns Hopkins, a man with a big ego and no bedside manner. She could forgive other physicians, whom she claimed had made errors in judgment because they accepted their responsibility. The Hopkins doctor put the blame on her, which infuriated her.

John Marsh had a severe heart attack on Christmas Eve 1945. Margaret sneered at one progressive-minded physician who wanted to get John out of bed and exercising. Instead he was bedridden for a year, and eventually quit his job at Georgia Power.

As she progressed into her 40s, Margaret got more "skeptical, distrusting, rigid, dogmatic and bitter," as had her father. She gained nearly 40 pounds.

**The Accident**

Margaret and John Marsh had almost a phobia about cars, driving and accidents. John never drove at all. Margaret finally bought a car in

1933 and the next year was in an accident, followed by three months of bed-rest with what sounded like whiplash and other symptoms.

Hugh Gravitt, who died in April 1994, rarely talked about the accident on August 11, 1949, wherein he was speeding on Peachtree Street and struck Margaret as she lurched across the far half of the street on a rainy night to attend "A Canterbury Tale" at the Arts Theatre (later the Weiss Cinema). He tearfully entered the Bellwood Prison, convicted of involuntary manslaughter, and served 10 months and 20 days, including two months on a chain gang. He subsequently lived in a small brick house near Covington. "I'd rather it had been me instead of her," he said. He was not sure that he had ever heard of her, the book or the movie at the time of the accident.

Gravitt was going between 35-50 miles per hour north on Peachtree, en route to "a pharmacy to pick up medicine for his stepson, ill at home with a fever." Margaret and her husband were standing in the middle of Peachtree Street. As Gravitt reveals "all of a sudden she snapped loose from him and broke running..." There were 67 feet of skid marks. Two officers testified that they smelled alcohol on his breath. Others at the scene saw no evidence that he was intoxicated. Gravitt couldn't remember whether he had had a can of beer or not. He had 16 prior traffic convictions in the five previous years, including speeding and reckless driving. "About all of them," he said, "was (sic) on Ponce de Leon, coming back from the hospital (with taxi riders) late in the morning. No traffic, no nothing."

Gravitt was the youngest of 10 children. He had dropped out of school at age 12 to help his dad transport chickens, eggs and calves to Atlanta from Cumming.

"It was an accident," he recalls. "I couldn't help it."

Noted Atlanta historian Franklin Garrett said that "exceeding the speed limit and striking and killing the most famous person in town" caused public outrage. A picture in the paper of Gravitt smiling in his cell (the photographer had just told him a joke) didn't help.

"I'll remember it till I die, I reckon," Gravitt said, "but I know I'll be haunted and hounded till I take my last breath."

Celestine Sibley, a friend of Margaret's, said that "Peggy was an extremely generous and forgiving woman. She had been darting in and out on that street. She would not have wanted that man to go to prison. She would not have wanted (him) to suffer."

Ed Lockridge, M.D., was the intern at Grady and about to get some sleep. His colleague was ill with gastroenteritis so Ed took his place on the emergency room call. His first mission was to ride the ambulance to the scene of Mitchell's accident. He didn't recognize her, but knew instantly who she was when John Marsh introduced himself. Margaret was admitted to Grady Hospital comatose from a severe head injury. President Harry Truman wired his concern. Atlanta Federal prisoners volunteered blood for their friend.

Death came several days later, despite the medical expertise of Drs. William C. Waters, Charles Dowman and Exum Walker. Her funeral was at 10 a.m.; Mayor Hartsfield asked that all activity in Atlanta be momentarily suspended as a token of admiration, love and respect.

## The Margaret Mitchell Museum

The apartment building where Margaret Mitchell lived while writing her epic novel was originally a single-family home, built in 1899 by Cornelius Sheehan. In 1913, the house was relocated to the rear of the lot. Six years later it was converted into the 10-unit Crescent Apartments. Margaret and her husband lived in the basement apartment, facing Crescent Avenue. According to Walker, the apartment had "...only two rooms plus a kitchen and a bath, had dark woodwork, dark, faded wallpaper, dark hardwood floors and an unpleasant musty odor."

The Margaret Mitchell House, Inc. organization was formed in 1989 to acquire and restore the house for public viewing. In the renovation plans, Mitchell's apartment was the only internal space of the home to be preserved and restored. The rest of the house was gutted and modernized for use as a rotating exhibit space.

## Epilogue

John March was found dead in bed in 1952 at age 56 of a cardiac arrest. Vivian Leigh developed tuberculosis in 1945 and died of an exacerbation of it in 1967 at age 54. Clark Gable died of a heart attack in 1960 at age 59. The plane in which Leslie Howard (who played Ashley) was a passenger, was shot down by the Germans en route to England from Portugal. The German intelligence had thought Winston Churchill was on board. Oddly enough, Olivia diHaviland, whose character Melanie was the only major one to die in the book, is the only main actor still living. Butterfly

*John Davis Cantwell, M.D.*

McQueen, who played Prissy, died in a house fire on December 22, 1995, in Augusta, Georgia.

On a beautiful Saturday morning one fall I visited Margaret Mitchell's grave at the west end of Oakland Cemetery. I didn't know exactly where to find it, but correctly surmised that it would have fresh flowers around it, narrowing the possibilities.

It was fitting that at her grave-side service the 103rd Psalm was read. Listen to it carefully:

> *"The days of man are but as grass, for he flourisheth as a flower of the field. For as soon as the wind goeth over it, it is gone; and the place thereof shall know it no more."*

Margaret Mitchell's days on earth, like grass and flowers, were all too brief, and gone with the wind. But her remarkable book endures, as does the building wherein she wrote it, fitting memorials to a special person.

*Adventures on Seven Continents And Other Essays*

# PEOPLE

*John Davis Cantwell, M.D.*

# 41

## William Heberden: His Life, His Times, and His Book

Among the treasures in our medical library is an 1803 edition of William Heberden's *Commentaries on the History and Cure of Diseases*. Heberden was a man for all seasons. Born in London in 1710, he was a friend of both Ben Franklin and King George III. As a physician, he was inclined to trust his own astute clinical observations and experience rather than merely follow the traditional, often dubious, medical practices of the day. He was the first to describe the symptom complex of angina pectoris, and the nodules in the distal aspect of the fingers which we associate today with degenerative arthritis. So in touch was he with his own persona that he declined a court appointment to be royal physician to Queen Charlotte because "it might interfere with those connections that (I) had now formed." He knew how to live and when to retire.

### Heberden's Times

According to Cambridge scholar, R. J. White, the era of King George III, was "the age of reason, of confidence, of elegance, of expansion, above all the age of the flowering of English civilization, which reached a height it has never surpassed." The era stretched from the end of the Seven Years War to the Napoleonic Wars.

*John Davis Cantwell, M.D.*

George III ascended to the throne at age 22. He ruled for 60 years "a period longer than any British sovereign, with the exception of the one who resembled him most closely, his granddaughter, Queen Victoria." His subjects were a talented lot. In literature there were Pope, Blake, Wordsworth, Coleridge, Sir Walter Scott, Samuel Jackson, Dickens and Jane Austen. Political figures included William Pitt, John Wilkes, Lord North, and "for a time," George Washington. In addition to Heberden, the medical community included William Withering (who introduced digitalis), the brilliant anatomist, William Hunter, and Edward Jenner (of smallpox fame).

During King George III's reign, the population of England doubled to 12 million. The great English country homes and gardens blossomed. There were "new methods of agriculture, of transport, of manufacture, of financial organizations." Little wonder that it seemed that "even God was an Englishman."

Unlike some of the flamboyant leaders of other countries in his time (the "greats" of Russia, Peter and Catherine, plus Frederick of Prussia and Napoleon in France), George III was rather bland. His tastes "ran to the conventional and the safe." He preferred "the substantial to the elegant, the practical to the theoretical, sentimentality to sentiment, humor to wit." One of his favorite pastimes was sitting for his portrait.

During his reign, George III had five major attacks of multi-systemic symptoms, including mental disturbances. They began usually in the winter with a cold, cough and malaise, followed by angina-like pains, abdominal colic, constipation, tachycardia, hoarseness, weakness and stiffness of the extremities, paresthesias, tremors, agitation, sensitivity to light and sound, and emotional lability ("he baffled all attempts to fix his attention, showed gross errors of judgment, and was (aimlessly) occupied adjusting his bedclothes"). Little wonder that the United Stated gained its independence during this period.

Ida Macalpine, noting that George III's urine turned darkish brown or purple when left in the chamberpot overnight, speculated that he suffered from an inherited medical condition called porphyria. In tracing the British royal family back to Mary, Queen of Scots (1542-1587), Macalpine noted 15 other members to have possibly also been afflicted. Geoffrey Dean has challenged this hypothesis, due to a lack of conclusive evidence in living descendants.

## Heberden: The Man and His Book

Heberden was educated at Cambridge and soon became one of the most remarkable clinicians of his day. He earned the respect of his colleagues and praise from his patients. One of the former, Dr. William Wells, noted that "No other person, I believe…has ever exercised the art of medicine with the same dignity or has contributed so much to raise it in the estimation of mankind." Heberden's patient, the poet William Cowper, penned this tribute to his physician:

> "Virtuous and faithful HEBERDEN,
> whose skill attempts no task it cannot well fulfil,
> gives Melancholy up to nature's care,
> and sends the patient into purer air."

*John Davis Cantwell, M.D.*

Like Plutarch, Heberden divided his career into three portions: 1) time spent learning the duties of a profession, 2) the practice of such duties and 3) teaching the nuances of the profession to others. He took notes at the bedside of the sick, written in Latin, over a 50-year career, to pass on to one of his sons, should the latter select a career in medicine. The notes were never intended for publication. Heberden reviewed them every month, adding such facts as "tended to throw off any light upon the history of a distemper (disease), or the effects of a remedy." He retired from his practice, "not from a wish to be idle" but rather before he could no longer "do justice to my patients."

William Heberden, Jr., did follow in his father's footsteps. He published the notes one year after the death of his 90-year-old father. The *"Commentaries"* subsequently became a prominent textbook of medicine, and Heberden, Jr. eventually became the personal physician to King George III. That he did not consider porphyria in the latter isn't to his discredit, for the disease wasn't identified until a century later.

We remember Heberden today mainly for the nodes he first described and for his observations on angina pectoris, which he wrote was "...a disorder of the breast, marked with strong and peculiar symptoms, considerable for the kind of danger belonging to it, and not extremely rare." he added the following:

*"They who are affected with it are seized while they are walking (more especially if it be up hill, and soon after eating) with a painful and most disagreeable sensation in the breast, which seems as if it would extinguish life, if it were to increase or to continue; but the moment they stand still, all this uneasiness vanishes."*

**Summary**

Heberden's contributions far exceed his original descriptions of osteoarthritic nodes and angina pectoris. He was a keen observer, a man so in touch with himself that he could turn down the lofty position of physician to the Queen. He relied heavily on personal experience, rejecting many of the then-popular therapies that we know today were worthless at best and harmful at worst. He also knew when to retire and left a book and a legacy of excellence that not only was of benefit to his physician-son, but to physicians for generations after.

King George III was less fortunate. He became hostile to his oldest son George when that latter was still a youth. His wife, "gracious, cultivated and pretty" in her youth became "fat and unpleasant" in later years. He lost the American colonies and suffered from incapacitating fits that had "all the appearance of progressively worsening mental illness." He spent the last nine years of his life in "permanent derangement and blindness," possibly from cataracts and porphyria, the latter disease that even his capable physician, William Heberden, Jr., could

*John Davis Cantwell, M.D.*

neither diagnose nor treat, as it wasn't identified until years after his death.

# 42

## PARKINSON'S DISEASE IN A MASTER SURGEON

Dr. Dwight McGoon was at the peak of his surgical career when I invited him to Atlanta in 1976 as our annual Mayo Clinic Alumni speaker. I had first met him during my medicine residency at Mayo, a decade before. While working up a new patient then at St. Mary's Hospital, I noticed someone waiting outside the door. I was surprised to encounter Dr. McGoon, and impressed with how patient he was, and how gentlemanly as well.

Several years after his visit to Atlanta I was sorry to hear that he had developed Parkinson's disease and had to give up cardiovascular surgery, for he was a master at repairing complex congenital defects as well as acquired adult defects. (The staff once baked a cake for him after his 100th consecutive aortic valve replacement without an operative death.)

While browsing through Majors' Scientific Bookstore I came upon *The Parkinson's Handbook*, written by Dr. McGoon as "an inspiring, practical guide for patients and their families." It is indeed that, and much more, a tribute to a remarkable man's tenacity and his faith.

In retrospect, Dr. McGoon feels that the disease came on gradually, over a two-year period:

*"I had no pep. It was taking me longer and longer to do the same things: shaving and showering, shoveling snow off the*

John Davis Cantwell, M.D.

> *sidewalk, eating a meal, even flipping through the pages of a patient's chart. My occasional sessions at the piano became more frustrating than fun. A three-hour operation could now take four hours."*

He became aware of a tiny tremor in his left hand and even made a little joke to his assistants about getting Parkinson's disease. Several months later the tremor and fatigue increased.

While visiting his son at Johns Hopkins Medical School, Dr. McGoon "...used some free moments to breeze through (his) medical books in search of more detailed information. As soon as I'd read the definition, I knew there was no doubt. I had a classic case of Parkinson's disease."

He subsequently consulted a neurologist and cut back on his surgical schedule, closely monitoring his symptoms. On May 7, 1979, his surgical career came to an abrupt end. He was doing a complex cardiac procedure on a young boy:

> "I didn't go into the operating room with the decision that this particular procedure would be the last one. But I remember that little boy; he had a rough time, but recuperated satisfactorily. I was very concerned about him...
>
> "I decided by the end of the operation on that little boy that that surgery would be the last one I would do."

That evening, during dinner, he announced to his wife that he had performed his last operation: "Even I, a seasoned doctor, could not avoid shedding tears." Several years later, Dr. McGoon received a phone call from a surgeon he'd never met, who indicated that he, too, would have to give up operating due to the same disease. The two vowed to keep in close touch and did exchange several letters. When several months went by without an answer to his most recent letter, Dr. McGoon sent another, asking how things were going:

> "His wife called and thanked me for my letter. Her husband, she said, had killed himself a few weeks earlier. I felt guilt and pain. If I'd known then what I know now about Parkinson's, I might have been able to give him cause for hope. I could have told him that the disease is really not as bad as one imagines at first. I could have sent him some notes about my personal experiences and observations; could have provided some basic information that might have helped dispel his depression. It would have been better yet, if I could have presented him with this book."

Indeed it would have, for the book is an excellent overview, written in lay terms, and divided into sections of 1) Onset, 2) Pathophysiology, 3) Treatment, 4) Fighting Back, and 5) The Importance of Attitude. I enjoyed the latter most, because it reflects the spirit of an exceptional man. Consider the following:

*John Davis Cantwell, M.D.*

> "...when I had to give up surgery, I suddenly had extra time to read long postponed classics in physiology, science, and history, a self-taught course in calculus, and even some fiction. And enough leisure, at last, to enjoy those accumulated records, tapes, and discs. There was time for unhurried phone calls to our children and their families."

> "...fear, in its cautionary role, also has a beneficial influence on health and survival. An alliance of fear <u>and</u> hope, when in proper balance, possesses immense value."

It wasn't an easy road, of course. How "humiliating, for a once-dexterous surgeon" to need your wife to tie your shoelaces. But Dr. McGoon set out to give himself lessons in shoe tying, "two-stage lessons:"

> "During the first stage, when medicated and eudopic, I studied in slow-motion detail how the fingers hold the strings; I memorized how they manipulate and transfer them through each step of the procedure. During the second stage of the lesson, when unmedicated, I practiced my new understanding of knot tying. Gradually, I'm relearning what I first learned as a child, retracing the same trial-and-error process."

The Parkinson's patient, writes Dr. McGoon, "...must search for the truth about the disease, examine its evil consequences, evaluate these challenges seriously, and then tackle them in an optimistic manner." *The Parkinson's Handbook* is an excellent source and a shining tribute to the author, who forged "a new life of singular enjoyments and significant little victories" before his death.

*John Davis Cantwell, M.D.*

# 43

## The Legacy of James Edgar Paullin, M.D.

He trained under Sir William Osler, during the "Golden Era" at Johns Hopkins. His reputation was such that he served as president of both the American Medical Association and the American College of Physicians, and was summoned to the bedside of a dying president.

**Early Years**

James Edgar Paullin was born in 1881 in Ft. Gaines, Georgia. He attended Mercer University, where he was a classmate of U.S. Senator Walter F. George. A chemistry professor at Mercer, Dr. James F. Sellers, kindled his interest in science, in lieu of the classics and a possible career in the clergy. Paullin did a year of graduate work in science at Mercer and then moved on to medical school at Johns Hopkins, graduating in 1905. He was greatly influenced by Osler.

*Adventures on Seven Continents And Other Essays*

James Edgar Paullin, M.D.

*John Davis Cantwell, M.D.*

According to an AMA resolution: "...the aims and ambitions of his great teacher were emulated throughout his professional career."

Dr. Paullin served an internship as resident pathologist at Rhode Island Hospital and then returned to Atlanta to do another year of post-graduate work at Piedmont Hospital. From 1906-1911, he served as pathologist for the Georgia State Board of Health and also as professor of pathology at the Atlanta College of Physicians and Surgeons (which became Emory University Medical School in 1915). In 1909, he started clinical work as an associate visiting physician at Grady Memorial Hospital, and in 1915 was appointed Professor of Clinical Medicine at Emory.

His early medical research interests were many, ranging from testing rabies serum and medications for diabetes to presentations on hookworm, typhus, and syphilis. He was the first Atlanta physician to prescribe insulin. In World War I, he was apparently "not robust enough" to go abroad with the Emory Unit, but did serve as a major in the Army Medical Corp.

**A Thriving Career - And Leadership Role**

After the war, Dr. Paullin's medical career began to thrive. He built a large practice and was much in demand as a medical consultant. According to Dr. R. Hugh Wood, Dr. Paullin had learned from Osler the four-lettered symbol for success, W-O-R-K: "despising mediocrity, he was never satisfied with less than excellence, and though he demanded much of himself and others, he maintained warm personal relationships."

His activity in medical politics began as President of the Fulton County Medical Society in 1915, and of the Medical Association of Georgia in 1935. He became one of only two physicians to serve as president of both the American College of Physicians (1942) and the American Medical Association (1943-1944). He was also one of the first physicians from this area to be invited as a member of the Association of American Physicians.

In 1935, he sponsored the organization of the Southeastern Clinical Club, composed of internists from Atlanta, Birmingham, Nashville and New Orleans. I was once a member of that group, which remains very active 67 years later. Dr. Paullin also sponsored a Study Club of young physicians in Atlanta, who met frequently in his home and "...absorbed the art of medicine and fellowship from the master." This organization developed into the Atlanta Clinical Society, which continues to meet for dinner, fellowship, and scientific exchange on a monthly basis.

**A Testimonial Dinner**

A testimonial dinner in his honor, sponsored by the Fulton County Medical Society, was held at the Piedmont Driving Club in July, 1942, with Dr. F. Phinizy Calhoun as toastmaster. Dr. R. H. Oppenheimer, Dean of Emory University Medical School, made the following comments on Dr. Paullin's qualifications as a great teacher:

*"First of these is a ready fund of knowledge. By this I mean that Dr. Paullin has been interested in medicine of the past, in the new things in medicine which have come to us in the present, and in the vision of things which are to come in the future. If you should*

John Davis Cantwell, M.D.

*call upon him in the evening you would undoubtedly find him in his library unless perchance, in latter years, he might be spending few moments at play with his grandchildren. Dr. Paullin's library is filled with medical books and journals, the study of which provided his evening's entertainment after a long day of work. His reading is never casual. Instead, it is done with a critical mind, which enables him to add to his knowledge those things which he feels worthwhile. By thus maintaining a constant renewed fund of knowledge, he is able to meet students with a vigorous, interested, and stimulating mind.*

*In a similar manner, he is a keen observer. He studies the symptoms, signs and other evidence of disease presented by patients with the same critical and analytical attitude he uses in his study of medical literature, arriving at thoughtful conclusions which are free from preconceived ideas and hunches. His work thus stimulates students to the development of an accurate approach to the problem of the patient and its solution.*

*Dr. Paullin has other valuable qualities. He is interested in the medical school as a whole, in its faculty and in its facilities for the education of students. He has taken an active part in planning and promoting its development in order to make it possible for all of us to do better teaching. His interest in the students does not cease with their graduation. He is concerned with their development as interns and residents and eventually as practicing doctors.*

*Finally, Dr. Paullin is interested in the conditions under which doctors are to practice. He is aware of the economic and social changes which will affect the place and work of the doctor in the community."*

Dr. Paullin's response reflected his own modesty and great respect for his profession:

*"I fully appreciate the fact that you are here tonight, not because of me, but because you wish to recognize and to honor something which is much greater and much higher than any man either living or dead. You are here to pay tribute to a profession which our forefathers founded and whose traditions you and I are attempting to carry forward and we hope that those who follow after us will uphold. We, along with a large group of our citizens, are still interested in demanding for all peoples Life, Liberty, and Freedom. You are here honoring a principle for which the medical profession has always stood for these hundreds and hundreds of years."*

## World War II and Early Aftermath

During World War II, he served as special consultant to the Surgeon General of the U.S. Navy. He helped organize the Finlay Institute of the Americas and for this work was decorated by Cuban President Batista in 1942. The award was given "because of your distinguished career in your chosen profession; because of your contributions to its development through ministry to the sick, through research, and through teaching; because of your statesmanlike guidance of its organized membership in a time of national crisis; because of the honor you have brought to Georgia, to Atlanta, and to Emory through your notable gifts of mind and heart and of professional skill." In 1944, the Atlanta

*John Davis Cantwell, M.D.*

Chamber of Commerce cited him for "distinguished achievement."

Immediately after the war, he was asked to study the medical care of natives in the Pacific Islands and promptly set off on a 25,000 mile trip. He met with Admiral Chester Nimitz, aboard the historic battleship *Missouri*, and found him to be "one of the nicest, kindest persons I've ever met," one who was intensely interested in medicine and well informed on tropical diseases. Paullin advised the establishment of extensive facilities for the medical care and education of the Pacific natives, who needed to be weaned from witch doctor rituals. He also advised that "…to keep our position in world affairs we must stay in the Pacific."

Dr. Paullin remained an honorary consultant to the Navy Bureau of Medicine and Surgery. In 1947, he was awarded the Presidential Medal of Merit, the highest award a nonmilitary person can receive. Other recipients included Irving Berlin, Henry Ford, Dr. Enrico Fermi, Francis Cardinal Spellman, and Dr. J. Robert Oppenheimer. In 1948, he was one of 10 authorities who presided at the First International Polio Conference in New York.

**Consultant to President Roosevelt**

Dr. Paullin was best known to the lay public as one of President Roosevelt's physicians. He had been asked by White House physician, Dr. Ross McIntire, to consult on the President during prior episodes of bronchitis and sinusitis. His advice was also sought as to whether or not the President should run for reelection to a fourth term. In rendering his opinion, Dr. Paullin used a comparison for

Roosevelt between the human body and an automobile:

*"Let's assume that you're setting out on a 10,000 mile trip - (in) a brand new machine. Hitting on every cylinder, you burn up the road for 8000 miles hitting a 70 mile-per-hour clip. By that time the tires are worn. The car, of course, is good enough to finish the journey, but not at top speed."*

The President laughed, "although a bit ruefully," and agreed to quit burning up the road - not down to 35 mph, but much less than 70 mph.

Upon his return from the conference at Yalta, Roosevelt was advised to spend a month relaxing at the Little White House in Warm Springs, Georgia. He was felt to be doing well, into his second week of vacation, and had regained 8 of the 15 pounds he had lost in recent weeks. Dr. McIntire (who was attending a conference in Washington) had just called Dr. Paullin on April 12, 1945, arranging for a routine consultation visit to Warm Springs. Shortly thereafter, he (McIntire) received an emergency call from his assistant, Dr. Howard Bruenn, who was attending the President. Roosevelt had been chatting gaily with his cousins, and with Mrs. Elizabeth Shownatoff, an artist who was painting his portrait: "...while a laugh was on his lips, he complained of a terrible headache and collapsed in his chair." McIntire summoned Dr. Paullin, requesting that he race to the scene, 76 miles from Atlanta, under police escort.

The escort was hardly necessary, for Dr. Paullin was "...a veteran of many a wild night's ride through the Georgia countryside. (He)

*John Davis Cantwell, M.D.*

knew all the back roads and shortcuts (and) made the 76 miles in 90 minutes." In his own words:

*"The President was in extremis when I reached him. He was in a cold sweat, ashy gray and breathing with difficulty. Numerous rhonchi in his chest. He was propped up in bed. His pupils were dilated and his hands slightly cyanosed. Commander Howard Bruenn had started artificial respiration. On examination, his pulse was barely perceptible.*

*I gave him an intracardiac dose of adrenalin in the hope that we might stimulate his heart to acting. However, his lungs were full of rales, both fine, medium and coarse, and his blood pressure was not obtainable. There were no effects from the adrenalin except perhaps for two or three beats of the heart which did not continue. Within five minutes after my entrance into the room, all evidence of life had passed away."*

In an editorial a few years later, entitled "The Modern Physician at His Best," it was said that Dr. Paullin's attendance at Roosevelt's final illness got headlines, but was "...one of the lesser incidents in his career." He was "...far more famous for the depth of his wisdom and the breadth of his skill. To laymen he was known as a doctor who gave every case the same thorough attention as he would give a stricken president."

## Later Years

Dr. Paullin gave up his teaching position at Emory in 1950, after 35 years of meritorious service. His "long and faithful service as a teacher was characterized by punctuality of attendance, exactness of knowledge, and clearness of exposition." He was admired, respected, and esteemed by medical students. Emory medical alumni honored him with a scholarship to aid medical students.

On August 13, 1951, while taking a medical history in his office, Dr. Paullin was stricken with chest pain, and correctly self-diagnosed the pain pattern as an aortic dissection. Among those in attendance was his son-in-law, William Minnich, M.D. Approaching the end, in true Oslerian spirit, he said, "My house is in order, and I am ready to go."

The funeral was simple, at his request, and devoid of flowers. Rev. Robert W. Burns presided, and mentioned how Dr. Paullin had given away hundreds of copies of Osler's *A Way of Life*. He also stated that in the recent months before his death, Dr. Paullin had cards printed, which he handed out to many of his patients, with a simple message:

> *"God, give me the serenity*
> *To accept the things I cannot change*
> *The courage to change all things I can,*
> *And the wisdom to know the difference."*

He closed with the following:

> *"Honor a physician according to the need of him with the honors due onto him.*
> *For verily the Lord has created him.*
> *For from the most High cometh healing;*
> *The skill of the physician shall lift up his head;*
> *and in the sight of great men, he shall be admired."*

*John Davis Cantwell, M.D.*

**Summary**

The legacy of the man lives on, years after his death. Physicians from his own hospital have held and will hold his former posts as president of the AMA and the American College of Physicians (Harrison Rogers and Nick Davies and Sandra Fryhofer, respectively). Organizations that he helped start, the Southeastern Clinical Society and the Atlanta Clinical Society, continue to thrive. His high standards of medical care continue from a grandson-in-law (David Watson) and great-grandson (Brooks Lide).

To quote from Dr. R. Hugh Wood's letter in 1951:

*"From the life of Dr. Paullin one may learn to better serve his profession and his country. Possessed of a keen intelligence, he took full advantage of his exceptional education opportunities, and with vigor and persistence, he lived a full life of service as physician, teacher, citizen, and friend."*

# 44

## Shackleton's Heart

Long before anyone coveted Antarctica's mineral wealth, the continent was the ultimate proving ground for explorers. While numerous turn-of-the-century adventurers joined in the race for the South Pole, one of the most heroic was Sir Ernest Henry Shackleton (1874-1922). Indeed, while the British commander never did reach the pole, (Norwegian Roald Amundsen first had that honor, in 1911), Shackleton's four Antarctic expeditions were accomplishment enough, together spanning half his adult life. Like many great explorers, Shackleton possessed unfailing optimism and courage - with one notable exception. Throughout his life he sustained such a phobia about his cardiac status that he only rarely allowed a physician to evaluate it. The man who willingly braved the harshest of polar adversities was terrified of the stethoscope.

### Early Warning

The eldest son of an Irish physician, as a schoolboy in England, Shackleton seemed healthy enough - although he became a cigarette smoker early on. While intelligent, he was a lackluster student, and he left college at age 16 to join the British Merchant Navy. Over the next 10 years his sailing stints took him to six continents.

Perhaps the young man's thirst for adventure stemmed from his certainty of an early demise. According to one colleague, Shackleton's

*John Davis Cantwell, M.D.*

boyhood nurse "had told him that he would die at age 48, and he believed this, he absolutely believed it." As it turned out, the nurse's prophecy was almost accurate; Shackleton died 41 days short of reaching his 48th birthday.

**Sir Ernest Shackleton**

In 1901, after a year of dabbling at business in England, Shackleton again longed for far-flung adventure. Getting wind of the upcoming Antarctic exploration headed by his countryman Robert Falcon Scott, Shackleton signed on as a member of the expedition. Soon after penetrating that icy, uncharted continent, however, Shackleton contracted scurvy, and to his great embarrassment - and disappointment - was sent back to England. En route, things got worse when he contracted "Mauritius fever" - an illness that was probably malaria or rheumatic fever.

After recuperating in Scotland, Shackleton was eager to try again. In 1907, pooling his resources, Shackleton formed his own expedition and returned to Antarctica. To allay the fears of his wife, he agreed to undergo a complete physical examination before leaving. Ironically, however, there are indications that while he kept the doctor's appointment, he refused to let the physician auscultate his heart. His fear, no doubt, was that he would be declared unfit for the adventure before him.

On that long and frosty foray, Shackleton and his small band trekked to within 97 miles of the South Pole - at which point harsh weather forced them to turn back. The party achieved distinction, however, by becoming the first to reach the South Magnetic Pole - about 18 degrees from the geographic South Pole - and the first to climb Mt. Erebus, a lofty, glacier-encrusted volcano. It was for these achievements that Shackleton would be knighted.

Due to the formidable conditions of the expedition, the accompanying physician finally talked Shackleton into permitting his heart to

*John Davis Cantwell, M.D.*

be auscultated. Dr. Eric Marshall detected a "pulmonary systolic murmur," which was still present on reexamination five weeks later. While all members of the party were under enormous physiologic strain, Shackleton's pulse seemed weaker than the other crew members'.

On one rigorous trek after months of severe cold and exertion, Marshall recorded that Shackleton's pulse was "thin and thready." By then the explorer had also developed a low-grade fever accompanied by shortness of breath and diarrhea. Dr. Marshall's diagnosis: a combination of asthma, altitude sickness and vitamin C deficiency. Only in retrospect did Marshall wonder if Shackleton might have suffered a mild heart attack.

In 1909, back in Sussex, Shackleton had an episode of chest pain and profuse sweating. While he himself shrugged it off as "acute rheumatism," one physician told him he probably had angina pectoris. No doubt fearful to have this truth confirmed, Shackleton steadfastly avoided a medical examination. Making matters worse, he lapsed into a lifestyle marked by overeating, alcohol and cigarette excesses, and minimal physical activity.

**Floe Chart**

Shackleton resumed command with his third expedition to Antarctica, in 1914. In preparation for the trip he reportedly placed an advertisement in a British newspaper that read: "Men wanted for hazardous journey. Small wages, bitter cold, long months of complete darkness, constant danger, safe return doubtful. Honor and recognition in case of success."

The trip's start was less than auspicious. Stopping off in Buenos Aires, Shackleton developed another febrile illness - this time tonsillitis and a boil on his neck. Once again he refused to let a doctor examine him with a stethoscope. One crew member commented: "It was as if the one fear he knew was what might be discovered in his heart."

Recovered and continuing stoically on, Shackleton faced other obstacles. After sailing 12,000 miles from England - including about 1000 through jagged ice floes - his sturdy ship *Endurance* became trapped in ice, was badly damaged, and had to be abandoned.

The 28 men then set out for a supply hut on Paulet Island, some 350 miles away. But more than a year later, stymied by fierce storms and a drifting ice pack that had steadily swept them backward, they found themselves stranded on uninhabited Elephant Island. The nearest source of help was a whaling station on South Georgia Island - some 800 miles away. In between lay the Scotia Sea, one of the most tempestuous in the world. But Shackleton rose to the occasion. With his party's provisions running dangerously low, he and five others set off for South Georgia Island in a 25-foot lifeboat, leaving a trusted crew member, Frank Wild, in command of the remaining 21 men on Elephant Island. Of course, Shackleton knew well the risk involved in tackling what he termed "hurricane force winds and mountainous seas."

Before casting off he slipped this note to Wild: "In the event of my not surviving the boat journey to South Georgia you will do your best for the rescue of the party…I have

*John Davis Cantwell, M.D.*

confidence in you and always have had. May God prosper your work and your life. You can convey my love to my people and say I tried my best."

Against all odds, Shackleton's group reached South Georgia Island three weeks later - albeit landing on the uninhabited side. This necessitated a trek over mountains and glaciers that were considered impossible to transverse.

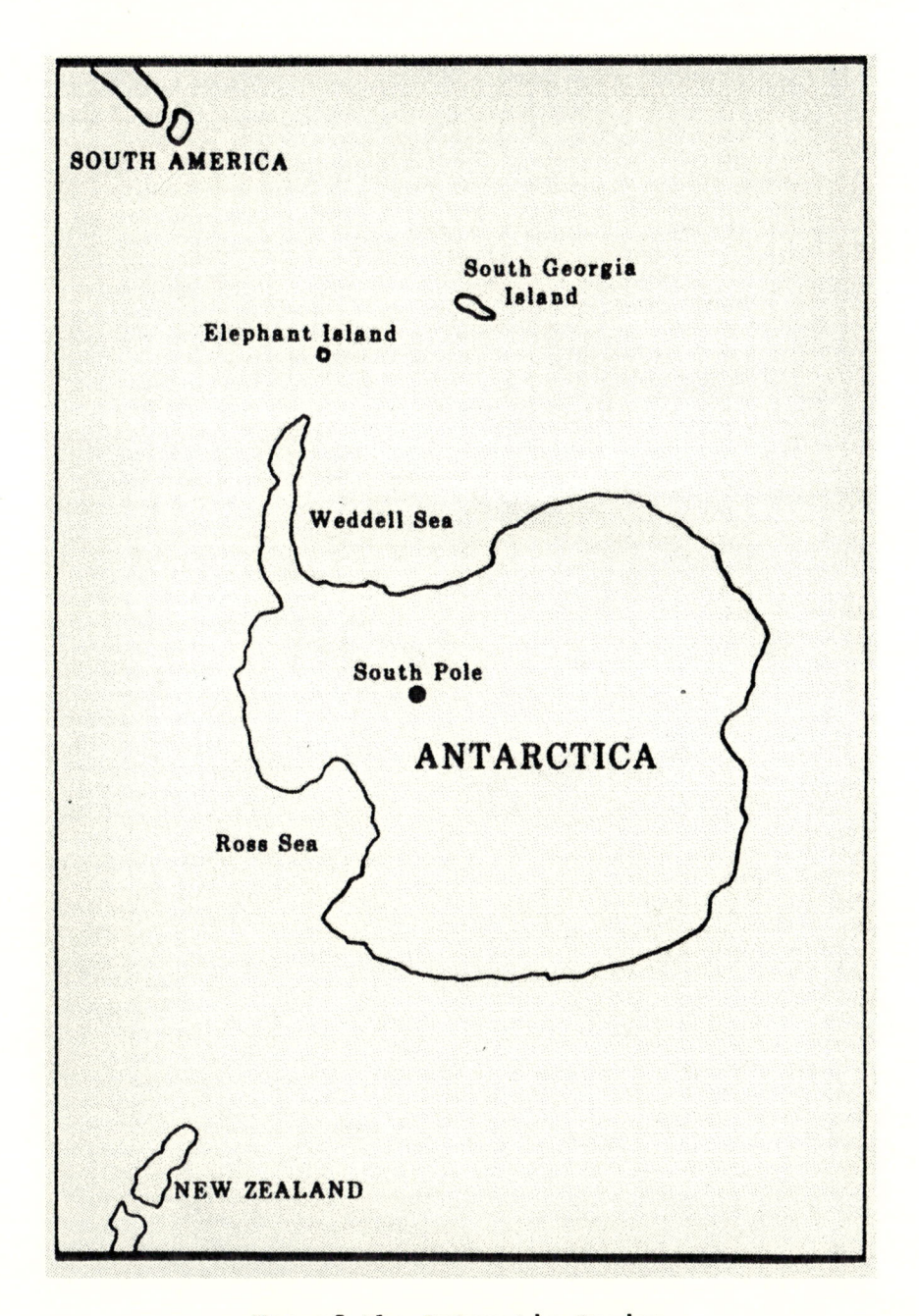

*Adventures on Seven Continents And Other Essays*

Map of the Antarctic Region

*John Davis Cantwell, M.D.*

By the time the small group reached the Grytviken whaling camp, they were caked in ice and snow, and wearing the same ragged clothes they had worn for over a year.

Shackleton's main concern was for the men left on Elephant Island. After four brave attempts he reached them, some four and a half months later.

Shackleton again returned to England a hero. Not one man under his leadership had been lost in the ordeal. Of the group, he later waxed: "It was a privilege to me to have under my command men who, through dark days and the stress and strain of continuous danger, kept up their spirit and carried out their work regardless of themselves and heedless to the limelight."

Shackleton's adventures – and health problems – continued. In 1918, having joined a British expeditionary force to northern Russia, Shackleton became ill. Although his physician suspected a heart attack, an ashen-faced Shackleton refused to undress and allow auscultation of his heart.

While he soon rallied, during the next three years in England Shackleton caught frequent colds and complained of intermittent pain between the scapulae – which he self-diagnosed as indigestion. He continued to smoke, overeat and drink alcohol to excess.

**Heart of the Matter**

In 1921, at age 47, Shackleton embarked on his fourth and final expedition to Antarctica. On the ocean voyage south he suffered another episode of severe chest pain. But after summoning the physician, A.H. Macklin, he perversely changed his mind and refused to be examined. In spite of this, based on what medical history of Shackleton's he was able to piece together, Macklin diagnosed angina pectoris. Shackleton remained an uncooperative patient, increasing his alcohol intake sharply to the point where (perhaps to relieve chest pain), he habitually drank champagne in the mornings.

On January 5, 1922, at 2 a.m., while lodging again at Grytviken on South Georgia Island, Shackleton called for an emergency visit by Dr. Macklin. His complaint: facial neuralgia. He seemed unusually quiet and complaisant to Macklin, who tucked an extra blanket around him and advised him to take things "very much more quietly." Shackleton responded to the physician: "You are always wanting me to give up something. What do you want to give up now?" According to Macklin, these were Shackleton's last words, for thereupon "he died quite suddenly."

Macklin's autopsy indicated "atheroma of the coronary arteries." The doctor added, "The condition was a long-standing one and in my opinion was due to overstraining during periods of debility." In retrospect we can surmise that Shackleton's cause of death was almost certainly ventricular fibrillation in the setting of severe coronary atherosclerosis. (The systolic murmur detected during Shackleton's cardiac auscultation was probably functional.)

He was buried on South Georgia Island, the site of his greatest triumph.

*John Davis Cantwell, M.D.*

Shackleton's cairn on South Georgia Island

*Adventures on Seven Continents And Other Essays*

**His Grave**

*John Davis Cantwell, M.D.*

Dr. Macklin also wrote: "What is remarkable is that in such an advanced condition he was able to carry on as he did. It shows, psychologically, a wonderful willpower and an underlying determination to overcome difficulties."

Indeed, in the figurative sense, Shackleton always had a great deal of heart. Courage and optimism were among his greatest assets as an explorer, along with an unwavering devotion to those under his command. His colleagues cited numerous instances when he gave up his gloves, boots, and food to members of his expedition during moments of greatest hardship.

A particularly fine tribute to Shackleton was made by Sir Edmund Hillary, who himself traversed Antarctica in the late 1950s. "For scientific discovery," Hillary wrote, "give me [Robert Falcon] Scott; for speed and efficiency of travel, give me Amundsen; but when disaster strikes and all hope is gone, get down on your knees and pray for Shackleton."

Actually, Macklin, in remembering "the boss" in his last medical report, may have said it best: "As a living organism he was wonderful."

# 45

## RENOIR'S RHEUMATISM

Renoir's rheumatism began a century ago, when he was in his late 40s. It progressed, over the remaining three decades of his life, to the point where he had to be carried in a chair to his outdoor studio, with brushes fastened to his gnarled hands. Nevertheless, he painted every day, despite the interruptions from paroxysms of pain. "He was aware of his decline and realized the seriousness of his condition, but generally he wouldn't talk about it," writes B. E. White, a Renoir scholar at Tufts University.

Dr. White sifted through nearly 1000 letters, published statements and interviews by Renoir, using 88 different sources. Her book, *Renoir. His Life, Art and Letters*, combines events and paintings from each era of his long career, supplemented by photographs which show the progression of his rheumatoid arthritis.

We learn that Renoir first showed artistic talent at age 15, when he used up ends of charcoal in his father's tailor shop to draw on the walls. He then spent a year copying the masters in the Louvre, and never lost his appreciation of his predecessors. In 1919, the year of his death, he traversed the long galleries of the Louvre in his wheelchair to view once again the masterpieces that had just returned from their wartime hiding place.

As a young man he enrolled as an art student in the studio of Gleyre, and was joined by other students such as Monet, Sisley, and

*John Davis Cantwell, M.D.*

Bazille. His first major break came at age 24, when two of his paintings were accepted by the prestigious Salon. His early works, like the Impressionists in general, featured vivid colors, with combinations of "real and imagined" hues and visible brush strokes. The emphasis was on people and their social relationships, the joyfulness he saw in the world of "…holidays, amusements, leisure and comfort." His attention to fashion detail was probably influenced by his father's occupation, along with that of his mother (a seamstress) and a brother-in-law (a fashion illustrator).

The happy times were interrupted by war against Germany in 1870, during which Bazille was killed. France surrendered in 1871, and Parisian life became more austere. A brief post-war boom was followed by an economic crash. Frustrated by the hard times, Renoir concentrated more on doing portraits of rich Parisians and deemphasized the Impressionistic movement. Not everyone appreciated his style (the critic, Wolff, suggested that someone "try to explain to Renoir that a woman's torso was not a mass of decomposing flesh with green and purple spots that indicate the state of total putrefaction in a corpse").

Still struggling into his mid-40s, Renoir travelled to Algiers and Italy, and the experience helped him become a more diversified painter. He gradually achieved success, thanks to buyers in America (late 1880s) and eventually in France (by 1890), but along with the success came rheumatoid arthritis, preceded by Sjogren's syndrome. There was a familial component, for his father had to relinquish his tailor shop in his 60s for the same disease.

As he became ill, Renoir's art seemed to almost compensate, as the figures became more active and sensuous. He required a cane for walking as he approached age 60. A nerve to his left eye became partially atrophied. His hands became more ossified and deformed. Treatment of the arthritis consisted of heat, mineral baths, sun, walks, rubdowns, purges, and insertion of heated needles. An aspirin-like drug was tried in 1899. There were exacerbations and remissions, but he became progressively more debilitated after each bout. He continued to find joy, however not only in his work but "…in growth and power of life itself."

To the very end his retained his "blithe love of nature, human beings, and art." His patron, Durand-Ruel, was amazed by Renoir's strength of character: "He has to be carried everywhere by two people. What torture! And still the same good humor, the same happiness when he can paint"

His fingers were virtually paralyzed by age 70, but with the brush fastened to his hand his stroke remained steady. A cloth was inserted in the hollow of his hand to keep the wooden handle of the brush from injuring his tender skin. When his hands became numbed from fatigue the brush was removed from his fingers, for he couldn't open them himself. He continued to paint, except for several months when a stroke rendered his arms immobile, and when rheumatoid nodules had to be excised.

Several days before his death at age 78 (from pneumonia and a myocardial infarction), he stated that he was "still making progress" in his work. He had begun a small still life and even in his pre-death delirium asked for his palette, so he could paint two woodcocks

*John Davis Cantwell, M.D.*

that his physician had casually mentioned earlier.

An admirer wrote at the time of Renoir's death that "it is as if the sun had gone out of the sky." He left us with a permanent illumination, however, in his 720 paintings. Although none brought him great financial success, they are so highly valued today that "The Boating Party" alone was insured for $10 million, when it went on tour (including Atlanta) in 1982.

In reflecting upon his life, Renoir simply compared it "to one of those corks thrown into the river. Off it goes, then it is drawn into an eddy, pulled back, plunges and rises, is caught by a grass, makes desperate efforts to get free and ends up losing itself, I do not know where." His "desperate efforts" to persevere, despite the ravages of early poverty, old age and disease, are at least as impressive a legacy as was the magnificence of his artistic works.

# 46

## THE ADVENTUROUS ELISHA KENT KANE, M.D.

Few recall his name today, but at the time of his premature death in 1857, Elisha Kent Kane, M.D. was one of the best-known physicians in America and in England.

The son of a prominent Philadelphia judge, Kane was born in 1820, the eldest of seven children. He was an "unpromising scholar" as a schoolboy. At age 15, he developed symptoms that were diagnosed as rheumatic fever three years later. He attended the University of Virginia briefly, but dropped out when his disease flared. His father picked him up at the school and advised him that "if you must die (of the disease), die in harness." The son's subsequent exploits would exceed his father's most extreme expectations.

At age 19, Elisha decided on a medical career and enrolled at the University of Pennsylvania Medical School. Ward rounds were conducted at Blockley Hospital (now Philadelphia General).

The senior Kane guided his son toward a medical career in the Navy, fearful that the rigors of private practice would be too strenuous for him. He vastly underestimated his son's tremendous physical capabilities.

Kane's naval duties took him to the North and South Atlantic Oceans, the Pacific and Indian Oceans and the Mediterranean and Adriatic Seas. During the war with Mexico in the 1840s, Kane was selected to deliver a message from President Polk to General Winifred Scott. He sailed to Veracruz and

John Davis Cantwell, M.D.

planned to ride on horseback to Mexico City, accompanied by a ragtag unit of 120 Mexican renegades. En route they encountered a company of Mexican Lancers. In the hand-to-hand battle with both sabers and pistols, Kane's group emerged victorious. The renegades wanted to execute the captured brigadier general and his son, but a seriously wounded Dr. Kane leveled his pistol at them and prevented it. He also took a piece of pack thread and ligated a severed artery of the major's, keeping him from exsanguinating.

Kane's next adventure was to secure him international recognition. In 1850, at age 30, the small, muscular physician was selected to be part of a U.S. Naval expedition to the Arctic, searching for British explorer Sir John Franklin and his 129 men. The Franklin expedition was seeking the Northwest Passage to India. They had left England in May, 1845, and were last seen by an English whaler in June. Several British expeditions had been sent to search for the missing explorers, to no avail. Responding to the pleas of Lady Franklin, and financed largely by Henry Grinnell, an influential New Yorker, the United States sent two ships, with Kane as the surgeon.

In collaboration with several other vessels, the explorers discovered three graves of Franklin expedition members on tiny Beechey Island, but no trace of Franklin or the rest of the men was found.

Although courageous and tenacious, Franklin hadn't been to the Arctic in 20 years, and was considered to have a "perchance for making bad decisions." He once burned down his own tent in 1820, trying to send smoke signals to some Indians. In 1821 Franklin lost ten of his men when he elected to put canoes into the freezing North Seas. The Copper Indians rescued him, semiconscious and several days from death.

## The Second Expedition

Kane was selected to lead a second expedition to search for Franklin and his men, sponsored again by Grinnell and using the ship, Advance. In May, 1853, he and 17 officers and crewmen sailed from New York. Some of the men were questionable. The ship's surgeon, Isaac Hayes, was only 21 and still just a medical student. Two crew members, William Godfrey and John Blake, were late additions from the waterfront bars and were of "unknown and probably discreditable" backgrounds. Over a three-year period Kane and his men ventured into previously uncharted Arctic waters, looking for both the Franklin expedition members and the "open sea" to the North Pole. They found neither, but endured a multitude of hardships in the process.

Food was scarce. Kane trapped rats and made a soup out of them, which no other crew member would imbibe. The temperature was as cold as -69.3ºF. When their boat became locked in ice, eleven of the crew members voted to abandon the vessel and set out on their own, against Kane's advice. They were later to return, unable to succeed on their own without his leadership. Godfrey and Blake were troublemakers. At times, the diminutive Kane had to confront them with his drawn pistol to maintain order.

On one occasion he pummeled Godfrey, aided no doubt by some brass knuckles concealed in his glove.

*John Davis Cantwell, M.D.*

Kane eventually abandoned ship and led his men on a sledge trip toward safety. In one 31-day period alone he covered 1,100 miles. Bonsall later wrote:

> "during our passage through the ice and open boat on that perilous journey of more than 80 days, by his judicious management he (Kane) not only cheered the dispirited and quieted the querulous and discontented, but he also dispensed the provisions as to give no one the slightest cause for complaint."

A relief ship had been sent to look for Kane. Among the crew was his younger brother, John K. Kane, M.D. The men were finally spotted by a Danish brig:

> "long-bearded and weather-beaten, they had strange wild costumes…Dr. Kane, standing upright in the stern of the first boat, with his spyglass slung around his neck, was the first identified."

Kane returned to a hero's welcome, despite the inability to achieve his goals. His book about the second expedition was a best-seller, with sixty-five thousand copies purchased in the first year. The Royal Geographic Society presented Kane with their prestigious gold medal for his courageous exploits.

The indefatigable Lady Franklin wanted Kane to head a third expedition, searching more to the south, around King William Island. Kane sailed for England and met with her, but was weakened due to fever and weight loss. He decided to seek warmer weather and sailed on to Cuba. While doing so, he had a recurrence of joint pain and swelling. Shortly after leaving St. Thomas, he had a left cerebral stroke, likely embolic and perhaps related to atrial fibrillation or possibly infectious endocarditis (in the presence of rheumatic valvular heart disease). Kane arrived in Cuba. His mother and his physician brother were summoned, and came as soon as they could. On February 10, 1857, Kane suffered another stroke. He was treated with leeches and with cold compresses to the head. Six days later he died, so quietly "that his mother, who was reading the Bible at his bedside, went on reading until the others told her that his life had ended."

Kane's body was taken from Havana to Philadelphia "on a funeral journey the likes of which Americans had never seen." At every town the steamboat passed, going up the Mississippi and Ohio Rivers, "people were standing on the levee and wharves to see her go by." The final trip was by rail. Only the processions of Lincoln (in 1865) and Robert Kennedy (in 1968) were of the same magnitude. People stood silently at every stop, and gathered at each railway station, amid tolling of bells. As the hearse arrived in Philadelphia and moved toward Independence Hall, seven members of the advanced crew (including the notorious Godfrey) joined in the procession. Kane's body lay in state at Independence Hall and he was subsequently buried in a cemetery in Philadelphia.

**Franklin**

In 1857, Lady Franklin persuaded the British Royal Navy to send one of its best young

*John Davis Cantwell, M.D.*

explorers, Captain Leopold McClintoch, in yet another search for her husband. He probed King William Island and found some abandoned supplies and skeletal remains of expedition members, along with two written notes. The latter told of Franklin's death on the ice-bound ship, Erebus, on June 11, 1847, probably of malnutrition and scurvy. His body was never recovered but, to date, about two-thirds of the expedition members' remains have been found.

In 1985, Canadian anthropologist, Owen Beattie, returned from an expedition to Beechey Island with a striking picture of the preserved body of John Torrington, a sailor on the Franklin expedition, whose body was discovered in an icy grave.

**The Northwest Passage**

Franklin had come close to finding the Northwest Passage to the Pacific. Had he gone to the west of King William Island instead of to the east, he might have found it. Although a monument in Westminster Abbey commemorates Franklin and his men for "completing the discover of the Northwest Passage," it wasn't actually found for 60 more years. In 1906, Norwegian explorer, Roald Amundsen, succeeded in taking a 70-foot-long ship from the Atlantic to the Pacific. Five years later he became the first man to reach the South Pole. He would later die in the Arctic when his seaplane crashed in a rescue attempt of a fellow explorer.

## Kane's Legacy

A recent novel, *Voyage of the Narwhal*, reintroduced Dr. Kane to a generation that had largely forgotten him.

His legacy included the mapping of previously uncharted lands and waterways in the Arctic. One of the latter, Kane Basin, bears his name on today's maps. His fair and kindly treatment of the Eskimos helped pave the way for future expeditions that ventured into the area. His use of smaller, more maneuverable boats, was emulated by future explorers such as Admiral Robert Peary and Amundsen.

Kane's books were read widely. At age six, Robert Peary was influenced by a story based on Kane's second expedition and became an explorer too, being first to reach the North Pole. A biographer of Kane's was intrigued by the Arctic and became a physician to the natives of Labrador. In 1878, the director of the Astronomical Observatory in Athens, Greece, named a moon crater after Kane.

As G.W. Corner aptly concludes:

"Although no memorial column or pedestal bears a sculptured likeness of Dr. Kane of the Arctic Seas, and his fate as a national hero barely outlived his days on Earth, he would no doubt deem it the greater honor that his name is still known to travelers and explorers in the distant regions of the sea and the sky."

*John Davis Cantwell, M.D.*

# 47

## THE PHYSICIAN WHO HELPED CAPTURE GERONIMO

In the fall of 1886, a 26-year-old Army officer came face to face with the Indian chief he had been pursuing for several months. According to one account, the Indian asked the officer if he could hold his gun. The officer obliged and the Indian took it, aimed and fired, narrowly missing one of his tribesmen. Greatly amused, the 57-year-old Geronimo fell to the ground laughing, after which he returned the firearm to the soldier.

Geronimo and Officer Leonard Wood had in common the fact that both were athletic, courageous and great leaders. Yet, in other respects they were quite different. Wood grew up in New Hampshire, the son of a doctor, and himself a graduate of Harvard Medical School. At 5'11", he had powerful arms and shoulders, owing to his fetish of physical fitness. Even in medical school he kept in superb condition by running every day and participating in strenuous athletic activities.

Geronimo, the fourth of eight children of an Apache warrior, never went to school. As a boy he was taught to run four miles while holding a mouthful of water and was not allowed to swallow any. He was encouraged to be a swift distance runner, capable of covering over 70 miles a day, and was also taught how to rustle stock, raid pack trains, ride, and to despise non-tribal Mexican neighbors. Dr. Wood practiced medicine at Boston City Hospital but

*Adventures on Seven Continents And Other Essays*

quit after a disagreement with the hospital administrator. He moved across town in Boston and tried private practice, but grew restless and volunteered for military duty.

When only 29, Geronimo's mother, wife and three sons were killed by a Mexican band. Geronimo was put in charge of the revenge battle and displayed tremendous courage, such that he became war chief of the whole Apache tribe, leading them in the Apache Wars with the U.S. military which lasted from 1860 until 1886. The war began when a drunken white man beat his half-breed son. The boy ran away and the father accused the Apache, Cochise, of kidnapping him and some stock as well. Cochise agreed to a conference, but discovered that it was a trap and barely escaped with his life by slashing a tent with a knife.

Leonard Wood viewed life as an adventure and wanted to show that he was more than just a "pill-pusher." The day after arriving at Ft. Huachuca, Arizona, he volunteered to accompany Capt. Henry Lawson and several others in a 30 mile ride, tracking the Apaches. This was the start of a four-month effort during which, with hardly any rest, Wood rode and marched over 3000 miles through some of the most rugged country in North America. It took 2000 soldiers to round up Geronimo and the last band of 30 Apaches. Only Wood and Lawton had the stamina to complete the entire campaign. Lawton wrote of Wood:

> "His courage, energy and loyal support during the whole time; his encouraging example to the command when work was hardest and prospects darkest; his thorough confidence and belief in the final success of the expeditions, his untiring efforts to

*John Davis Cantwell, M.D.*

make it so, has placed me under obligations so great that I cannot express them."

Wood later received the Congressional Medal of Honor for his efforts. The citation read:

"Throughout the campaign against the hostile Apaches...this officer serving as medical officer with Captain Lawton's expedition, rendered specifically courageous and able services involving extreme peril and displayed most conspicuous gallantry under conditions of great danger and hardships. He volunteered to carry dispatches through a region infested with hostile Indians, making a journey of 70 miles in one night and then marching 30 miles on foot the next day. For several weeks, while in close pursuit of Geronimo's band and constantly expecting an encounter, Wood exercised the command of a detachment of Infantry to which he requested assignment and that was without an officer."

Geronimo and his renegade band were put on a train and sent to Florida, subsequently transferred to Alabama and eventually to Oklahoma. A bitter man, he always regretted the final surrender rather than fighting it out in the Sierra Madre mountains of the Southwest. He did become a shrewd capitalist, one Indian who exploited the exploiters better then they could him. He became a farmer, joined the Dutch Reformed Church (and even taught Sunday school until expelled for gambling) and was a tireless self- promotor, "hawking photographs, bows and arrows, and posing for pictures at various fairs and expositions." In the winter of 1909, at age

80, he went to a nearby town to sell one of the bows he was invariably making. He got drunk on the money from the sale and, on the way home, fell out of his buggy and lay all night on the road in a freezing rain. He died shortly thereafter in the military hospital at Ft. Sill. Had an autopsy been done, it would have revealed gunshot wounds to the right leg (above and below the knee), to the left forearm, the left flank, the back and lateral aspect of the left orbit, along with a saber wound to the right lower leg and a head scar from the butt of a musket.

Leonard Wood became the Surgeon General of Ft. McPherson in Atlanta. He enrolled in Georgia Tech and, at age 33, became their first football captain in 1893. In the big game against the University of Georgia, Wood played guard on defense and fullback on offense. Carrying the ball about 80% of the plays, Wood blasted into the end zone for a four-point touchdown and led two other scoring drives, staking Tech to an 18-0 halftime lead. During intermission, the Georgia fans started throwing rocks at the Tech players and Wood was struck above the right eye by a stone propelled from a slingshot.

*John Davis Cantwell, M.D.*

Leonard Wood, captain of Georgia Tech's 1893 football team

*Adventures on Seven Continents And Other Essays*

Undaunted, he led Tech to a 28-6 victory and later stitched his own wound in front of a mirror. Tech halfback Hunter said:

"After the game we were greeted by a shower of rocks, sticks and missiles. Most us were badly scared but Wood calmly walked off the field and made his way to the (train) station."

Wood's career had just begun. He became a favorite of Theodore Roosevelt, who said of him:

"No soldier could outwalk him; could live with greater indifference on hard or scanty fare; could endure hardship better or do better without sleep."

In 1898, for the Spanish-American War, Wood was commissioned to recruit the Rough Riders. Wood selected 1200 from 23,000 applicants, with Roosevelt as his assistant. In only 21 days after receiving the commission, he had the men ready to march.

Leonard Wood subsequently became Governor of Cuba. Yellow fever was rampant and Wood was impressed with the theory of a Doctor Finlay, who practiced in Cuba, that mosquitos were the disseminators of the disease. He got a board of Army Surgeons to investigate this, and the work of Dr. Walter Reed and his associates is now medical history.

After completing his term as Governor of Cuba, Wood subsequently was appointed military commander and civil governor of the troubled Philippines. In 1914, he became Chief of Staff, the highest office in the Army.

*John Davis Cantwell, M.D.*

Wood's later years, like Geronimo's, were filled with a few disappointments. He was precise in speech and somewhat harsh or sarcastic when irritated by the stupidity of his inferiors. This earned him a few bitter enemies to go along with his close personal friends. He had hoped to lead the expeditionary forces in World War I, but John J. Pershing was selected instead. President Woodrow Wilson felt Wood was too domineering and too amenable to discipline. Wood got into the battle anyway and, characteristically, was one of the first American officers to be wounded.

In 1920, he was a leading Republican candidate for President, but Warren Harding won the nomination on the 10th ballot. Seven years later, Wood died (at age 67) and is best remembered today by the Army base in Missouri which was named after him.

# 48

## OSLER: A ROLE MODEL FOR TODAY'S PHYSICIAN

While I was contemplating whether or not to accept a position as Director of Internal Medicine at Georgia Baptist Medical Center, a physician friend gave me a copy of Cushing's two-volume biography of Sir William Osler. I had always intended to read it, but heretofore had not had the opportunity to do so. I set about the task with some trepidation, as I would with any 1400 page book. I quickly became immersed in the man, his ideas, and his role as a teacher par excellence. I was impressed with the timelessness of his dictums and found him to be a perfect role model for the challenge I finally decided to accept.

Osler, the youngest son of an Anglican missionary living on the edge of the Canadian wilderness, was born in 1849. Expelled from public school (for apparently shouting abusive remarks through the keyhole of the headmaster's door), young William entered boarding school where he came under the influence of Rev. William Johnson, a minister and natural scientist. Osler pursued a similar interest in biology and also excelled as an athlete. He participated in all the school sports, winning a prize for kicking the football and once threw a cricket ball an estimated 115 yards, a record for an amateur. He also competed in the hurdles, dashes, and the steeplechase, until his athletic pursuits were curtailed by osteomyelitis. At Trinity

John Davis Cantwell, M.D.

College in Toronto, Osler encountered Dr. James Bovell, a physician and biologist who was in the process of switching to the priesthood. Bovell opened his home to Osler, sharing his personal library of classical and medical books and was to become a lifelong influence on him. When he entered McGill Medical School, Osler met Dr. Palmer Howard, the third man (along with Johnson and Bovell) who influenced him so. Like Dr. Bovell, Howard also gave Osler ready access to his library, something that in years to come Osler would do for his own students.

After graduation, Osler joined the staff at McGill as a pathologist, and remained there until 1884, when at age 35 he was summoned to a professorship in medicine at the University of Pennsylvania. Five years later he accepted the position as Chief of Medicine at the new Johns Hopkins Medical School. Within three years he had written a textbook of medicine (dedicated to Johnson, Bovell and Howard), married the widow of a physician friend, and established a method of clinical teaching which still exists today. He remained at Hopkins for 16 years, finishing his career as the Regis Professor of Medicine at Oxford.

Osler's value system is as relevant to medical education today as it was at the turn of the last century. He believed in punctuality, stating that it is "the prime essential of a physician. If invariably on time, he will succeed even in the face of professional mediocrity." He advocated the importance of being organized, encouraging his students and housestaff to divide their lives into 24-hour compartments, focusing on each day's work. He believed in scholarship and the necessity for daily study, reminding us that "it is astonishing with how little reading a doctor can practice medicine, but it is not astonishing how badly he may do it." He encouraged the students to obtain a well-rounded education, insisting that they "rest not satisfied with...professional training, but try to get the education, if not of a scholar, at least of a gentleman." Osler thought that the young medical house officer should "seek knowledge for itself without a thought of the end, tested and taught day by day, the pupil and teacher working together on the same lines, only one a little ahead of the other." His home became "Open Arms" to the residents, who were given keys to his private study. Osler met with these "latchkey" students one evening each week, seated around the dining room table, reviewing interesting medical topics and items of historical and cultural importance.

Osler taught clinical medicine for 45 years. A multi-talented man, he could have excelled in many vocations. According to an editorial in a Baltimore newspaper, "Dr. Osler would have had been great in any field - in the pulpit, in politics, in literature, in law - because God gave him a great and many-sided mind and spirit which such minds often lack - the inspiration, the courage, and the honesty of the prophet who had walked on the mountain-top and swept the whole world with his eyes, and who can deliver a message that is as unbounded as his vision."

His health began to fail after the untimely death of his son, Revere, on the battlefields of Flanders. Osler remained a clinician to the very end, following his own case with careful observation. He knew that pneumonia in a 70-

*John Davis Cantwell, M.D.*

year-old was usually fatal, and it proved to be in his case.

He had such an influence on his profession and his peers that, according to Dr. A. G. Gibson of Oxford "...Some continue to test their conduct in a dilemma by asking the question, what would Osler have done." Indeed, his example influenced me as a medicine program director more than 70 years after his death and is likely to continue to do so as long as I continue to practice medicine.

His photograph near my desk, a gift from distant kin, is a daily reminder of his standards of excellence, and a measuring stick for me to assess my own performance.

# 49

## AN ENCOUNTER WITH PAUL DUDLEY WHITE

Ogelsby Paul's biography on the late Paul Dudley White, M.D., brought back memories of an encounter I had with Dr. White, years ago. I was a medical intern, attending my first medical meeting at the Plaza Hotel in New York. Dr. White was one of the featured speakers. After registering at the hotel, I moved to the elevators, only to discover that they were malfunctioning. A small crowd had gathered, seemingly perplexed by the dilemma. Just then, Dr. White also appeared, two heavy suitcases in hand. Told of the situation, he merely shrugged his shoulders, and said something to the effect that it really wasn't a problem, for he was only on the 14th floor. Up the stairway he charged, dragging his bags along, refreshingly vital at age 79!

Dr. White was a role model for me during my formative years because of his interest in medical areas of importance to me, such as preventive cardiology, sports medicine and international concerns. Paul's biography captures the essence of the man, and his vast contributions to the medical world.

He was probably the first pure cardiologist in the United States. Early in his career, in the 1920s, he was advocating the importance of regular exercise and of preventive medicine. In a lecture to the U.S. Public Health Service personnel, he said:

*John Davis Cantwell, M.D.*

"You can all do something towards keeping your hearts and arteries in good condition. Most of you are careless of health even though you are intelligent in other matters…

Exercise to keep fit. To be indolent physically is worse than to be excessively athletic; there is a happy mean…

Use your arms and legs more, and your stomachs and automobiles less."

He later cautioned that "the period of 20 to 40 is a critical age…when the rusting process in the artery walls… begins. The rust piles up year by year until at the age of 45 or 50 the over-nourished man of our day comes to a doctor with angina pectoris, a heart attack, or a little stroke, or he may die suddenly. It is the end result of a long period of accumulated disease."

What made him such a great physician? Dr. Paul's book offers at least six strong attributes:

## 1. HARD WORK

He was probably influenced by his physician-father, who died of a heart attack while making a house call at age 69. A colleague, who shared a room with him on a medical trip, was surprised to see a light on at 4 a.m. and Dr. White hard at work on a paper (paradoxically on the evils of overwork). When stricken with his first heart attack at age 84, Dr. White insisted on stopping at his office, en route to Massachusetts General Hospital, to pick up a briefcase full of work. He was a firm believer that the one most important means to improve and to maintain the health and happiness of our older citizens is to keep them working both mentally and physically.

## 2. THOROUGHNESS

Like all great clinicians, he was a stickler for being thorough. While in Los Angeles once, at age 67, to receive an honorary Doctor of Science degree at U. S. C., he was asked by a former resident to see one of the latter's seriously ill patients, mainly to placate the family. Dr. White appeared at the hospital after the festivities, still in his tuxedo, at 11:30 p.m. The former resident thought that he would give just a brief sketch of the elderly patient who was obviously dying, later to recall:

> "That didn't do for Dr. White. He had to talk with and examine the patient, go through every item on the chart, every item in the laboratory data, write them down in his own records, and then spend a great deal of time with the patient and the family discussing everything with them. Dr. White did that not just for the patient and the family - he also did it for me."

## 3. ENTHUSIASM

This was one of the traits "that made him a wonderful teacher," according to a former resident. A finding on physical examination, which he had no doubt encountered many times before, could still generate enthusiasm, and this would be shared by both the housestaff and students alike.

*John Davis Cantwell, M.D.*

## 4. OPTIMISM

The title of Dr. Paul's biography, *Take Heart*, concerns this aspect of Dr. White's personality. It comes from *The Pirates of Penzance*, by W.S. Gilbert ("Take Heart, Fair Days Will Shine").

According to Dr. Edward Bland, a long-time colleague of Dr. White, the latter excelled at making the patient feel that "…this wasn't the end of the road. He would take the most dismal situation and look at the bright side, and the patient would leave his office happy. He just had a knack of convincing the patient and you and himself that perhaps things weren't as bad as they appeared."

## 5. COMMON SENSE

Several examples illustrate his common-sense approach to clinical matters. One concerned an 18-year-old Yale College swimmer whom Dr. White saw because of a four-year history of recurring tachycardia. The ECG showed a short P-R interval and a wide QRS complex, something never previously reported. Dr. White carefully evaluated the young man, studied his cardiac response to running up flights of stairs, and eventually cleared him to continue swimming. Fifty-six years later the man was still swimming, and doing well with a condition that came to be known as the Wolff-Parkinson-White syndrome.

Another example of his practical approach concerned his advice to his most famous patient, President Eisenhower. Serious questions were raised about the latter's ability to withstand the rigors of a second term, following a heart attack in 1955. Dr.

White felt otherwise, and encouraged Ike to push ahead. Eisenhower successfully served a second term and went 10 years before experiencing a recurrent myocardial infarction.

## 6. A SENSE OF ADVENTURE

Dr. White brought his medical skills and knowledge to remote parts of the world. He visited Albert Schweitzer's hospital in Africa and, in his mid-80s, lectured in China. It was his whaling expedition along the Baja Peninsula, however, which I feel best reflects his adventurous spirit. The purpose of the trip was to record an ECG on this largest of mammals. The mission failed because of technical reasons, and one of the boats was damaged and nearly capsized by a mother whale guarding her young. Nonetheless, the stirring account of the whole affair (*National Geographic*, July, 1956) is a tribute to Dr. White's scientific tenacity at age 70.

Paul Dudley White authored a major cardiology textbook and hundreds of scientific articles in his career, and played a role in founding the American Heart Association and the National Institute of Health. He treated the rich and famous, along with those lower down on the social scale, and was "as courteous to the lowest as the highest…there was no difference." He remained physically active well into his 80s, once walking from the airport in Washington, D.C., to the White House for a meeting with President John F. Kennedy.

He developed a slight murmur of aortic regurgitation at 78, confirming the diagnosis by self-auscultation. At age 81 he first

*John Davis Cantwell, M.D.*

experienced angina pectoris while hurrying to see the finish of the Boston Marathon. He lived six more years, finally succumbing to a stroke.

# WILLIAM STOKES, M.D.

Throughout the first half of the nineteenth century, most of Ireland (including the city of Dublin) was in a state of decay. The culmination of this was the potato famine of 1845-9, wherein over a million Irish men, women and children died of malnutrition and starvation; countless others, including my great-grandfather, emigrated to other countries. In the midst of these most trying of times, a remarkable group of internists, including Stokes, Graves, Corrigan and Cheyne made the Dublin School of Medicine famous. To paraphrase Herrick, they were not only practical physicians but also men with investigative spirits, gifted lecturers and bedside teachers, authors of now classic articles and books and founders of journals and medical societies. One of the most talented was William Stokes.

## FAMILY BACKGROUND AND EARLY YEARS

The Stokes family came to Ireland in 1680. William's great-grandfather, an engineer, devised a system for supplying piped water to the city of Dublin. Whitley Stokes (William's father) was a physician and initially an ardent member of the United Irishmen. He was eccentric, but very able, and became Regius Professor of Medicine in Trinity College. He helped establish the College Botanical Gardens and the Zoological Gardens, and also

*John Davis Cantwell, M.D.*

published, at his own expense, a translation of the New Testament in Irish.

William was born in Dublin in 1804. His academic beginnings were less than auspicious. He left formal schooling after only one day, "after having drawn blood by sending a slate at his master's head." He initially seemed shy, lazy and incompetent, and lacked interest in either sports or education, preferring to read the ballads of Walter Scott, lying in a field, his head "propped on the neck of a red cow." He began to reform, stimulated by his mother's tears. He joined his father on long walks in the woods and developed an interest in the archaeologists, painters, lawyers and doctors who dropped by his father's study. He wasn't admitted to Trinity College, perhaps because of his father's nonconformity or prior connections with the United Irishmen, but a tutor helped him learn the essentials of Greek, Latin and math, and his father instructed him in science. William began working in the laboratories of Trinity College and the Royal College of Surgeons, and walked the wards of Meath Hospital with the students and Dr. Robert Graves. He subsequently attended medical school in Edinburgh, where he spent the days in lectures and the nights making house calls with Professor Alison. He graduated in 1825, and promptly published a 269 page treatise on the use of the stethoscope. It was the first English publication on this new technique, took him three months to write, and earned for him the sum of 70 pounds. It also helped establish his academic reputation.

After graduation, Stokes began working in Dublin's General Dispensary. In a subsequent letter to Mary Black (his future wife) he wrote: "In the course of my practice here I meet with instances of want and wretchedness that wring my very heart, and I wish for the fortune of a prince that I might relieve them." In 1826, he joined the staff at the Meath Hospital (a year after John Cheyne was forced to limit his own practice there due to ill health) and became immersed in treating victims of the typhus epidemic.

**EVENTS IN HIS CAREER**

Stokes spent 50 years working at Meath Hospital, including 30 years with Robert Graves. The latter was eight years older, and died 25 years before Stokes. According to Herrick they were colleagues, but not rivals, unusually effective lecturers and bedside clinicians, prolific writers (and often co-authors) and active participants in medical societies. Of Graves, Stokes wrote, "He was once my teacher, later my colleague, always my friend."

In 1837, Stokes published the first of his three medical texts, *A Treatise on the Diagnosis and Treatment of Diseases of the Chest*. It was considered the best book on the subject since Laennec's. In it he referred to a case described by Cheyne in 1818, a bedridden 60-year-old man who was flushed, speechless and hemiplegic:

> "The only peculiarity on the last period of his illness, which lasted only eight or nine days, was in the state of his respiration. For several days, his breathing was irregular; it would entirely cease for a quarter of a minute, then it would become perceptible, though very low, then by

*John Davis Cantwell, M.D.*

degrees it became heaving and quick, and then it would cease again."

Stokes observed this in other cases, and linked it to a weakened heart. He commented that in this condition (the apneic phase) "The patient may remain as such a length of time as to make his attendants believe that he is dead..." The condition is now known as Cheyne-Stokes respiration.

In 1845, Stokes became Regius Professor of Medicine at Dublin University. The next year, writing in the Dublin Quarterly Journal, he described two of his cases with syncopal episodes and a slow pulse, and mentioned five other case reports, including one that fellow Dubliner Robert Adams (a surgeon) had published in 1827. The latter case was a 68-year-old man who had multiple apoplectiform seizures over a seven-year period. Adams noted "the remarkable slowness of the pulse which generally ranged at the rate of 30 per minute." The patient subsequently died during a similar attack and the autopsy showed a dilated right ventricle, a soft and thin-walled left ventricle, "specks of bone" in the aortic valve and fatty changes in the myocardium. Stokes described cannon waves in the neck of his two patients, noting that "the pulsation of veins is of a kind of which we have never before witnessed." He mainly wanted to draw attention to the combination of the cerebral and cardiac phenomena, "of which our knowledge is still imperfect." The condition today is recognized as the Adams-Stokes attacks (or Morgagni-Adams-Stokes attacks, for Morgagni had mentioned a prematurely slow pulse in 1760).

Stokes published his second medical book *Disease of the Heart and Aorta* in 1854, aimed at helping the general practitioner and featuring experience gleaned from case histories. This book "carried the renown of the Dublin School throughout Europe and became a classic in the United States schools as well." Stokes stressed the importance of a murmur in diagnosis, and the difficulty in distinguishing the existence of functional and organic disease (which can "occasionally baffle the powers of even the most enlightened and experienced physician"). He also cautioned against overreliance on the stethoscope, for "too many depend on it alone to ascertain the disease." He recognized that the efficiency of the heart muscle could be improved with graduated exercise: "The symptoms of debility of the heart are often removable by a regulated course of gymnastics, or by pedestrian exercise." He was aware of angina pectoris, but felt that "obstruction of the coronary arteries much be considered as but a remote cause of angina."

**PERSONAL ATTRIBUTES**

Stokes had an attractive personalty, was modest and courteous, and possessed an "intermittent exuberance of almost childlike spirits."

He had a multitude of interests beyond medicine, including archeology, music, art and literature. His closest nonmedical friend was Petrie, an archeologist and collector of Irish music whom Stokes memorialized in a biography. The Stokes' home in Merrion Square was open to friends every Saturday evening, for fellowship and stimulating conversation. A country home

*John Davis Cantwell, M.D.*

near the seaside provided a brief respite from his large private practice, hospital work, and teaching duties. In his typical day:

> "I rise early, write until breakfast, then go to the dispensary where I sit in judgment on disease for an hour; then to the hospital, where I go around the wards attended by a crowd of pupils. From the hospital I return home, write again until two, then go around and visit my patients through the various parts of the town attended by a pupil."

As an educator, Stokes believed that medical doctors and surgeons should get the same basic training ("The constitution is one; there is no division of it into a medical and surgical domain"). He felt that medicine was not a single science but "an art, depending on all sciences." and that a liberal education could give a student the moral character so necessary for medicine:

> "...the still prominent evils among us are the neglect of general education, the confounding of instruction with education, and the giving of greater importance to the special training than to the general culture of the student."

This emphasis on the advantages of a liberal education for medical students "was exemplified by his own life." One can see why he was such a popular teacher, for "his great object in teaching medicine was to make his pupils practical men, to stimulate them to original investigations, and to make them feel that he himself was in all cases their fellow student."

## LATER YEARS AND HONORS

Stokes was elected physician to the Queen in Ireland in 1861. In 1867, he served as President of the British Medical Association. His last book, *Lectures on Fever*, was published in 1871, the same year the University of Dublin established the Diploma in State Medicine (at his urging) for those who wished to emphasize preventive medicine. In 1874, because of his interest in patronage of the arts, he was elected President of the Irish Academy. In 1875, Stokes resigned as physician to Meath Hospital and as Regius Professor of Medicine. The following year the German government honored him with the Prussian Order of Merit. In November, 1877, Stokes had a stroke, and died on January 10, 1878. He was buried at St. Finlans, in Howth.

Thus ended the life of not just an outstanding clinician, teacher and writer, but of a cultured man and prominent citizen of Dublin, one "ever conscious of the unique position of a doctor in society." His obituary stated it best:

"Stokes did not obtain any title. He never coveted any; he never sought any. He was a prince from birth of the aristocracy of intellect. His name is crowned with the triple coronet of the gratitude of the poor, for whom he tenderly and piously cared; the confidence of the public, whose approbation he universally secured; and the love and esteem of his profession, whose honour and interests he unflinchingly upheld."

*John Davis Cantwell, M.D.*

# 51

## AN EVENING WITH DUTCH

**The Event**

The invitation arrived unexpectedly. President and Mrs. Ronald Reagan were inviting my wife and me to a cocktail buffet at the White House. It was to be a gathering of consultants to the President's Council on Physical Fitness and Sports.

We debated about going. We had three young children and not a lot of extra money to spare. Babysitters were hard to come by. It was a long way to go for a brief event.

On the other hand, how many opportunities does one get in a lifetime to meet the President in his own home?

We decided to go. We flew to Washington and whiled away time in the Dupont Plaza's hotel lobby before attending the party.

*Adventures on Seven Continents And Other Essays*

> The President and Mrs. Reagan
> request the pleasure of your company
> at a reception to be held at
> The White House
> on Tuesday afternoon, February 2, 1982
> at five o'clock

**Invitation to a White House party**

After hailing a taxi, I tried not to appear smug as I instructed the driver where to take us. He dropped us at a special gate, we presented our invitations, and walked up to the White House entrance. A military band was playing. We soon mingled with cabinet members like Caspar Weinberger, notable athletes such as Tenley Albright (former Olympic gold medalist in figure skating and now a physician), former Miss America, Colleen Hutchins, "Suzie Chapstick" (an attractive former Olympic skier and now a television pitch woman), and author Jim Fixx.

President Reagan joined us toward the end of the event. We presented him with a set of sterling silver weights, which he promptly lifted, to our applause. A receiving line was forming and we queued up for a personal greeting. I was interested in his hair. Some wag once said, "He doesn't dye his hair; it is just prematurely orange." It was described

*John Davis Cantwell, M.D.*

later as being "so dense and fine as to amount to a Marvel Comics helmet, slicked with Brylcreem and water to a blue-black sheen, diffusing any hint of gray."

While awaiting my turn, I noticed that if you weren't a pretty woman or didn't have something notable to say, the Secret Service agents whisked you by the President in an instant.

*To John Cantwell
With best wishes,
Ronald Reagan*

**Meeting President Ronald Reagan**

As I shook his hand I blurted out, "Dr. Loyal Davis," who was a neurosurgeon at Northwestern Medical School and one of my professors. He also happened to be Ronald Reagan's father-in-law. We visited briefly

*John Davis Cantwell, M.D.*

about our common bond and I mentioned that I still carried Dr. Davis' reflex hammer in my little black bag. Dr. Davis disliked the triangular-headed hammer and had designed his own, insisting that each medical student obtain one.

It was a thrill to wander through the Green Room and the Blue Room, studying oil paintings of the great men who had inhabited the place, especially Washington, Jefferson, and Lincoln. Pretty soon it was time to go. Nobody wanted to leave. The lights flashed from bright to dim several times and the Secret Service men in dark suits and "hearing aids" circulated about, guiding us toward the door.

It had started to rain, fairly hard as I recall. The walkway back to the entry gate was long. No umbrellas were around. We ducked into a nearby pub, shook ourselves dry like a dog does, and reflected upon the incredible event over glasses of wine. We then took a cab back to the airport and were home before midnight, mere mortals once again.

**The Controversial Book**

Memories of that evening and of President Reagan came flooding back recently when I read Edmund Morris' authorized biography of Reagan (entitled **Dutch**) and listened to Morris speak at the Atlanta History Center's Livingston Lectureship. I had read the Morris biography, **The Rise and Fall of Theodore Roosevelt**, a fine book which won the Pulitzer Prize. I expected a similar effort in **Dutch**, but was disappointed.

Morris chose to insert his fictionalized self as a contemporary of Reagan's from his childhood to the presidency. In the lecture,

Morris said that he did this because Reagan was opaque, a man who was an interplay of fiction and nonfiction, an actor who was happy on either side of the screen, a man who resisted orthodox analysis. Given the liberty of this fictionalized alter ego, Morris proceeds to do a number on Reagan. Consider the following statements he makes:

- He had an attention span which an exasperated aide would compare to that of a fruit fly.
- Preferred the *Readers' Digest* for its indiscriminate accumulation of facts, whether sterile or significant.
- Reagan was not by nature appreciative (he merely accepted favors, as he did the mail).
- Horrified some by his encyclopedic ignorance.
- Lacked intellectual energy. His brain was resistant to detail. He was an apparent airhead.
- He was disturbed by the relentless banality, not to mention incoherence, of the President's replies in interviews.
- Viewed Reagan as a pleasant, if purposeful mediocrity.

In the Livingston lecture, Morris was much kinder to Reagan. In spite of his cornball stories and hokey ways, Reagan was a majestically certain person, the strongest person in every room he entered, a man who was naturally fearless. Good at everything that he did, Reagan was an extremely effective president.

He had enormous personal power and was personally sweet and irresistible. His faith was strong and simple. His magnetic personality attracted people who wanted to serve him.

Reagan was egocentric (the center of his own universe), but not vain (praise didn't particularly matter to him). His journals were devoid of self-congratulations, although he tabulated the number of times various talks were interrupted by applause, much like an actor evaluating his performance.

His leadership style was compared to that of a conductor who beats time imperceptibly, often with eyes closed, before a band of players, few of whom even look up from their desks. Somehow, a concerted sound emerges.

The first evidence Morris observed of Reagan's cognitive frailty occurred during his 82nd birthday celebration in 1993. Margaret Thatcher was in attendance and Reagan toasted her in a fine speech. Shortly thereafter, Reagan got everyone's attention again and stated that he would like to propose a toast to Thatcher, and proceeded with an almost word-for-word repeat of his earlier speech.

The diagnosis of suspected Alzheimer's disease was confirmed the next year at the Mayo Clinic. On November 5, 1994, Reagan published his hand-written letter to the American people, ending with "I now begin the journey that would lead me into the sunset of my life. I know that for America there will always be a bright dawn ahead."

After reading the letter, Edmund Morris stated that, "for the first time in my life I felt love for Ronald Reagan, and overpowering sadness." Those of us who have had relatives with dementia could certainly echo those sentiments.

# 52

## LEILA DENMARK, M.D.: PRACTICING MEDICINE AT AGE 103

After a busy morning in the office several years ago, I drove to a northern suburb of Atlanta to spend part of the afternoon with Dr. Leila Denmark, a pediatrician who at age 100 then was the country's oldest practicing physician. It was an uplifting experience for me, given the current complaints of managed care and the threats of early retirement of some close colleagues who are being driven from the profession by the bureaucratic morass.

Dr. Denmark grew up on a farm in south Georgia, the third of twelve children. As a child, she writes, "I did not know a woman could become a doctor, but I loved to see things live, I would pick up flowers that had been thrown out as dead and put them in water and see them come back to life.

I would help a little sick chicken, or get a grasshopper out of a spider web, or help my father doctor a sick cow. I would make salve for the sores of my little brothers and sisters and the little colored children on the farm."

After college, she taught for two years, and then applied to medical school at the Medical College of Georgia. Her application wasn't acknowledged. The day classes began, she went to the school and asked to be admitted, only to be told that they already had 52 students in the class and had room for only 36. "I

*John Davis Cantwell, M.D.*

asked them to just fix me a place in any corner and take me on a trial basis for a few days," she writes. They agreed to do so, placing her with the "one married man and a Yankee boy." The three shared a cadaver, and soon were taken in by the whole class and by the administration.

**Leila Denmark, M.D., age 100**

She practiced pediatrics in Atlanta for many years. In 1953, she was named Atlanta's "Woman of the Year," especially for her work at the Central Presbyterian Church's Mission Clinic.

Her office today is in a refurbished farmhouse adjacent to her beautiful antebellum-style home. The office didn't have a receptionist or even a nurse. Patients are seen on a "first come, first served" basis. With office hours posted, Dr. Denmark spends as much time with each patient as she needs to, seeing 15 to 25 a day. She doesn't belong to a health maintenance organization ("They have wrecked the medical profession"). She writes down pertinent information on patients, but doesn't dictate lengthy notes to satisfy third-party personnel.

I asked her how much longer she planned to work. She stated she has never worked: "Anything on earth you have to do is work," she said. "My husband made the living. I do this because I enjoy it, not because I have to." In her book she writes that children "...must be taught that work is truly a gift of God and is something to be thankful for, not something to be feared; something we should want to do, not something we have to do; it is not a punishment but a pleasure." She adds, "The happiest people are not necessarily those who have made the most money, or made the headlines in the news, but they are those who have done the best they could with what they had in an effort to make a better world."

I inquired as to the secret of her longevity. Did she exercise? "Yes," she said, "I used to play tennis. I try to walk now, to a lake and back, three miles round trip. Often I get so busy in the office, until 8 p.m. some

*John Davis Cantwell, M.D.*

nights, that I don't have the time. I know I should."

Her parents died relatively young, her mother from some type of cancer at age 45 and her father from "a heart problem" at age 65. Her oldest sister lived to 86. Two brothers are still alive at 82 and 80. One sister died in her 20s. Two siblings lived into their 70s, and the rest died in their 50s and 60s.

She has never been overweight. She eats "good food," including meat, and doesn't eat between meals. She only drinks water. She gave up coffee over 35 years ago, when she developed some arthralgias, and the symptoms subsided thereafter. She takes a daily vitamin.

How has she dealt with stress through the years? According to her 67-year-old daughter, her only child:

> "Mother does not seem to have a 'worrying' nature. Or if she does, she doesn't let it show. I think she handles stress by working at something - in the office or around the house - all the time. She cannot stand boredom and I believe that is why she has no desire to retire. She enjoys puttering in the yard and that is always a stress reliever."

She did think of retiring once, at age 91, when her husband died, but changed her mind after only two weeks. "When I go," she comments, "I hope it will be right here in this office." In an era sometimes burdened by the bureaucracy of managed care and the threats of stiff fines and even imprisonment for Health Care Financing Administration evaluation and management guideline violations, I was inspired by Dr. Denmark's example. It has given me a new perspective of my own medical practice. With my children married and on their own, and having saved enough money through the years, I really don't have to continue working. I do so, and plan to continue indefinitely, because, like Dr. Denmark, I enjoy it, especially the "sacred space" between doctor and patient that my father and grandfather so cherished.

I hope that my son, an internist, and my daughter, a nurse, will one day feel likewise.

*John Davis Cantwell, M.D.*

# 53

## A LIFETIME OF FITNESS

An 88-year-old retired real estate attorney and former college dean, who was born in Georgia, was seen as part of a research project on physical fitness and aging. He has been unusually active during his life. His father took him on daily hikes as a child. He learned to walk on his hands while performing in a Y.M.C.A. circus and once walked down the Washington Monument in this fashion. In college, he ran six to eight miles every morning with two-pound weights in each hand, training for boxing. He later ran five miles daily with his youngest son, when the latter was training for college tennis. His most astounding feat was to bicycle around the world, from Norway to Saigon, in his twenties (The one-speed bike, "Bucephalus," is in the Smithsonian Institute). En route, he had encounters with a scimitar-wielding Iranian (whom he dispatched with his fists) and was tracked by wolves in the Sinai desert and a tiger in the Far East. Three years later he bicycled 12,120 miles around North America. (The second bicycle, "Pegasus," is also in the Smithsonian Institute). At age 63, he hiked the Appalachian Trail with his physician-son. Three years later, he did the Inca Trail.

Beginning at age 71, he built a huge stone wall (up to 16 feet high) around his two-acre lot. He did most of the work himself, over a five-year period, loading and hauling the rocks in an old car and lifting the equivalent of 72 boxcars of boulders into place. He has contemplated a climb of Mount Kilimanjaro.

He had surgery for colon cancer and associated bowel obstruction while in the military in 1945, a prostatectomy for localized cancer in 1979, and an inguinal hernia repair in 1955. He never used tobacco or alcohol and was not on medications other than a multivitamin. His father died of pneumonia at age 87, as did his mother at 90. A brother died of a brain tumor at 68. Three of his four children are physicians, and one is an engineer.

He follows mainly a vegetarian diet, eating "a little baked chicken or fish to keep my meat-eating wife happy." He avoids fried foods, soft drinks, and caffeinated drinks, preferring water, decaffeinated tea, and a self-made blended drink of vinegar, chicken broth, tomato juice, brown sugar, garlic, soy sauce, basil and oregano.

He arises at 5 a.m. daily and begins with a series of situps. He walks two miles with his wife before breakfast, and later spends up to three hours at the local Y.M.C.A., walking up to five miles on the treadmill, using the Cybex strength machines, and swimming a mile or so in the pool.

He has an upbeat personality, which he attributes to the "gift of life" after surviving his abdominal cancer operation. He feels that it is "my duty and pleasure to keep myself as physically and mentally fit as possible so that I can take care of my wife, if she ever gets old." His wife of 62 years is no less remarkable, exercising with him every day and joining him on hiking trips throughout the world. For their honeymoon, they biked

*John Davis Cantwell, M.D.*

4,500 miles on a tandem cycle in Cuba, Jamaica, Central America and South America.

His blood pressure was 138/62 mmHg and his pulse was 72 beats per minute. His height was 65 inches and his weight was 141 pounds (body mass index 24 kg/m$^2$). Other than actinic keratotic skin changes and abdominal surgical scars, the physical examination was normal. His serum total cholesterol level was 213 mg/dL and the low-density lipoprotein cholesterol was 145 mg/dL, the triglyceride was 71 mg/dL, and the high-density lipoprotein was 54 mg/dL. His resting electrocardiogram was normal. On the Bruce treadmill test, he had a duration of 14.5 minutes, and could have gone longer had he not developed atrial fibrillation.

**Fred Birchmore and his wife, on their honeymoon**

His ST segment response was normal to a peak heart rate of 153 beats per minute. The oxygen uptake was 41.9 ml per kg per minute, placing him on the borderline between the high and very high fitness categories for all men his age.

An electron beam computed tomography scan of the heart showed a calcium score of 996, mainly in the left anterior descending (574) and right coronary arteries (363).

The patient was given atenolol, and had a repeat electrocardiogram the following morning, which showed a return to sinus rhythm. In view of the high coronary calcium score, he was advised to have a dual isotope exercise stress scan if he intends to climb Mount Kilimanjaro (to date he has not done so), and to reduce his blood lipid levels, aiming to get the serum total cholesterol well below 200 and the low-density lipoprotein under 100 mg/dL.

This remarkable man continues to be an inspiration to his family, friends and physicians as he enters his 9th decade. His joints seemed to have held up well, despite the lifetime of strenuous physical activities. Multiple studies have shown that physically active individuals are no more (and possible less) prone to degenerative arthritis than are sedentary persons. Decades of exercise have not prevented him from developing coronary atherosclerosis, as implied by the electron beam CT scan, but he has not experienced any clinical evidence of coronary artery disease.

The exercise-induced atrial fibrillation seems like an isolated event by history, although prolonged electro-cardiographic

*John Davis Cantwell, M.D.*

monitoring would be necessary to be sure. It may have been triggered by the surge of adrenalin that can occur during exercise testing.

   He keeps active driving friends to doctors' appointments and church events, lecturing to civic groups, clubs, and schools, and tends to the many plants in his garden, mowing his two-acre lot with a push-mower. He also pursues a multitude of interests, ranging from Native American artifacts to bird watching.

   As a tribute to his "generosity and indomitable spirit," his city and county dedicated a 2.5 mile nature trail in his honor, and chose him to run the Olympic torch through the city when the Olympic Games came to his home state.

*Adventures on Seven Continents And Other Essays*

# TRAVEL AND PLACES

*John Davis Cantwell, M.D.*

# 54

## WANDERING LONELY AS A CLOUD: AN ODYSSEY IN MID-CAREER

**INTRODUCTION**

A few years go, the United States Sports Academy asked me to lecture on the primary and secondary prevention of coronary heart disease in the Middle East. I agreed to do so, but stipulated that I might renig if the Persian Gulf area was teeming with Lebanese militants. I planned the itinerary so that I could visit southern Greece on the way over, and return via London and the lovely Lake District of England. In the midst of preparing for the trip, I seriously considered several job opportunities in other states. The decisions were difficult ones. In spare moments during the lengthy trip, I had occasion to reflect upon my final choice as well as to consider a multitude of other happenings, both current and far removed in time. These I recorded in the following diary.

**August 23**

En route to Bahrain, an island country in the Persian Gulf where I will lecture for a week, I spend a few days in Greece. There, in a crowded outdoor cafe near the Parthenon, which is silhouetted by a full moon, there is time to contemplate events of a recent mid-life crisis and attempt to put it into perspective with happenings of times past. To move or not to move is the big question. Is it

John Davis Cantwell, M.D.

better to accept a job in another city with an appreciable increase in income and a great promise for future advancement, or should I stay in Atlanta and continue to build upon a concept I had worked hard to develop de novo. The tide swings in favor of the move. I sit down and write a farewell letter to my patients, explaining my decision. Overcome by emotion, it is difficult to complete the letter, but I finally do. I think if Willie, an elderly black man whom I have come to know and appreciate, and Dorothy, a refined lady in a nursing home for whom I have deep feelings. They can do without me, I feel sure, but can I get along without them?

Several events cause a change of mind. Farewell parties turn into "welcome back" ones. I have an enhanced appreciation of friends, colleagues, home and city. Legal action is threatened by a doctor in the other city over a contact we signed concerning his home. I am appalled that he would threaten such retaliation on anyone, let alone a fellow physician.

Meanwhile, the local Greek wine goes well with the veal and rice, and I reflect upon my first day in Athens. The cab driver at the airport was young and not long for this world, I fear, in view of his recklessness. He somehow delivers me to the hotel, where I again discover that the travel agent has overestimated my financial resources. I sign up for a half-day tour of the city and eagerly view the Academy, where Socrates taught Plato, Plato lectured to Aristotle, and Aristotle instructed Alexander the Great. I climbed a hill to the monument of Philopappas and finally located the cave where Socrates was imprisoned prior to being given the fatal cup

*Adventures on Seven Continents And Other Essays*

of hemlock. A nonconformist and critic of the State, Socrates was guided by his own conscience. At the same time he felt it his duty to submit to the law of Athens, even though his trial was likely to be biased against him. How minuscule my legal problem now seems, compared to his, considering that his life hung in the balance. I am intrigued that Socrates never published a word, a marked contrast to the "publish or perish" mentality of certain academic institutions today.

In the National Archeological Museum, the guide was pointing out the differences in Archaic, Classical and Hellenistic sculpture. Suddenly I became aware that my pulse was rapid. Shortly thereafter I was diaphoretic and vertiginous. I sat at the base of a statue but was waved away by an angry attendant. Soon I was on the floor, the vertigo worse, feeling that I might pass out. A crowd gathered and some offered water while others rubbed an oil on my forehead. A man bent down, identified himself as a doctor, and asked if I had epilepsy, diabetes or chest pain. He was Greek, but spoke fluent English. I answered his questions, told him that I, too, was a doctor. He asked where in the United States I was from, and smiled at my answer, for he likewise lives in Atlanta and was also visiting Greece. I appreciated his tender care and concern.

**August 25**

The sidewalk cafe in Nauplion overlooks the Aegean fortress of Bourzi. I am saturated with ruins - Corinth, Mycenae and Epidaurus. I have seen the rostrum in ancient Corinth where Paul lectured to the populus. His comments on love

*John Davis Cantwell, M.D.*

(I Corinthians 13:4-8) are among my favorite Biblical passages. I marveled at Schliemann's tenacity, for who really thought that Homer's Iliad was other than fictitious? The cult of Asklepius in Epidaurus emphasized the comprehensive approach to healing, interweaving compassion with physical activity, music and poetry.

Pressed against the bus window were faces of Greek children. I think about a similar face I encountered on my front porch a month ago. The six-year-old girl rang the doorbell and asked for my daughter, who was away. With front teeth missing and eyes wide open, she directed her next question at me, having seen the "for sale" sign in the front yard:

"Why would you ever want to move?" she asks. "Don't you like it here?"

I study her innocent face, searching for an answer, suddenly aware that down deep I don't want to move, but that would be too complicated:

"A better job," I mumbled.

She nods, satisfied momentarily with my answer, but still wondering, as am I.

**August 26**

For the long drive across the Peloponnesus Mountains, I pull *Plutarch's Lives* from my backpack and read about Pericles, leader of Athens during her Classic Era. I am impressed by his self-composure. One day he was "reviled and ill-spoken of" by an obnoxious fellow in the open market. When Pericles returned home that evening, the man followed him, "pelting him all the way with abuse and foul language."

Pericles said nothing in return, but upon entering his house asked one of his servants to take a light and escort the man safely back to his home.

We reach Olympia where I positioned my feet in the starting blocks and imagined that I am Koroibos, from nearby Elis, attempting to win the 200 yard dash over 2700 years ago. My arms pumping furiously at my sides, I surge into the lead in front of the priestess of Demetra, the only woman allowed in attendance. The spectators, seated on the sloping embankments, roar in delight as I maintain the lead and capture the olive wreath.

I learn from my book on Greek mythology that the Olympic Games were founded by Heracles, the son of a god (Zeus) and a mortal woman (Alcemene). The latter must have angered the goddess Hera, who sent two tremendous snakes to kill the child. Hercles, incredibly strong despite his youth, "caught the snakes by their throats, one in each hand, and strangled them." When he later founded the Olympic contests, Heracles decreed that the winners would receive only olive wreaths, rather than riches, since he (Heracles) had received no pay for his labors (which included killing the monstrous Hydra).

Turning to Plutarch once again, I learn that Alexander the Great was a fine runner, but never participated in the Olympic Games because he didn't have other kings to run with. Alexander "seemed to look upon the professed athletes with indifference, if not dislike."

Not far from the ancient Olympic site, I study the monument containing the heart of Baron de Coubertin, the Frenchman who dedicated his life to reviving the Olympic

*John Davis Cantwell, M.D.*

Games in 1896, about 1500 years after they were stopped. As with Schliemann, I am again impressed with the accomplishments of a single, determined individual.

**August 27**

Taking a rest break along the Ionian coast, on the way to Delphi, I learn that Demosthenes, like a lot of gifted people, had to work hard at developing his talent. Because he was weak and of "delicate health," his mother forbade him from exerting himself. He sought to emulate the much admired orator, Callistratus, and overcame "inarticulate and stammering pronunciation" by talking with pebbles in his mouth and by reciting speeches while running or climbing up steep places. He also built an underground study and shaved half his hair to force himself to study for two or three months at a time.

As I scrambled up to the sanctuary of Apollo at Delphi, I found it hard just to breathe, let along practice my recitation. The oracles at Delphi were delivered by an ordinary middle-aged peasant woman who was obligated by the honor to abandon her husband and children. I wondered how the people accepted the edict of Theodosis, who prohibited this cult and all other pagan customs (including the Olympic Games) in 394 A.D. The last oracle was a fitting epitaph:

> "Tell ye the King: the carven hall is fallen in decay: Apollo has no chapel left, no prophesying bay, no talking spring. The stream is dry and had so much to say."

*Adventures on Seven Continents And Other Essays*

In a tiny shop I study the Oath of Hippocrates (see chapter 20), engraved in bronze. Parts of it I don't adhere to (for instance, I don't "swear by Apollo" and do get paid a partial salary for teaching medical housestaff). Other aspects of the oath I still find applicable.

The story of Hippocrates is well known to most physicians, but the myth of Asclepius is much less so. Artemis, upset at the death of Orion, blamed Apollo and got even by shooting the latter's wife, Coronis. Artemis did have the decency to let Coronis give birth to a son, whom Apollo named Asclepius and carried to Mt. Pelion. There, the child was raised by Cherion, King of the Centaurs (who were half men, half horses). Cherion, who had tutored the likes of Heracles and Jason, taught Asclepius about the alphabet, archery and astronomy. The boy was most interested in medicine, however, and soon became the best doctor in Greece. He not only cured dying people but also, according to legend, restored several dead patients to life, using a magical herb which a snake had shown him. King Hades complained to Zeus that Asclepius was stealing his subjects, and receiving money for his efforts, no less. Zeus fired a thunderbolt at Asclepius, killing him to please Dionysis. Apollo was enraged at this misdeed and reacted by shooting all the cyclops, who had forged the thunderbolts of Zeus. Zeus had the final word, making Apollo serve as a common herdsman for a year.

*John Davis Cantwell, M.D.*

**August 29**

The sun sets across the Mediterranean Sea as my plane makes an intermediate stop in Beruit, just hours after an unsuccessful assassination attempt on our ambassador. The machine-gun laden solder gives me a once over as I rush to make a close connection. There is no time to contact a Lebanese cardiologist with whom I trained at Emory.

I arrive in Bahrain, reeking of cigarette smoke as 95% of the passengers, or so it seemed, had been smoking. Representatives of the U.S. Sports Academy hastened my passage through customs, and I was taken to a house near the hospital. Everything in Bahrain is expensive, I was told, except for gasoline, which sold for 40 cents per gallon.

Bahrain is considered by some to be the original Garden of Eden, and has over 100,000 ancient burial mounds to help support this claim. The first country in the Arabian peninsula to produce oil, its daily output has now dwindled to 50,000 bbl, far below Saudi Arabia's 9,500,000 bbl. Little wonder that the country has turned to other ventures, such as becoming the banking capital of the Middle East.

The next day's dawn beamed into my bedroom at 5 a.m., and I rose to dress. The early sunrise is compensated by an equally early sunset, making the temperature barely tolerable at night, unlike during the day when it can reach 115ºF.

Word has spread through the Royal Family that an American cardiologist is in the country (Bahrain has only three). I was asked to consult on a seven-month-old with an apparent ventricular septal defect, a middle-aged woman with probable angina pectoris and a separate pain of chest-wall origin, and a young sheik with multiple coronary risk factors. Subsequent ward rounds revealed an interesting spectrum of diseases, ranging from typhoid fever to mitral valve prolapse. That evening I lectured to the Bahrain Medical Society on cardiac rehabilitation. The questions and discussions afterwards were stimulating, and I found a real need for both primary and secondary coronary prevention in the country.

Almost as the clock struck 12, ringing in the new month of September, I developed shaking chills, averaging one every half minute for the next three hours. Fever then set in, followed by cramping abdominal pain, explosive diarrhea, nausea and vomiting. The mind of a sick physician plays tricks on him in the dead of night. I am concerned about typhoid, amoebic dysentery, and similar maladies that might confine me in Arabia for a prolonged period. I suddenly become even more empathetic with the American hostages once held in nearby Iran. I know that my lecture series is over. I am more concerned about the chances of dying from a strange infection, far from loved ones, as my body temperatures exceeds 104°F.

Because of weakness, weight loss and dehydration, my medical hosts insist that I be hospitalized. I resist, but finally agree as my condition is deteriorating, and I am hopeful that hospitalization will speed my recovery. I must be ready for a flight to London two nights hence - I must!!

The admitting house officer does an inadequate history and physical, but my attending physicians turn out to be fine

*John Davis Cantwell, M.D.*

doctors, combining sound judgment with compassion. When frontal and occipital headaches develop, the internist carefully examines the eyegrounds and elects not to do a spinal tap. An aspirin-like compound is prescribed, which helps.

I am awake during the night, having slept fitfully for the last 24 hours. I want to be discharged the next afternoon in time to make the flight. The ticket agent in the Athens airport had told me I was returning on the Concorde, which will cut the flying time in half.

I set about to build up my strength. As I prescribe for post-coronary patients, I began by sitting up for a while and then walk back and forth across the room and perform some flexibility exercises. Initially I can make only 15 round-trips in the room but by daybreak it is up to 25. I must be on the Concorde! The following day the fever has subsided, the diarrhea is better, and the headache is only mild. I request to be released. Several British-trained nurses are strongly opposed, feeling I am too weak to make it to London without problems. The doctors give me more credit, cognizant of my athletic background. We double check the flight schedule and find it is not the Concorde after all but a regular British jet that will stop first in Rome. I will go anyway.

I have been hearing soft background music during my illness. There are popular tunes from the last three decades, classical pieces (I recall Beethoven's "Für Elise"), Hungarian rhapsodies, and melodies unknown to me. I assume it is stereo music, piped into my room, but now wonder if I am imagining it. I hear it en route to the airport and ask my Arab driver if he has a stereo in the car. He looks back with a puzzled expression and states that the car doesn't even have a radio. I say no more. Later, on the plane, the stewardess asks if I would like a headset so that I can listen to music. I smile, a private joke, and tell her that I don't need a headset. She thinks I'm trying to be cute and spins away down the aisle.

**September 9**

Somehow, nine hours later, the plane arrives in London's Heathrow Airport. I am pale, wobbly and weak, but drag my suitcase to the subway, find a hotel, and sleep for a day.

Wandering lonely as a cloud in the Lake District of England, my body regains strength and my mind is enriched, filled with thoughts of Wordsworth. I hiked partway up Mt. Helvellyn, which he last climbed at age 70, and spent hours walking around Grasmere Lake and Rydal Water, where he used to ice skate in wintertime. A visit to Dove Cottage showed me his study, although he rarely worked in it, preferring to compose his romantic poetry while on his walks, frightening children and strangers half to death with his shouting.

His friend, De Quincey, once estimated that Wordsworth walked over 180,000 miles during his lifetime. Was this why he remained in such excellent health until his death, at 80, of "nothing serious?" After studying his biography I find there were other factors which contributed:

*John Davis Cantwell, M.D.*

- He was loved and catered to at home by three devoted women (his sister, wife and sister-in-law).
- He was spartan in lifestyle, avoiding strong drink and rarely eating meat.
- He was not vindictive, didn't harbor grudges, and accepted vicious criticism of his poetry with the feeling that his work would bring joy and comfort to people in years to come.

The walking did "soothe and sustain his soul and feed the wellspring of his poetry."

**September 7**

The plane touches down in Atlanta. I return from my odyssey, disguised not as a beggar (as was Odysseus) but as a teenager, clad in jeans, a T-shirt and running shoes.

It has been a marvelous trip, despite the illness. My mind has touched on a wide variety of things - lawsuits, Socrates, Plato, St. Paul, Olympic athletes, the oracle at Delphi, Alexander the Great, the impact of Arabian oil on future world developments, sickness, dying, my family, the compassion of physicians, Asclepius and Hippocrates, rehabilitation and Wordsworth. I embrace my wife and children and turn toward the second half of my life and career, hoping it will bring the same challenges, joys and satisfaction as the first. The examined life is, indeed, worth living.

# 55

## MEDICINE AND ADVENTURE IN THE HIMALAYAS

> "Everest was a symbol;
> it was metaphor...
> the ultimate goal,
> the boldest dream."
> - Ridgeway

**INTRODUCTION**

Through the windows on the left side of the airplane one could scan practically the whole Himalayan range - all 1250 miles of it - with views of Annapurna, Dhaulagiri, Ama Dablam, and finally Everest herself, a triangle of black granite with a plume of snow and cloud, peering over the ridge of Nutpse. Our goal was to reach the Base Camp of Everest and to climb Mt. Kala Patar, elevation 18,100 feet.

It began during a casual conversation with architect Herb Lembcke and his wife, when I discovered that the latter shared my long-term ambition, that of visiting Nepal, land of the Sherpas, eight of the world's 10 highest mountain peaks, and the exotic capital city of Kathmandu.

My wife agreed to go along, although she had never camped out. Not that I qualify as an outdoorsman, for my only experience was 25 years ago at a Boy Scout Jamboree, where my fellow scouts and I learned to drink beer and pull tent stakes late at night.

Our trekking party gradually expanded to eight with the addition of attorneys Jim Landon and Al Campbell, the latter's wife, and

John Davis Cantwell, M.D.

plastic surgeon John Griffin. Landon seemed a promising addition, with his past experience of rafting down the Colorado River. I knew we were in trouble, however, when he asked me (a noncamper) about the right type of boot to purchase and when he expressed fear that our sleeping bags resembled coffins.

Griffin looked good on paper too, having climbed the Matterhorn, but his idea of a regular fitness program was to occasionally climb a flight or two of stairs. Lembcke and I have run marathons, but on the negative side, I disliked heights and am petrified about most of the rides at Six Flags.

## NEPAL

Nepal, about the size and shape of Tennessee, has a population of 12 million scattered throughout its mountainous terrain and is the birth place of Lord Buddha (563 B.C.). Kathmandu, the capital and principle city, has a population of 200,000 and a latitude similar to Florida. The city bustles with market vendors, rickshaw drivers, sacred cows and monkeys, and a blend of Hindus and Buddhists.

It is a city of the new (the Royal Palace, the Yak and Yeti Hotel) and the old (pagodas and Swayambhunath stupa, which dates back over 2000 years), a noisy place because of the bells on the rickshaws, the horns on the cars, and the voices of the shopkeepers.

## THE TREK

We flew from Kathmandu to Lukla (elevation 9000 feet) on a tiny plane geared to short runways. The sky was clear and the view magnificent. Suddenly the airstrip at Lukla was visible, a one-fifth mile gravel runway carved out of the mountainside by Sir Edmund Hillary, the New Zealander who first climbed Everest (along with the Sherpa, Tenzing Norgay). Wreckage from previous unsuccessful landings were seen along the runway and did nothing to bolster my confidence.

After deplaning, we were met by our team of 20 porters, four Sherpas, and a dozen yaks, and were soon on the first of our 11-day trek to and from the Everest Base Camp. We met our sirdar (head Sherpa), 29-year-old Nima Tsering, a veteran of the 1971 International Expedition to Everest, and quickly began to experience what Hillary had described earlier:

> "In Nepal the tempo is slower. As you walk, the body gets strong: the mind has time to dwell on the beauties of nature and gain refreshment; you meet the local people, the Sherpas; and enjoy their cheerful friendliness and admire their toughness and strength."

We ascended to Namche Bazar, a trading village at 12,000 feet. That evening as I unzipped my tent, I was overcome by the stark beauty of my environment - brilliant stars, with a background of clear sky, outlined by shadows of majestic peaks. My enjoyment was interrupted by concern over my inability to walk a straight line, an early sign of mountain sickness.

I staggered back into the tent and climbed back into my double sleeping bag, worried that I might have to descend in the morning. Fortunately I felt fine the next day and we set out for Thangboche, the beautiful Buddhist

*John Davis Cantwell, M.D.*

monastery that houses 50 lamas and sits atop a 14,000 foot mountain, affording a view of peaks such as Ama Dablam, Thamserku, Kangtega, and a glimpse of the Everest summit.

We left Thangboche the following day, bidding farewell to the terraced hillsides, rhododendron leaves (curled up to protect the buds), and evergreens as we ascended to Pheriche. Along the way I periodically examined one of the porters, 42-year-old Ang Rita, who carried a load of over 80 pounds on his back. Despite the latter, his pulse rate was consistently under 100, at least 20 beats per minute slower than John Griffin's. Ang Rita received the equivalent of $2.00 per day for his efforts, about half the salary of our head Sherpa.

**VISITED HOSPITAL FOR MOUNTAIN SICKNESS**

While in Pheriche, Dr. Griffin and I visited the Himalayan Rescue Center, a one-bed hospital founded by a Japanese surgeon for the purposes of 1) supplying emergency medical care to climbers and trekkers who succumb to mountain sickness, 2) providing medical care to the local Sherpas (and their yaks), and 3) conducting research on altitude sickness. The resident physician had arrived two weeks ago and will spend a total of three months at the outpost before returning to his surgical training. I was sobered to hear that a 28-year-old woman Japanese trek leader died in this hospital only three weeks prior of pulmonary edema (fluid buildup in the lungs).

We resolved to walk even slower, averaging 1.5 miles per hour, in hopes of avoiding the same fate. The physician described how patients are transported to his hospital from higher elevations, tucked in sleeping bags and carried in a basket on the back of a strong Sherpa. (I wonder if this is how the term, "basket case" was derived?)

At the outpost of Lobuche, 17,000 feet, Dr. Griffin and I treated a Sherpa and an Australian trekker for respiratory ailments. We then pushed on to our final campsite, Gorak Shep (or "Crow's Cemetery"), and advanced through the terrain of rocks and ice formations to the Everest Base Camp. The next morning we decided to climb up Kala Patar and get a good view of Everest, the Khumbu glacier, and the icefall. After a two-hour climb, several of us reached the rocky peak of Kala Patar, dwarfed even at 18,100 feet by surrounding giants as Pumori, Cho Oyo, Nuptse and Everest.

As I studied the latter, I couldn't help but remember the brave souls who lost their lives trying to climb the "Mother Goddess of the World," including Mallory, who disappeared near the summit back in 1924.

*John Davis Cantwell, M.D.*

**With Marilyn at the Mount Everest base camp**

*Adventures on Seven Continents And Other Essays*

**On the Mt. Everest Trek**

*John Davis Cantwell, M.D.*

Other people came to mind, because of memorials we passed on our way to the Base Camp; names such as John Brietenbach (American Expedition, 1963), and Mick Burke (British Expedition, 1975). I thought also of my visit with Jim Whittaker, the first American to climb Everest, and of his climbing partner, Tom Hornbein, M.D., who reached the summit from the West Face, only to discover fresh footprints (Whitaker's).

**CONSULT WITH SHERPAS**

On the return trip, John Griffin and I visited the Hillary Hospital in Khunde, where we consulted on cases of pulmonary embolism and facial lacerations (the Sherpa had been attacked by a bear). I also held blood pressure clinics for the Sherpas.

## Checking the Sherpas' blood pressures

Our 11th and final campsite was back in Lukla. We sipped Napoleon brandy around a roaring fire, told dirty jokes, reminisced about the highlights of our trek, and expressed hope that the next morning would be clear, allowing our plane to land and take us back to Kathmandu, the hot baths and tasty food of the Yak and Yeti Hotel, the warmth of the sun in the valley.

The morning fog lifted. The sirens sounded at the airport, indicating that the plane had taken off from Kathmandu. We bid a fond farewell to Nima, our three Sherpas, to the cook, and to several of the porters. We were soon airborne and would relinquish our sleeping bags for feather beds, our yaks for automobiles, our bed tea for coffee and Danish rolls. I left with mixed emotions, grateful for some of the latter amenities but sorry to give up the brightest stars, bluest skies, highest mountains, and swiftest rivers that I have ever seen.

Why did we make the trip? Perhaps we were just following the dictum of Hillary, who said that man should "wander through the forest, play in the lakes, climb mountains, and sail across the seas, trying our strength against the uncompromising hand of nature. Only through testing and tempering can we come to know who we are and what we are capable of doing."

*John Davis Cantwell, M.D.*

# 56

## ON THE INCA TRAIL TO THE LOST CITY OF MACHU PICCHU

> *"Then up the ladder of the*
> *earth I climbed through the*
> *barbed jungle's thickets until*
> *I reached you Machu Picchu.*
> *-Pablo Neruda*

Amid talk of typhoid and yellow fever shots, gamma globulin injections, pills to prevent high altitude sickness, diarrhea and malaria, and threats of terrorist guerrillas (known as the Sendero Luminosa, or Shining Path), my daughter Kelly, then 14, asked the obvious question:

"Dad, why can't we take a vacation like normal people do - perhaps to the beach...?"

I guess it's because I prefer expeditions over vacations, active experiences which teach me about other cultures, trips which require physical and mental preparation and which help to shrink the world so I can better appreciate what is happening in Nepal, Israel or even Antarctica.

The trip this year was to Peru and would include rafting a tributary to the Amazon, hiking the Inca Trail to Machu Picchu, and exploring the jungle near Puerto Maldonado.

## PREPARATION

The physical preparations included jogging over hilly terrain and climbing hospital steps to toughen my legs. There were also chin-ups, weight lifting sessions, and push-ups for enhancement of upper body strength.

The mental preparation included reading Prescott's classic, *History of the Conquest of Peru*, poems by Pablo Neruda, Bingham's *Lost City of the Incas*, and Theroux's *The Old Patagonian Express*. I also packed Read's book *Alive*, (about survival in the Andes). I stayed away from *War and Peace*, which was much too heavy reading during my trek to the Mt. Everest Base Camp. (It wasn't Tolstoy's fault; the book was just inappropriate for the occasion).

## TO GO OR NOT TO GO

Six weeks before we were to leave, an article in *Time* stated that over 1000 people had been killed in guerrilla fighting in the mountains. Two weeks before departure, President Belaunde suspended civil rights and declared a 60-day state of emergency after guerrillas blew up the Bayer chemical plant outside Lima.

I called Mountain Travel, the California-based agency which organized our expedition and spoke with May Ling. She is not easily phased by bad news. I told her that an Eastern Airline pilot was arrested in Lima for photographing a military installation from the air ("maybe he was." she said). I next tried the bit of news that a bazooka was fund trained on the United States embassy ("Oh," she said, "they are always aiming something at

*John Davis Cantwell, M.D.*

our embassies in South America"). I then called Coca-Cola International. After checking with their head man in Lima, they assured me that the situation was under reasonable control. We will go! Given the uncertainties, perhaps we will better appreciate the risks taken by the Spanish Conquistadors.

**THE TRIP**

We flew to Lima and, after the usual delays in Third World countries, caught an Aero Peru flight to Cusco, the oldest continuously inhabited city in America and former capitol of the Inca Empire. This was the City of Gold, sought by Pizarro, site of the Temple of the Sun. Since the elevation is nearly 12,000 feet, we took Diamox to minimize symptoms of altitude sickness.

The following morning we went by bus to the Sacred Valley of the Incas and began our two-day raft trip down the Urubamba River. We visited the Inca ruins at Pisac and Ollantaytambo and stayed at a local inn near Chilca. The second night at the inn the lights suddenly went out. The guerrillas had detonated several power stations near Cusco, causing a two-day blackout in the city and surrounding area.

Undaunted, we read by candlelight and departed early the next morning for Chilca to begin our five-day trek on the Inca Trail. After only 30 minutes of hiking, my son, Ryan, was felled with severe vomiting. A horse was obtained, and we rode past the ruins of Llactapata to the little schoolyard above the mountain of Huayllabamba (9700 feet) where we made camp for the night.

*Adventures on Seven Continents And Other Essays*

Our group included a physicist from the University of California, a Mormon physician and his wife from Utah, a public health physician from California, an Arizona State University coed, living in Chicago, and an anesthetist who was also from Chicago. Our guide was Lindy Farley, a Canadian girl who married the son of Peruvian missionaries.

Our 24 porters, all Quechua Indians, carried loads of up to 80 pounds. They earned about four dollars per day for this laborious work, made easier by the centuries-old custom of chewing coca leaves. At the top of Warmiwanusga ("Pass of the Dead Woman," at 13,776 feet, the highest point on the Inca Trail), I tried on one of the loads. The porters laughed uproariously at this, especially my attempt to descend the steep path on the far side of the mountain.

After an overnight near the ruins of Runkuraguy, we hiked along stretches fringed with blue lupin, yellow orchids, and multi-colored begonias. Passing by the ruins at Sayajmarca, we camped at Phuyupatamarca ("town in the clouds," at 11,906 feet), cooling off in the still-functioning Inca baths.

Along the trail, I thought of the Inca couriers (chaskais) who were stationed at intervals along the route.

*John Davis Cantwell, M.D.*

**With Ryan atop the "Pass of the Dead Woman"**

They carried messages on the run, averaging a 6-7 minute mile pace. At this rate, they could bring a message (on quipa strings) from Cusco to Quito, a distance of 1250 miles, in five days. They could also transport fresh fish from the coast to Cusco for the Incas' supper.

We kept an eye out for condors, but to no avail. Our guide subsequently told us that she sees only about two per year on her 75-acre farm in one of the valleys southwest of Cusco. The final approach to Machu Picchu took us through some high jungle, infested with snakes (bushmaster and coral) and a hoard of bees. We didn't see the former and managed to elude the latter.

**Kelly and Ryan at Machu Picchu**

Finally, we arrived at the original gate to the "lost city." Approaching the target of our journey, I had an eerie sensation. The city was deserted, except for two llamas and an Indian woman. Where were the tourists? And why was smoke arising from an area of ruins? Had the Shining Path struck in this Peruvian mecca for tourists?

The answer was soon forthcoming. The trains were on strike, so tourists could not arrive the easy way, a four-hour ride from Cusco. The smoke was from brush, being burned off one of the Inca terraces.

I could imaging Hiram Bingham's excitement in 1911 when the Yale explorer happened upon the site, aided by Indians who lived nearby:

"Without the slightest expectation of finding anything more interesting than the

*John Davis Cantwell, M.D.*

ruins of two or three stone houses...I finally left the cool shade of the pleasant little hut and climbed further up the ridge..."

"Hardly had we left the hut and rounded the promontory when we were confronted with an unexpected sight, a great flight of beautifully constructed stone-faced terraces..."

"It fairly took my breath away...surprise followed surprise in bewildering succession...suddenly we found ourselves standing in front of the ruins of one of the finest and most interesting structures in ancient America."

We descended the switchback road by bus, camping in the canyon below. The following day we had the ruins virtually to ourselves, exploring the nooks and crannies and climbing up Huayna Picchu (9000 feet).

We were treated to dinner, hot showers, and a nice bed in the Machu Picchu Hotel and informed that we must walk 20 miles along the rail line the next morning as the strike was still on. We were joined by Greg (an artist and mountain climber), and Martin (an archeologist). We also encountered a group of high school students (from Athens, Georgia, of all places) and a family of six. The former had had luggage stolen along the trail. The latter had experienced altitude sickness and a strike by their porters.

It took almost 10 hours to traverse the 20 miles (over an estimated 50,000 railroad ties) back to Chilca. We were met by a truck and transported to an area where roads permitted penetration by bus. We stopped along the way for dinner, washed down with Cusquena beer, and then motored on to Cusco.

*Adventures on Seven Continents And Other Essays*

The final leg of our Peru adventure involved a flight to Puerto Maldonado, a gold-mining town deep in the jungle, near the Bolivian border. Motorized dugout canoes transported us three hours up the Tambopata river to the Explorers Inn. There we searched for the cayman, shining flashlights from our boat, and fished for piranha. The airport in Puerto Maldonado was uncommonly busy. Further inquiry revealed that the last plane in (a military aircraft) had crashed into the control tower five days prior, killing nine passengers. Sombered by this news, we waited patiently for our flight to Cusco, which was considerably late, as usual ("after all, this is Peru," our guide reminded us). We stayed on the same plane for the connection into Lima. Halfway down the runway, the Aero Peru jet decelerated to a halt. The tail-wind, which on takeoff had read 8, abruptly increased to a dangerous reading of 12, causing the pilot to abort the takeoff. It would simply not be adequate for the craft to clear the mountains at this elevation. After a hasty lunch the wind died down and we lifted off for Lima, the "City of Kings," founded by Pizarro. We viewed the latter's bones and the Gold Museum and then had our farewell dinner in a suburban restaurant, near the "Bridge of Sighs."

It was time to bid goodbye to Howard, the physics professor from Berkeley, who had taught us so much along the way about energy, astronomy, and anything else we wanted to know. Bye to Virgil and Jackie, the physician-wife couple from Utah, whose vitality was a good advertisement for the Mormon lifestyle. So long to Jim and Kim, the young folks from Chicago who were strangers when they met and a romantic duo in just two weeks. Adios to

*John Davis Cantwell, M.D.*

Alvin, the bachelor physician who specialized in preventive medicine and public health. Salute to Manuel, our trusty porter, who diligently watched over Ryan during his illness on the trail. And farewell to Lindy, our lovely guide, who combined femininity with physical toughness.

We had traveled by raft, mountain trail, truck, bus and dugout canoe, mingling with the Quechua Indians, many of whom still live in stone houses with thatched roofs just like their Inca ancestors. I took away from Peru an appreciation of the latter's durability and creativity and a feel for the Conquistadors' courage and brutality. As I surged with the mobs in Lima, I couldn't help but wonder about the political future of South America.

In all, it was a grand experience...possibly even better than a week at the beach, my daughter would concede.

# 57

## STALKING HEART HEALTH MYSTERIES IN KENYA

After strapping on my backpack, weighted down with selected books by Ernest Hemingway, I pulled my safari hat low over my eyes (in the spirit of "Indiana Jones") and ventured into Kenya. I hoped to learn about the Masai tribe (who are spared clinical coronary disease despite a diet high in cholesterol and saturated fat), to do some climbing on Mt. Kenya, and to view the migration of animals from the Serengeti to the Masai Mara Game Reserve. I also wanted to feel the pulse of Africa through my hiking boots.

Accompanied by my wife and son Ryan, then age 14, I flew to Nairobi, stopping along the way in Senegal, Liberia, and Nigeria. Our "base camp" was the Norfolk Hotel, where in recent times one was likely to encounter Brooke Shields, Charleton Heston, Meryl Streep and Robert Redford.

We entered Masailand 100 years after the first white man - Joseph Thomson - passed through. Thomson was impressed with the Masai, calling them "splendid fellows." He succeeded while others failed, because of a unique blend of courage, humility and intuition, plus an extreme coolness when under fire. Once, when surrounded by hundreds of Masai warriors who "…grasped their spears as if only waiting for a signal to precipitate themselves on our small party," Thomson merely folded his arms and laughed derisively, "…a piece of acting I have always found to have a remarkable effect

*John Davis Cantwell, M.D.*

on the natives, who at once concluded that I have supernatural powers."

**With a Masai warrior**

The Masai are still a nomadic tribe, now numbering approximately 100,000, and living in a 10,000 square mile area in southern Kenya and northern Tanzania. Their diet consists largely of milk, fresh cow's blood, and the meat of cattle, goats and sheep. Their daily fat intake is high (averaging 300 grams), as is their cholesterol intake of 600 mg. Yet, their blood cholesterol level is low, averaging 135 mg/dl. Clinical coronary disease is virtually unknown in this tribe, despite their diet. This was confirmed by my review of cardiac catheterization data at Kenyatta National Hospital and from visits with various medical personnel at that center. Autopsy studies are sparse, because the Masai dead are usually left in the open "...to be cleared away by wild animals." Biss and associates did perform 10 autopsies and found a paucity of atherosclerosis. They explained this on the basis of metabolic studies, which showed that the Masai suppress their bodies' production of cholesterol with this high-fat diet, unlike Americans. Mann and associates, however, studied the hearts and aortas of 50 Masai men and did find atherosclerosis. They also found that the diameters of the coronary arteries were enlarged, increasing with age, and speculated that this was due to their exercise habits and physical fitness.

I conclude, based on personal observation and a review of the medical literature, that the Masai are generally free of clinical coronary disease. They have low blood cholesterol levels, despite a high-fat diet, probably due to dietary fat suppression of their intracellular production of cholesterol. I'm uncertain as to whether or not they have atherosclerosis, based on conflicting autopsy reports. I'm surprised that the physical fitness of Masai elders ("elders" being 26 and older, warriors less than age 26) is as high as reported, because they didn't seem that physically active to me, especially those above age 26. I'm not convinced that their large coronary arteries are exercise-related. In general, coronary diameter varies directly with cardiac weight. Hence, an exercised animal or an athlete with a "heavy" or enlarged heart might tend to have larger coronary arteries than a sedentary animal or person. However, the Masai heart weights averaged 300 grams, less than those of American and Englishmen of similar age.

*John Davis Cantwell, M.D.*

I departed from Masailand, concerned for the future of these once proud people. Described just 100 years ago by Thomson as "Warriors, aristocrats, lion killers, herdsmen, drinkers of blood and milk...carriers of tall spears (with) a dignity of attitude beyond all praise, "they are now in a Catch-22 position. As Isak Dinesen observed, they are "...fighters who had been stopped from fighting, a dying lion with his claws clipped, a castrated nation." Saitoti, himself a westernized Masai, summarized their plight best:

"The Masai are a people whose time has passed. The industrialized world is closing in upon them like a flood out of control, and they must move to higher ground to save themselves...they must adapt to the realities of the modern world and become a part of it for the sake of their own survival."

One of the prices of becoming part of the modern world, however, will be the development of clinical coronary heart disease.

# 58

## TO ANTARCTICA: A JOURNEY INTO THE SELF

> *The dreamers of the day are dangerous men, for they may act their dreams with open eyes, to make it possible.*
> *- T. E. Lawrence*

A medical colleague stopped me in the corridor shortly after hearing that I had just returned from Antarctica. "I just wanted you to know," he said, "that if I were to make a list of the 1000 places I would like to visit, Antarctica would *not* be on it."

Hardly any of my friends were envious of the trip my wife and I made to the seventh continent. At first thought, you could hardly blame them. Antarctica is the highest, driest, coldest and windiest place in the world. (Upon reaching the South Pole, Scott's entry in his diary read: "Great God! This is an awful place.") The average wind speed is 55 mph, with gales exceeding 200 mph. The temperature has been as low as -129.3ºF., and doesn't get above freezing even in the summer months. The average annual precipitation on the continent is two inches, about the same as the Sahara Desert. Little wonder that the only permanent inhabitant of Antarctica is a wingless fly.

Antarctica has an area equal to that of the United States and Europe combined, with a transient population of only 1000 in the winter months. It was named by Aristotle and the ancient Greeks, who noted that the northern hemisphere was under the constellation of Arktos, "the bear," and

John Davis Cantwell, M.D.

reasoned that there must be land to the extreme south, an "antarkticos." In 1773, Captain James Cook circumnavigated the continent without even seeing it. He did become the first man to penetrate the Antarctica Circle (66º 3'), a feat we also celebrated with a champagne toast in the wee hours of a January morning.

Most of my fellow passengers, 96 in number, were veteran travelers. They had been almost everywhere else, including Tibet, and this was a logical new place to see. Many had heard glorious tales of the natural beauty from friends on other voyages. After all, there are not many places where one can see glaciers a mile thick, calving in front of your very eyes, or icebergs the size of Connecticut. Not to mention humpback whales, singing out in the water in preparation for a magnificent dive, and penguins by the thousands, hovering over their chicks to protect them from sea lions and aerial predators.

My reason for going was a little different, for I certainly had not been everyplace else. I wanted to experience, in some small way, what the explorers encountered in the early part of this century. I have always thrilled to the thought of Shackleton's optimism and the incredible devotion of his men, to Scott's perseverance, to Amundsen's mastery of detail, and to Byrd's cool daring. I wanted to better appreciate their accomplishments by actually visiting the land of their triumphs, and their tragedies. I rationalized that the cost of the venture would be covered, in part, by royalties from a recent softcover book.

We flew to Patagonia, and boarded our ship in Punta Arenas, a surprisingly large city of 100,000 located along the straits of Magellan, discovered in 1520. Our passage through the latter and down to the Beagle Channel (named after Charles Darwin's boat) was uneventful. The Drake Passage, a 600-mile stretch of the world's roughest seas, separates Tierra del Fuego from Antarctica. We entered the Passage at night, not knowing what to expect over the next 36 hours. My wife and I awoke feeling well the next morning, until we tried to assume a vertical position, when suddenly waves of nausea and vomiting drove us back to bed. I pawed through my duffle bag like a drug addict searching for the transdermal scopolamine and Dramamine I had thrown in just in case. I subsequently substituted Bonine for the Dramamine and did much better on the return trip (until I foolishly watched a videotape of a sailboat trip to Antarctica - our ship had a lateral rock of 30º while the film had a vertical pitch even greater).

The first land we spotted was Smith Island, where the great British mountaineer-sailor, H.W. Tilman, wanted to spend his 80th birthday. Unfortunately he was lost at sea en route, but on thinking about it I surmised he might have chosen that mode of death over a lingering illness in a nursing home. Our first landing was Deception Island, just off the Antarctica peninsula. We motored ashore in Zodiac rafts, to be greeted by penguins and fur seals. The latter weigh as much as pro football lineman and move twice as fast. They attack upright foes and mount prostrate ones (so either way one loses).

Over the next week we explored the nooks and crannies of the Antarctica peninsula. We made 18 more landings, visiting the Argentinian, Chilean, Russian, British and American research stations. We talked with the basic

*John Davis Cantwell, M.D.*

scientists, most of whom were studying either weather patterns or the crustacean-like organisms known as krill (potentially a tremendous resource of protein, for man as well as whales). We mingled with the physicians at several bases and inspected their medical facilities, the best of which was the Russian base. We learned how resourceful some of these physicians had to be. At a Russian base, near the South Pole, the physician had to remove his own appendix, using a mirror and Xylocaine.

We saw how quickly the weather could change, as katabatic winds suddenly swept down off the glaciers. We encountered icebergs city blocks in length, some of which had to be nudged out of the way so our ship could penetrate rather narrow channels and straits.

As I studied the lives of several explorers, I became even more impressed with man's great inner resources and tenacity. From Amundsen I learned the importance of meticulous planning and of personal experience. He listened to natives from the Arctic, tested and improvised on clothing and equipment, and his reward was to be the first to the South Pole. He was not a man to waste words, as evidenced by his telegram to Scott indicating that the race was on ("Scott - Heading South. Amundsen").

Scott has gone from hero to chump, in some circles, owing to a scholarly biography by Roland Huntsford which was depicted on Masterpiece Theatre. I will concede that his wife may have manipulated his memoirs, to make him appear more heroic, but will not deny his courage and inner drive. What father can help but be touched by Scott's last letter to his wife, Kathleen, expressing his hopes and aspirations for their infant son:

*Adventures on Seven Continents And Other Essays*

"I had looked forward to helping you bring him up, but it is a satisfaction to know that he will be safe with you…Make the boy interested in natural history if you can. It is better than games…Try to make him believe in God, it is comforting…Guard him against indolence. Make him a strenuous man. I had to force myself into being strenuous, as you know - had always an inclination to be idle."

What fellow countryman and human being is not deeply moved by his final entry:

"I do not regret this journey, which has shown that Englishmen can endure hardships, help one another, and meet death with as great a fortitude as ever in the past."

Ever the scientist, Scott's sleds had over 30 pounds of geological samples, which added an extra burden to his waning energy stores.

They still speak of Shackleton with awe on South Georgia Island, even though he last set foot there in 1921. From him, I learned the importance of optimism, and of devotion to those for whom one is responsible. He certainly did not make false promises. For him difficulties were "just things to overcome." He inspired his men as they drifted 497 days on an ice pack, before finally reaching Elephant Island in 20-foot wooden boats. (See chapter 44). He then set out with five others for the nearest whaling station on South Georgia Island, facing "hurricane force winds and mountainous seas" and a distance of 800 miles! Upon reaching the island, he then had to trek over unnamed mountains and glaciers,

*John Davis Cantwell, M.D.*

previously felt impossible to traverse, to reach help. It took him four attempts, over 4½ months, to rescue the 22 men he had left on Elephant Island, but he did it without the loss of a single man. The essence of the man can be found in his comments upon finally reaching the whaling station, heavily bearded, caked in ice and snow, dressed in rags:

> "That was all of tangible things; but in memories we were rich. We had pierced the veneer of outside things. We had suffered, starved, and triumphed, grovelled down yet grasped at glory, grown bigger in the largeness of the whole. We had seen God in his splendors...we had reached the naked soul of man."

From Byrd I saw the importance of having dreams, and the value of self-mastery. He was not always heroic in all of his ventures (after all, while in Virginia, in 1907, he did fumble a punt during the game against Washington and Lee). However, his "competitive nature, his insistence that he must succeed in the conquering of heavy odds, was far beyond that of the average man; it was what would make him a great adventurer." A "creature of dreams and impulses, a man of direct action," he was respected by his men even though some did not particularly like him. They all knew that his most outstanding characteristic (like Shackleton's) was his concern for their safety.

Byrd became the first to fly over the poles, and was the third to fly across the Atlantic Ocean. His account of the seven months he spent alone in the heart of Antarctica, which nearly cost him his life, is an intimate portrayal of man's incredible spirit. Several years after, he wrote:

> "Part of me remained forever at Latitude 80º 08' South: what survived of my youth, my vanity, perhaps, and certainly my skepticism. On the other hand, I did take away something that I had not fully possessed before: an appreciation of the sheer beauty and miracle of being alive."

On our trip back from Antarctica we rounded Cape Horn, an event that took sailing ships in years past three months (if ever) to accomplish. We were fortunate to encounter the Cousteau turbo sailboat and delighted in having Jean-Michel come aboard for an informal educational session. When we reached Chile there were rumors of an explosion, some even said involving the space shuttle. We studied several Chilean newspapers and saw front page accounts of a bus that had exploded after catching fire, near Valparaiso. It was not until we reached Miami that I learned the other rumors were correct, and instantly remembered that the schoolteacher, Christa McAuliffe, was on that flight.

I thought a lot about the Challenger Seven over the next few days, and saw commonalities in their triumphs and tragedies with those of the Antarctica explorers of times past. I learned still more about man's pioneer spirit in reading about the two women, the black man, the Japanese-Hawaiian, and the three whites, the very embodiment of what America is all about. The words of columnist, Joyce Maynard, could have applied to Robert Falcon Scott as well as to Christa McAuliffe:

*John Davis Cantwell, M.D.*

"...Nothing is worth much that comes without risk. Giving someone your heart. Having a child. They all leave us open to danger and loss. The more you risk, maybe, the more you have to gain. The more you have, the more you have to lose.

And still, it's for all of us to push on, not shrink back. Who can forget those last words spoken by Mission Control the moment the sky exploded? Full Throttle!"

In the final analysis, my trip to Antarctica, a continent thousands of miles away, became more of a journey into the self. In reflecting upon the lives of past and recent explorers, I learned a good deal of man's heroic potential, of qualities that too often lie dormant in most of us. It is the actualization of this potential that sets man apart from all other creations. It is reflected in the words of Tennyson, on the stone carving that marks the grave of Robert Falcon Scott and his men:

"To strive, to seek, to find - and not to yield."

# 59

## FROM RUSSIA WITH LOVE (OR AT LEAST GOODWILL)

**INTRODUCTION**

It seemed like a rather innocent act, snapping a picture of the emergency room corridor of Moscow's Botkin Hospital. Granted we didn't have formal permission to be there, but who would care? We found out in a hurry! Before the camera was lowered hospital personnel appeared, seemingly out of nowhere. We were taken into an office, where our cameras were seized. Before giving his up, however, Dr. John Griffin slipped the roll of film out and passed it behind his back to my wife. It wasn't the emergency room picture we were trying to protect, but rather a series of Christmas card-type poses in front of beautiful St. Basil's cathedral. After an hour of interrogation we were released, together with cameras and film. Although not a pleasant experience, it did give us a feel as to life in a totalitarian state.

I was in Moscow as a physician to the Goodwill Games. Initially, it was to provide medical services to the American athletes. However, terrorist acts and the Chernobyl episode caused the sponsoring organization to back out. Each athletic team was to provide their own physician and/or trainer. I was about to make other plans for the summer when suddenly the opportunity arose to be the physician for Turner Broadcasting Company's (TBS) 1000 personnel and special guests. My wife would get to join me, as would my

John Davis Cantwell, M.D.

surgical counterpart, John Griffin, and his wife and three nurses.

**PREPARATION**

The first task was to assemble a list of the medications we would need, as we had to supply all our own. The Soviet government officials would have to approve the list, so we could get the items through customs. I was to underestimate the amount of drugs needed to treat upper respiratory infections and vastly overestimate those for vaginal infections. In looking at the drugs we brought back unused, we probably could have handled an epidemic of vaginitis in the entire city of Moscow. In addition to the various drugs, I also included a small ECG machine and lightweight electrical defibrillator (for cardiac emergencies). I didn't know the response time of the Moscow ambulances nor how well-equipped they were. I was to find that the response time was slow, for bureaucratic reasons, but that the cardiac-type ambulances did have defibrillators.

In addition to the medical preparation, I was also undergoing physical preparation, after finding out that one event, the marathon, was open to a few athletes of just average talent. What a thrill it would be, I thought, to exit Lenin Stadium, in the presence of world-class runners, stimulated by the cheers of perhaps 100,000 fans. I continued my habit of running five miles on weekdays, and added weekend runs of up to 15 miles, struggling through 99-100ºF Atlanta temperatures.

One of the nurses, Chris Dismukes, preceded me in Moscow by several weeks, to cover the small core of TBS employees doing preliminary work. A special telephone line was set up in the TBS headquarters (in Moscow's Cosmos Hotel), facilitating calls to the United States. Chris and I could communicate about any medical matters she had questions about.

To assist me in advising her, I read the book *Inside Russian Medicine* by an American physician. Some of his observations, made in 1981, were as follows:

- There are one million physicians in Russia, one per 222 people (only Israel has a ratio approaching this). There are also one half million feldshers ("physician substitutes"), introduced by Peter the Great, who got the idea from Germany.
- Moscow has a citywide emergency care system with 800 emergency ambulance teams, reached by dialing 03 (if the phone worked, I'd say).
- Intravenous needles are saved and re-sterilized. Thick rubber tubing is used in transfusions, after which it is washed, wrapped in gray cloths, and baked in an oven.
- Russian physicians are quick to recommend hospitalization for patients, especially those with abdominal pain. An estimated 25% of Soviet citizens get hospitalized each year, often unnecessarily.
- Soviet dentistry is crude, and to be avoided by visitors with acute dental problems. Russian citizens in many areas have to bring in their old jewelry to be used for gold fillings.

John Davis Cantwell, M.D.

- Russian physicians tend to recommend surgery excessively, using it sometimes as a substitutes for more expensive diagnostic tests that aren't available.
- Orthopedic surgery is poor. "Cast, and get out of the country," was the recommendation for care of visiting Americans who develop orthopedic problems.

I read the latter late one evening. I was awakened the next day by a phone call from Chris, at 6 a.m. One of the TBS employees, a former semi-professional basketball player, had injured his ankle in a pickup basketball game. The Russian physician advised surgery. What did I think? "Cast and get out," was my reply, so Chris arranged a flight to a hospital in Finland. In all fairness to the Russian doctors, the patient did eventually have a surgical procedure there, drainage of a hematoma in the area of his severe ankle sprain.

A hint of Soviet bureaucratic problems came with the difficulty in getting our Russian visas. The latter are issued only when the Russian Embassy in Washington decides to do so, no matter who calls or what the situation might be. Ours arrived one day after our original flight left, and just 15 minutes before a rescheduled departure to the Atlanta airport.

**THE GOODWILL GAMES**

We did arrive just in time for the opening ceremonies, one of the most spectacular shows I have ever seen. There were dancing bears, legions of synchronized gymnasts of all ages, a precise card section, trick riders on horseback, and a variety of high-wire acts.

The marathon was to start at the unlikely hour of 5 p.m. I spent several hours just trying to get my passport and visa back from the cantankerous lady at the Cosmos Hotel office. "Nyet," she said, our group leader had these. After another hour I finally discovered who our group leader was. No, he didn't have the documents, the lady I had just spoken to did. I took him with me to converse with her in Russian. After still further delay and denials, she finally opened a box, promptly found the items, and handed them to me.

I hurried to obtain transportation to the Rossyia Hotel, headquarters for the athletes, to get my pass card (so I could get back to our hotel) and race number. It was now just several hours before race time. After contacting numerous officials, a list of marathon entrants was located, and my name wasn't on it. I would have to go upstairs to register. I quickly filled out a form.

    Coach - Jeff Galloway
    Club - Atlanta Track
    Prior International Competition - Boston Marathon
    Best Time - 3:23 (I was afraid the official would roll his eyes, but he didn't.)

At least 10 phone calls were made, and various people consulted in person. It was now little more than an hour before race time. A number would be waiting for me at Lenin Stadium. The Intourist guide was helpful; she would take me back to our hotel, on the north end of town, to get my running gear. She sent

*John Davis Cantwell, M.D.*

an aid to pick up the number at Lenin Stadium (south end of town) and to bring it to me at the hotel. He never appeared. I watched the start of the event on television, feeling like I had already run a marathon. I could empathize with Solzhenitsyn and with Jewish dissidents, who spend years getting jerked around by the Soviet system, trying to get on "the list."

My journal entry, dated July 7th, must have reflected my post-race feelings.

> "A.M. - city tour - bad news.
> Afternoon and evening on call - boring. No calls. Only medial problems were a case of ankle swelling and dermatitis and a mild sore throat.
> Evening dinner on my own. The chicken was inedible.
> I did observe why Russia doesn't have unemployment problems. Each job is done by three or four people (checking passes at the hotel entrance, manning the reception table of the restaurant, watching the elevators on each floor of the hotel)."

As the games commenced, and the TBS guests rolled in, our days and nights became action-packed and at least my attitude improved markedly. We worked in shifts, doctor and nurse, on call every other 24-hour period. One member of each team was always in our hotel, while the other was on the beeper. During the spare moments we attended the athletic events, thrilling to the masterful performances of Edwin Moses, Jackie Joyner and Evelyn Ashford, of Russian gymnasts (several of whom scored rare prefect 10s), and of Stanford figure skater Debby Thomas. The badges we wore enabled us to walk about at courtside where we could almost intercept one of Cheryl Miller's basketball passes or pat Olympic wrestling champion, Dave Schultz, on the back.

**With Marilyn in Red Square**

There were a multitude of cultural things to do, such as viewing the treasures in the Armory and the Pushkin Museum, viewing the contemporary art of the Russian painter, Glazunov, and visiting the homes of great Russian writers such as Tolstoy and Chekhov.

Our only excursion outside Moscow was a four-hour drive to Tolstoy's beautiful country home, Yasnaya Polyanna, where I was

*John Davis Cantwell, M.D.*

overwhelmed by browsing through his extensive personal library.

**MEDICAL PROBLEMS**

We were intermittently busy, treating mainly gastrointestinal and upper respiratory problems. The only medical emergency developed late one evening when the abdominal discomfort of seemingly gastroenteritis localized to the right lower abdominal quadrant. The pain had started several days before, and had intensified, now accompanied by fever. Physical examination revealed guarding and rebound tenderness. There was no time to consider flights to Sweden, Finland or Germany, our three back-up hospitals, because it would delay things another estimated 14-18 hours, risking perforation of the appendix.

I notified our "group leader" that I wanted to transport the patient to the hospital emergency room (the very place we had been held in for questioning less than six hours previously). It turned out to be another bout with "red tape." We couldn't just take the patient to the hospital, he had to go by ambulance. Before the latter could be called, the patient would need to be examined by the hotel doctor. My protests not withstanding, protocol was followed. The hotel doctor informed me that the man had appendicitis, and needed to go to the hospital (how do you say "So what else is new" in Russian, I wondered). Before the ambulance would take him, however, the ambulance doctor would have to examine the patient in the hotel. After further delay this was done. The ambulance doctor informed me, through his interpreter, that the patient had acute appendicitis, and needed to have surgery right away. My frustration mounted.

I insisted that I be allowed to ride in the ambulance. We drove off at high speed, curiously to a hospital far away, in the south part of Moscow. En route, my beeper went off. Seeing a phone in the ambulance, I asked if I could use it. No, that wouldn't be necessary, I was told. A little while later the ambulance squealed to a stop, on the edge of what looked to me like a small forest. I was told to get out.

They led me into the woods. Before I even had time to worry, I was told there was a telephone there that I could use. Indeed, a pay phone was attached to a small wooden fence. I inserted two kopeks and called the hotel operator. The message was from TBS headquarters, informing me that a patient was being taken to the hospital.

The emergency room was a bit dirty. A physician with a deep scar across his face, dressed in a bile-green wrinkled scrubsuit, examined the patient. Acute appendicitis, he concluded, and advised that we go straight to surgery. I requested at least a blood count and urinalysis, which was done. I also insisted on viewing the operative suite, and talking with the head surgeon. The latter was a pleasantly plump woman, probably in her late 40s. She and her assistant had been operating at that hospital for a number of years. She showed me about the operating room, and the ward where the patient would be postoperatively. The facilities were adequate. The blood count was consistent with the suspected diagnosis. We would go ahead with surgery, I said. It was now 4 a.m., five hours after the start of this charade.

*John Davis Cantwell, M.D.*

The surgery was successful. The only surprise to me was when the IV was removed as soon as the incision was closed. Antibiotics would be all given intramuscularly, as is the Russian custom.

The patient was moved directly to a private room. I didn't see another patient on the whole ward. I requested that I be allowed to stay in the empty four-bed room across the hall. After some discussion I was told that I could.

The nurses were very attentive, but clearly upset by my presence. They would not be able to give me any food ("okay," I said, "a cup of coffee later in the morning would be fine"). I was later told that I'd have to leave, as they might be getting more patients. This seemed ridiculous, as all of the rooms about me were vacant.

I subsequently learned that this particular hospital ward had been reserved for any visiting Goodwill Games participants who needed serious medical care. Our patient was the only one they had seen in the two-week period.

**REFLECTIONS**

For someone interested in medicine, athletics, liberal arts and foreign travel, the Goodwill Games experience was one I will always treasure. I won't forget the friendliness of the average Russian people, who were eager to be of help when we groped about in the marvelous metro system. I'll remember the head-to-head battle in the high jump, when the USA's Doug Nordquist topped the world-record holder, Igor Paklin of the USSR. I'll think about the stern glances of the

Russian guards as my line moved closer to Lenin's tomb, and my fear that my beeper might be detected or, worse, go off as I passed the bier itself.

I'll recall the fun-loving American fans, holding up clever signs and trying to keep a wave going, amid a somber Russian audience, during the women's basketball final. I'll benefit from the example of Edwin Moses, who focused on the job at hand rather than dwelling on the inconveniences and flaws of the host country. I'll also remember the cold reality of confrontation in the Botkin Hospital emergency room, when I got just a small taste of what Solzhenitsyn, Sakarov and countless others have experienced.

I have been fortunate to travel to many parts of the world. As much as I enjoyed the Goodwill Games experience, I have never had such an urge, when our flight landed in this country, to kneel on the ground, kiss it, and say without any embarrassment, "Thank God I'm an American."

*John Davis Cantwell, M.D.*

# 60

## SEARCHING FOR NOAH'S ARK

**INTRODUCTION**

It is the Fourth of July, one day after our military shot down a civilian plane, killing 290 Iranians. We are in the eastern Turkey town of Dogubayazit, a mere jog from the Iranian border. Two Iranian men are in our hotel room posing as police officers. It is not an ideal situation, but more on this later.

Dogubayazit is the starting point for expeditions to climb Mt. Ararat, a snow-capped peak of almost 17,000 feet on which Noah's Ark is said to be located. Accompanied by my wife, Marilyn, and two children, (Kelly, at the time a college junior, and Ryan, a rising college freshman), I hoped to climb the mountain, look for evidence of the Ark, and visit with people living in the region about their thoughts and experiences.

Turkey did not seem to be the ideal place to spend one's summer vacation. After viewing the old movie "Midnight Express" on the VCR, I decided to leave most of my medical equipment home, especially any needles and syringes. Turkish customs appeared rough, and prison life even more so. Eleven days before we were to depart, a gunman tried to assassinate the Prime Minister of Turkey. Mr. Ozal was wounded in the hand, had a white cloth wrapped around it, and returned to the lectern to finish his speech. A week before departure a mud slide not far from the region we were visiting buried 100 people under tons of mud and rocks.

Several days later a U.S. military attaché was killed in a car bomb blast in Greece, seeming in retaliation for the United States' failure to prevent Turkey's 1974 invasion of Cyprus after an Athens-inspired coup there. Perhaps these were warning signs that the area was too volatile for a family outing, but it was too late to reconsider.

**READING ABOUT THE ARK**

According to the book of Genesis, the earth was flooded for 150 days. On July 17th, the Ark, "came to rest on the mountains of Ararat." One assumes that it settled on the highest peak, but that may be incorrect. The Koran mentions Mt. Al Judi as the resting place of the Ark. A mountain of this name is only 7700 feet, and located south of Lake Van. Al Judi, however, means "highest" in Arabic, leading some Islamic scholars to believe that it refers to Ararat. Marco Polo wrote that "...it is this country of Armenia that the Ark of Noah exists on the top of a certain great mountain on the summit of which snow is so constant that no one can ascend." This certainly sounds like Ararat.

Mt. Ararat was first climbed by Dr. Frederick Parrot, a German-Russian scientist in 1829. The volcano erupted in 1840, "exposing Ararat's great granite heart" and creating the Ahora Gorge on the North side of the mountain. In 1876, Viscount Bryce made a solitary climb of Ararat and found pieces of hand-tooled timbers at 13,900 feet. Two years later he described his find to the Royal Geographic Society in London, amid great skepticism. In 1887, John Joseph, the Prince of Nouri (from India) was exploring on Ararat

*John Davis Cantwell, M.D.*

in search of the source of the Euphrates River and claimed to have seen the Ark. He estimates it to be 300 yards long and 100 feet high, with one end broken off. Nouri sought investors to have the Ark disassembled and transported to the Chicago World's Fair, but was denied permission by the Turkish government. George Hagopian, an Armenian shepherd, climbed to the Ark in 1905, at age 10. A drawing was made, based on his description, and coincided with what a pilot saw in an aerial view (also on the northeast side of Ararat) years later.

In more recent times, an industrialist from Bordeaux, France - Fernand Navarra - spotted a long dark mass under the glacier ice in 1952. He discovered hand-tooled wooden beams, and took a piece to the archeology section of the Cairo museum. The beam was of oak (some feel that gopherwood is white oak), but carbon dating showed vast discrepancies. In an aerial survey in 1959, a hull-shaped form was spotted 17 miles south of Mt. Ararat. The dimensions - 500 feet by 150 feet by 45 feet - roughly coincided with Biblical dimensions of the Ark. In a research expedition in 1960, dynamite was set off in part of the structure and the residue was felt to be merely solidified lava. In 1984, an American investigator, Marvin Steffins, took rock samples from the site, but geologic analysis was unimpressive.

The most celebrated "arkologist" was former astronaut James Irwin, who made multiple visits to Mt. Ararat in the 1980s. On his way down from the summit, in 1982, he was apparently struck in the head by a falling rock, and had to be evacuated to an area hospital. Irwin never saw evidence of the Ark, despite continued searches.

*Adventures on Seven Continents And Other Essays*

**EN ROUTE TO ARARAT**

We arrived in Istanbul and had a pre-dinner briefing by our Mountain Travel guide, Paul Williams, an attorney from the Seattle area. Our group of 13 ranged in age from 18 to 69 years and included another physician, an aerospace engineer, a tax attorney (who had argued cases before the Supreme Court), a geologist, a high school teacher, a pharmacist, a neurophysicist and a driver's education instructor. The latter had dreamed about climbing Ararat five years beforehand, and had saved up to fulfill that dream.

I was glad that our guide was experienced in mountain rescue, because the description I read of the climb sounded ominous:

> "...the quest is a serious one, fraught with dangers, seen and unseen, that test the mettle and the ingenuity of the most experienced climbers. The unexpected midsummer storms, and always the instability of authentic governmental permits which are often revoked at improbable times, avalanches and falling rocks, hurricane-force winds, slippery scree and 'widow-maker' boulders that often hurtle past the climber's head, tantalizing and inaccessible canyons, separated by razor-sharp ridges only a mountain goat would dare to scale, are but a few of the challenges that face all serious explorers who venture onto Ararat's unpredictable higher slopes."

On the lower slopes, "deadly vipers are a constant menace, and swarms of mosquitos can make camp life miserable." Higher up one might encounter mountain lions, "hardy" goats, and

*John Davis Cantwell, M.D.*

even an occasional great Russian bear. Some say that Ararat is actually a creature of moods, and like the temperamental prima donna to which she might be compared she can assume at a moment's notice "the most awesome and terrifying roles." To the Kurdish natives, the upper part of the mountain is inhabited by the evil "djinn." Climbing to this region "hath seemed not to be the pleasure of the Most High," according to a 14th century friar.

Assuming these to be overexaggerations, we flew via Ankara to the Anatolian city of Erzerum, spent the night, and then drove to Dogubayazit. En route, we were informed about the Iranian airline tragedy.

Around 11 p.m., my son and I were startled by a knock on the door. "Police," they said, and I foolishly opened the door. One of the two intruders flashed a badge and searched the bathroom and the balcony. They mumbled something about things being done differently in this country than in ours. After probing about, they apologized and left the room. I chased after them, down to the hotel lobby, and sought assistance from the desk clerk and from our native guide, Mustafa (who happened to be nearby). The two men, identified now as Iranians, seemed to apprehend a third party from near the TV set and headed out the door and into the streets. I followed them to a nearby hotel, where Mustafa managed to corral them and bring them back to our hotel for questioning. They claimed to have had too much to drink, and that they were in our room searching for an Iranian woman. Furthermore, they said they had stayed in our very room the night before, but had moved to a cheaper hotel in the morning. They denied posing as police, and flashing a fake police badge. We debated about taking the occurrence to the Turkish police, knowing that it would be an all-night ordeal, so we decided not to pursue the matter, especially after a review of hotel records verified that the men had actually stayed in our room previously. Ryan and I slept fitfully that night, concerned that the men, or the Iranians in the streets, might come back to our hotel. We were glad to depart the next morning, first to visit one Ark site 17 miles south of Ararat, and then to go via dump truck to a drop-off site, from which we would hike to base camp.

The geologist in our group wasn't too impressed with the Ark site we visited, feeling that it was a natural erosion of sandstone and lava. The spot was difficult to reach, because of dirt roads that periodically wash out and erode. That may change, however, as a tourist building is being constructed on a nearby hill.

We hiked up to base camp, at 9300 feet, accompanied by Kurdish families on horseback and by the Turkish military personal, armed with machine guns. Terrorists roam about the mountain, stealing valuables from the climbers, and sometimes even their cold weather gear (one group I read about had to descend in their underwear). That evening we experienced one of the most torrential rainstorms I have ever seen, with frightening thunder and lightning. It almost seemed as though we would need an ark of our own to survive the night. It was easy to envision a mud slide, rock fall, or a direct hit of lightning on our metal tent pole. The rain partially flooded a little town at the base of the mountain, and washed out areas of the road

*John Davis Cantwell, M.D.*

we had come up on, making our eventual descent more laborious.

## THE SUMMIT BID

We had one day to acclimatize, before heading up to high camp at 13,500 feet, Our mountain guide took us up onto a snowfield and taught us the essentials of using an ice axe to keep from sliding off the steepest portions of the mountain.

That evening, and again the following morning, I developed episodic abdominal pain and severe vomiting. I was weak and dehydrated, and unable to replenish the fluids because of extreme nausea. It was the worst possible time for this to have occurred, for there was no option to delay a day. My summit bid was over, as was any search on my part higher up on the mountain for the Ark.

Kelly and Ryan carried on. They reached high camp in the mid-afternoon and readied their gear for the summit attempt. There was no sign of an Ark, but this was predictable as we were confined to the southwest side of the mountain (the northeast side, around the Ahora Gorge, is closed to climbers at present as it faces Russia).

Our Turkish guide abandoned our group, claiming to be ill, taking the ropes (and return airline tickets) with him. The American mountain rescue expert was also forced to turn back, so my children and several others were pretty much on their own, fighting high altitude, thigh-deep snow, and partial white-out conditions. There was no time, and certainly no surplus of energy, to search about for the Ark. It became a matter of synchronous breathing and climbing, focusing on the summit and a rapid safe descent thereafter.

An aggressive German couple, and their Turkish guide, were ahead of our group. They refused to wait, or to share the expertise of their guide, in their focused ascent on the peak. As they descended, and met our group, the guide notified our members that they were not allowed to go up to the summit, as per orders by walkie-talkie from the Turkish commandoes, because they lacked a guide. One member - the driver's education instructor who was living out his dream - rebelled and eventually did reach the top.

Upon our return to Dogubayazit, I had ample time to inquire about the Ark. My main source was Ahmet Turhan, a veteran mountain guide with over 25 years of experience on Ararat. "Yes," he said, "there really were Russian bears, and terrorists, on the mountain." In regards to the Ark, he had yet to see hand-tooled timbers, or hull-shaped objects below the glacier ice. Did he believe that the Ark existed? "Sometimes yes, sometimes no," he answered. "So many people come looking of it, I suppose there must be something to it."

**REFLECTIONS**

Our group met for a farewell dinner at a seafood restaurant in Istanbul, overlooking the Bosphorus. One climber read a humorous poem he had written, mentioning an episode or characteristic of each group member. Our mountain rescue guide spoke briefly, telling us what a diverse, yet cohesive group we were. He said that we would promise to look each other up in the future, but in all likelihood we never would. He also stated that mountains

John Davis Cantwell, M.D.

tend to expose both our strengths and our weaknesses, and bind us in close harmony if we are honest about both.

For me, the trip was disappointing in the sense that I didn't have a chance to experience the summit attempt. On the other hand, I was extremely proud of how well my children did, in a new situation, together, meeting the mountain head-on and holding their own.

Does a remnant of the Ark exist? I think not. Stories of previous discoveries seem too much like UFO-type sensationalism in my judgment. I prefer the view of Charles Berlitz, author of *The Lost Ship of Noah:*

> "The Ararat Ark is a reminder of man's possible fate, but this time it is not the vehicle of salvation. For there is another Ark which may serve. All we have to do when we find it is to repair it and make it safe for a long journey. It is far from legendary, but in a place so obvious that no one has realized where it is. It is already provisioned with food and water, is as yet uncontaminated, and there is space for a crew much larger than that which boarded the Ark on the other survival ships of legend. The animals, those that have survived, are already on board. The Ark is built to weather great storms, as tumultuous as any encountered by the Ark of Noah. There will be no need to send forth a dove to find out if the Flood has abated since the catastrophes that this other Ark must surmount are of a different kind from the Flood of Noah. The Ark too is different. It is essentially a vessel, but it navigates in

an ocean vast beyond measure. For this time, the Ark is the Earth itself."

*John Davis Cantwell, M.D.*

# 61

## ADVENTURES OF A HARVARD DROPOUT

Norman Vaughan is a character, the type of unique personality one is fortunate to encounter in a lifetime. I first met him at an Atlanta regional meeting of the Explorers' Club, where he was lecturing on a) his participation with Admiral Richard Byrd in an expedition to Antarctica in 1926 and b) his dogsled trip to Greenland, during World War II, to recover top-secret information on bomb sites that were on a U.S. B-17 bomber which crash-landed. Through several additional encounters with Norman I learned a great deal more about him and could see why he is literally a folkhero in Alaska, where he lives most of the year. A recent publication of his, *With Byrd at the Bottom of the World,* will enable many others to learn of his fascinating life.

Vaughan entered Harvard in 1925, more interested in football than studies. He withdrew from college for a year and spent time with Sir Wilfred Grenfell, a British physician working as a medical missionary with the Eskimos in Labrador and Newfoundland. From Grenfell he learned techniques of dogsled transportation, which were to have a profound impact on his life.

Back in college, Norman and several classmates were studying at a table in a Harvard dormitory:

*"Hearing the outside door open, I glanced up, always ready for a disruption from my*

books. The other four, deeply involved with their assignments, paid no attention to the paperboy who tossed me the **Boston Transcript.** I unfolded the paper, intending to read only the headlines before resuming my studies. In large bold letters I read five magic words that would change the direction of my life: BYRD TO THE SOUTH POLE."

Vaughan once again left Harvard, joined by two of his studymates, and volunteered to work as a doghandler for Byrd, without pay for the first year. His first encounter with the admiral was a memorable one:

"Byrd wore his Navy uniform and appeared friendly. I immediately liked his looks. A thin, medium-sized man, he exuded power. Even when speaking quietly, his low voice demanded attention, and his appearance suggested a man in his early 30s, 10 years younger than his real age.

A bright, highly energetic man, Byrd never asked any of us to do anything he was not willing to do himself. He was also cautious and refused to take unwanted risks with human lives."

Byrd dubbed Vaughan and his two classmates "the three musketeers," and assigned them to work under the chief doghandler Arthur Walden, a veteran of "mail and freight sleddings in the Yukon." According to Vaughan, Walden became resentful of the more educated and wealthier youths and gave the impression he might use his pistol on Vaughan. The latter was forced to sleep outside in a hidden tent, despite temperature drops to −60ºF, until

John Davis Cantwell, M.D.

several Norwegian members of the expedition managed to take the gun away from Walden.

The two-year expedition, dubbed "Little America," was a big success. The geological portion, involving 1600 miles of dogsledding, resulted in a survey and mapping of a new mountain range. Vaughan and his classmates, Crockett and Goodale, each had a mountain named after them. Byrd, who in 1926 had been the first to fly over the North Pole, succeeded in making the historic first flight over the South Pole.

In 1934, Byrd made a second Antarctic expedition. Vaughan was initially scheduled to go along, spending several months with Byrd and two others on the Ross Ice Shelf. Byrd changed his mind and decided to spend the months alone, seemingly (to Vaughan) to reap the glory for himself. Vaughan decided not to participate. Byrd almost died from carbon monoxide poisoning and was ill for 72 of the 130 days. He was in such poor condition upon his rescue that he had to remain at the outpost another 64 days before he was strong enough to survive the overland journey. His reflections on the experience (Byrd RE. *Alone*. GP Putnam's Sons, New York, 1938) is a classic in expedition and adventure literature.

Vaughan's life has been a series of adventures since the 1928-30 trip. He joined a semi-professional football team in Philadelphia, but was forced to quit to preserve his job with an advertising company. In 1932 he represented the U.S.A. in the Olympics (Lake Placid, N.Y.), the only year dogsled racing was an official event. He finished 10th. In 1942 he received the Legion of Merit for his dogsled trip across Greenland to retrieve the vital information from the B-

17 bomber. He has gone fox hunting with the Prince of Wales, played polo with the Shah of Iran, taught the Pope to drive a dogsled, and crashed the Carter Inaugural Parade in 1977 with his dog team. He competed in the gruelling 1100 mile Iditarod Dogsled Race across Alaska and has finished five times since turning age 70, and most recently in 1990 at the age of 85.

Several years ago I arranged for him to speak at the Atlanta Clinical Society meeting, along with Carolyn Muegge, an Atlanta woman half his age whom he trained in the art of dogsled racing. He astounded me at the end of the talk by announcing that he and Carolyn were getting married that December. I subsequently received an invitation to the wedding, held in Trapper Creek, Alaska, approachable by private plane and, appropriately dogsleds. It was just after Christmas and, unfortunately, I wasn't able to attend.

Later, I received a note from Carolyn and Norman, inviting me to participate in the Polar Bear Project on Wrangel Island, a remote spot in the Chukchi Sea belonging to Russia. The island is normally closed, not only to foreign travelers but also to Soviets. The objective is to assist in doing research on the habits and movements of the denning polar bears.

After the Polar Bear Project, Norman would like to airdrop dogs and supplies to the Little American base in Antarctica and follow Amundsen's route to the South Pole and return via Scott's route, climbing the mountain named after him en route. Carol Phillips, an Anchorage writer, captured the spirit of the man when she wrote:

*John Davis Cantwell, M.D.*

> *"Norman Vaughan is fighting for a cause. It's the cause of older people, but also the cause of youth and exuberance. He is still excited about life, and he still has a lot of plans for his life. He still has eyes full of dreams. If you asked him, he would say the best is yet to come."*

Vaughan had periodic contact with Admiral Byrd through the years. A Christmas note from him, dated 1952, said "...18 years later, as I am traveling down the other side of the mountain, I...have found that my old friends, whether I see them or not, become more valuable to me year by year."

Byrd died of heart failure in 1957. Norman Vaughan was the only expedition member able to attend the funeral:

> "I stood at attention, listening to taps while vivid memories flashed through my mind. I thought of my first meeting with Byrd, when he inspected my dogs...my carrying him by sled to Little America...our walks along the barrier in Antarctica...his parting words when he left for his second expedition, back to Antarctica.
>
> In my mind I saw him again on the frozen continent as we hastened to board (the ship) in the Bay of Whales after our year at the bottom of the world.
>
> `It's over, Norman,' he had said. The smile - I saw the smile again. `We did it!'"

## 62

## THE CITY TOO BUSY TO HATE

In 1980 I almost moved from Atlanta. It would have been a terrible mistake. I would have missed our many friends and my local medical colleagues, five trips to the World Series with the Atlanta Braves, summer evenings of candlelight dinners at Chastain Park, an inside view of the Olympic excitement, Atlanta's multitude of wonderful restaurants, the rebuilding of the Margaret Mitchell House, and many other people, events and places.

I have lived in Atlanta for 33 years. Like so many others, I have been rather busy and haven't taken much time to reflect upon what has transpired here during those years. Three fine books have been published that offer us the opportunity to do just that.

In *Atlanta Rising*, Frederick Allen looks at the phenomenal growth and development of the city since 1948, up through the Olympic bid, and reflects upon a colorful array of characters, ranging from the political scene to the movers and shakers in business and development. I was amused at the description of former governor Eugene Talmadge as a "self-made illiterate," and the political skills of former mayor William B. Hartsfield. During one campaign, Hartsfield's rival had discovered that Hartsfield was overdue on several debts, including an $86 doctor bill, and had made this public. Hartsfield adroitly turned the coin by merely requesting the votes from

*John Davis Cantwell, M.D.*

everyone in Atlanta who owed money to a doctor.

On the bombing of the Jewish Temple on October 12, 1958, Allen wrote:

> "Random bombings had pockmarked the South for many years, but rarely in Atlanta. The city's confident, almost carefree presumption that it stood above the vulgar violence of the rest of the section - an attribute conveyed nicely in Driving Miss Daisy - was rattled to the bone."

Pulitzer Prize-winning editor, Ralph McGill, stands out, as does Ivan Allen, Jr. McGill, like Allen, "struggled with change, just as so many other white Southerners had. He did not start off `better,' he bettered himself along the way. Change did not come easily to him, which made his evolution all the more admirable."

Melissa Fay Greene, author of the previously acclaimed *Praying for Sheetrock*, focuses her book, *The Temple Bombing*, on that event in 1958, and especially on the Rabbi, Jacob Rothschild, and his quest for racial justice. Rothschild, she writes:

> "...looked somewhat the four-eyes, the egghead, the bookworm. But he had seen bloodshed on Guadalcanal and had sat with dying boys, Jewish and Christian, in hospital tents as bombs fell, the first Jewish chaplain to come under fire in World War II. What stood behind the logic and the quiet revolutionary actions was a clarity of mind and a history of having not flinched under fire."

Rothschild wanted his congregation and others as well "to see the holy Jewish texts as a moral blueprint for their lives." As we see in Greene's fine book, he succeeded admirably, but at a price, one that his prophet role models - Isaiah, Jeremiah, Ezekiel and Amos - had also paid generations ago.

I found the third book, *Where Peachtree Meets Sweet Auburn*, to be my favorite. Author Gary Pomerantz traces the family roots of two former mayors, Ivan Allen, Jr., and Maynard Jackson, Jr., - one white, tho other black - and in so doing, tells us much about how the city evolved since Civil War times.

Ivan Jr.'s grandfather joined the Confederate Calvary at age 14. His father came to Atlanta from Dalton to sell typewriters, and founded a family business that flourishes today. I was familiar with the rest of the Allen story, including the tragic suicide of Ivan Allan, III. I knew less about the Jackson heritage.

Maynard Jr.'s great-grandfather, John Miles McAfee, was a white physician and a Georgia state senator who had participated in the vote in 1843 to change the name of the city from Terminus to Marthasville (it was subsequently changed again to Atlanta, so it would fit better on railroad tickets).

I have seen the street sign for John Wesley Dobbs Avenue many times, but never knew who the man was until he comes to life in Pomerantz's writing. Dobbs was Maynard Jr.'s grandfather, a remarkable person, well-known to the black community centered around Auburn Avenue. I would like to have been present on June 3, 1952, when this marvelous orator

*John Davis Cantwell, M.D.*

addressed the Metropolitan Atlanta Planning Committee and said:

> "I make no apology for being a colored citizen in this community. God saw fit to send me into this world as a member of the colored race and I have never seen fit to ever attempt to question the wisdom of God's plan. My job is to do the best I can with the tools God gave me to work with. My father, grandfather, and great-grandfather have all lived and died among the red hills of North Georgia. I feel rather proud of that kind of heritage…The sweat from the brows of my ancestors have fallen in rice fields, cotton plantations, railroad carts, in the forests and along the mountainsides. In times of danger we have answered every call and spilled our blood for American ideals whenever it was necessary to do so. In this way I find that we have purchased the right to equal citizenship and all opportunities to go along with it under the law."

I can imagine the drama for those in attendance that Friday evening in March, 1961, when 1000 blacks and a handful of white leaders (including Ivan Allan, Jr.) met at the Warren Memorial United Methodist Church to discuss the proposed agreement between white merchants and black leaders. Rev. Martin Luther King, Sr., had tried to emphasize moderation, to the jeers of more radical colleagues. After three hours of rancor, his son finally rose to speak. MLK, Jr., "had seen his father's humiliation; it had affected him deeply." In "a voice familiar to everyone in the church," he delivered a 20 minute

*Adventures on Seven Continents And Other Essays*

masterpiece, reminding the audience that misunderstandings are not solved "trying to live in monologue," but rather "in the realm of dialogue." By the time he had finished, the soon-to-be Nobel Peace Prize winner "had achieved a unity of spirit among the crowd's disparate groups."

I would like to have been a silent observer when Maynard, Jr. came upon the tombstone to his slave ancestor. As Pomerantz describes the event:

> "By coming to the grave…Maynard, Jr. had come to a place that represented the blood of his family and provided proof about ancestors lost to time. He thought to touch the stone, but drew back his hand, disturbed for a moment by the reminder of slavery and its consequences still today…
> 
> He had come a distance to this graveyard, a distance measured in generations. The first black mayor of Atlanta had come to the grave of an $800 slave who had been his great-great-grandfather. Bending to the stone, Maynard Jr. touched it again, this time moving his finger across the cuttings that spelled out the name Wesley Dobbs. Below the name he felt the words there. Died February 5, 1897. Now he laid both hands atop the stone."

Perhaps one error in the book can be corrected in the reprinting. The first black man to attend the University of Georgia was, of course, Hamilton Holmes, not Hamilton Hunter. The friend of Ivan Allan, III, Dr. Ladd Jones, was an orthopedist, not a cardiologist, a minor point.

*John Davis Cantwell, M.D.*

The focal point in the story is when the great-grandchildren of John Wesley Dobbs and Ivan Allen, Sr., attended the same public grade school, Warren T. Jackson Elementary, free at last to do so, after decades of segregation and prejudice.

A nice aftermath occurred at the City Grill when members and friends of the Dobbs and Allen families gathered en masse for a dinner of shrimp, oysters, crab cakes and fried quail, amid singing, laughter, and reminiscence. At the function, Ivan Allen, Jr., said of the Pomerantz work, "It's a remarkable book, very well-researched and well-documented. I learned things about the Allens I didn't know myself." The latter was echoed by Maynard Jackson, Jr., when I visited with him at the opening of the Olympic Stadium.

I highly recommend all three books, as each has something special to offer, namely different perspectives of this great city of ours, a city that has been too busy indeed to hate, or to tolerate hatred, thanks to men such as Jacob Rothschild, Ivan Allan, Jr., and John Wesley Dobbs.

# 63

## FROM EVEREST TO ANTARCTICA - TRAVELS ON SEVEN CONTINENTS

> 'Tis not too late to seek a newer world
> ...for my purpose holds
> To sail beyond the sunset, and the baths
> Of all the western stars, until I die.
> - Tennyson

The monastery at Thangboche is one of the most beautiful sites on earth, a breathtaking spectacle midway between the airstrip at Lukla and the Everest Basecamp. After a hard day's trek, at an elevation of 14,000 feet, one finally arrives at the sacred site and camps uphill, with panoramic views of the Himalayan peaks. You can see Everest, Mother Goddess of the World, peaking between Lhotse and Nuptse, with a plume of snow fanned by 100 mile per hour winds.

I began to travel when our children were young. There were places I wanted to see before I became too elderly or debilitated. I was motivated to begin early, during my medicine residency, when a colleague developed leukemia and died three months later, his dreams and goals unfulfilled. I also encountered patients who desired to travel after retirement, only to develop a stroke or cancer that made such plans unattainable. I would try to seize the moment, avoid procrastination, and learn all that I could in journeys to the seven continents.

*John Davis Cantwell, M.D.*

I found that travel was a wonderful way to shrink the world. When I read of events in Berlin, I think of Wolfgang Barth, a physician-colleague in the former East Berlin. When troubles flare in Bosnia, I reflect on a beautiful day in Mostar, viewing young daredevils diving off the Stari Most Bridge, built in 1566 by Suleyman, the Magnificent. The splendid stone structure had lasted for 424 years. It would exist for only three more years before it was destroyed by a mindless Croatian bomber, a symbol of the destruction that was permeating every facet of that country's society. When Apartheid ended, I was happy for Dr. Tim Noakes, a friend in Cape Town, and for the residents I met in Soweto, outside Johannesburg, who now had the potential to be truly free.

Travel has also been a stimulus to learn about the history of a country and about different cultures. Before the trip to South Africa, I read Michener's *The Covenant*, which gave a good background on the turbulent history of this beautiful country. I read about the Inca Empire before I trekked to Peru, along the very trail these remarkably developed people walked centuries ago. A trip to Paris was enhanced by reading Cronin's biography of Napoleon, and Hemingway's delightful *A Movable Feast*. The trip to Antarctica was more meaningful after reading about Shackleton, Scott, Amundsen, and Byrd, heroic explorers from the early 1900's.

Sometimes a book will stimulate a trip, as it did last fall. I was intrigued by the dust jacket of Paul Theroux's, *The Pillars of Hercules*, depicting a pastel-colored village, plastered against a steep hillside, vineyards and olive groves above, the glimmering sea below. The village was eventually identified as Manarola, one of the five towns in the Cinque Terra, in Northwest Italy. We hiked from village to village, in the Romantic region where Byron wrote "Don Juan" and Shelley composed "To a Skylark," pausing for long lunches, dipping homemade bread into olive oil and savoring each bite.

Memories linger from all trips. I will highlight a few, usually shared with my wife, Marilyn, and children, Ryan and Kelly.

## Africa (See chapter 57)

We are staying at the Masai Mara Game Reserve, during the migration of the wildebeests, having climbed the third highest peak on Mt. Kenya, toured native villages and reviewed medical records of Masai patients in Nairobi.

Marilyn shouts at Ryan, during the night, to stop grinding his teeth. The noise is keeping her awake. He is mad that she aroused him and hollers back that he doesn't grind his teeth. The next evening I heard the sound again, emanating from near Ryan's cot. I tiptoed over to his bed and realized that the sound was coming from the outside. I lifted up the tent flap and quickly rolled it down, startled by a 3000 pound hippopotamus, the size of an army tank, grazing about a foot from Ryan's head. I'm glad I didn't know then that the hippo kills more people each year than lions, leopards, Cape buffalo, and elephants combined. Possessed of a jittery, skittish temperament, the behemoth can outrun a man and has canines two feet in length. Fortunately he was satisfied with the tall grass surrounding our tent that evening.

John Davis Cantwell, M.D.

## Antarctica

The Drake Passage, from Patagonia to Antarctica, has some of the most treacherous, turbulent waters in the world.

I had looked forward to this trip (chapter 58) for several years, a chance to see the areas traversed by Shackleton and others, the site where explorer H. W. Tilman disappeared, at age 80, an explorer to the very end.

I have never been exposed to rough seas, and didn't know if I was prone to sea sickness or not.

Marilyn and I slept well the first night. I felt well in bed and decided to get dressed and head up for breakfast. She would come later. Within a minute or two after leaving our room, I dashed back, my head spinning, very nauseated, and headed to the bathroom to vomit. After lying down for several minutes, I felt better and tried again, with the same result.

Marilyn observed all this, indicated something to the effect that I was a wimp, got dressed and ascended the stairs to the breakfast room.

With a wicked look on my face I lay in bed, checking my watch. In one minute and twenty-five seconds she came bursting back into the room and headed for the bathroom. I prudently refrained from making a comment.

We took some Dramamine, which helped, and I added a transderm scopolamine patch on the return trip. Overall, we fared better than some. One of our waiters at dinner mentioned that on prior cruises they had been at sea for up to ten days, only to see a new face at the dinner table, a seasick victim who only then had felt well enough to venture out of his or her cabin.

Antarctica is one of the last frontiers. I shall never forget the site of penguins, marching past me on a narrow path to the sea, like a procession of college graduates. Nor will I forget the huge iceberg, teal blue in its interior, calving in front of our Zodiac raft, sending a small tidal wave in our direction. Memories linger still of the whale, which submerged near our cruise ship and finally burst out of the water, twisted in mid-air, and dove deep, not to be seen again.

**Germany**

At a seminar in Sweden, in 1971, I befriended Dr. Barth, a preventive cardiologist and a marathon runner - a man of mutual interests. Several years later I took my family through "Check- Point Charlie" to visit him. The unsmiling border guard hassled Kelly because the sweater she was wearing wasn't the same one she had on in her passport picture.

From Dr. Barth's flat we could see the Berlin Wall, a menacing reminder of the constraints of communism. Dr. Barth preferred to speak of it as "the border," rather than "the wall." I didn't blame him.

I kept in touch with him through the years, sending Christmas cards and occasional medical books. I never received a reply, nor did I necessarily expect to. I never believed that the wall would be toppled in my lifetime.

On November 8, 1989, another East Berlin physician friend of mine, Klaus Heinze, was sitting in a little apartment with his wife, who was reading the newspaper. Something in

*John Davis Cantwell, M.D.*

the news caught her eye. As her husband recounted to me years later, at the Olympic Games, she told him that they should go to the wall that very night, for she believed it was going to come down. He chided her, stating that there was no possible way that would happen.

He was wrong! And so was I!

A few weeks after the border opened I received an eight-page letter from Dr. Barth, along with a piece of the Berlin wall. He thanked me for staying in contact with him. My letters and packages had gotten through, mainly because the postman was a friend of his. He could not write back, for fear of getting in trouble with the authorities.

One day I hope to return to Berlin, to visit Dr. Barth and his wife, and to take a special gift - the 1936 Olympic book, in German, with glossy pictures (including those of Jesse Owens and Lutz Long) pasted in - as a token of our friendship, one that endured despite walls, border guards, and years of unanswered letters.

**Ireland**

In the mid 1980s I took our family on a two-week driving tour of Ireland, home of my paternal great-grandparents. I was to serve as our tour guide, choosing the places we would visit and sharing with the family what I had learned about each. At the end of the day, Kelly and Ryan gave me a grade, based on my performance.

They loved Killarney, as I knew they would. The horseback ride through the Gap of Dunloe was adventurous. The Torc Waterfall was most beautiful and the Ross Castle enchanting. I especially enjoyed the singing pubs, always tearing up with each moving rendition of "Danny Boy" or "Mother Macree." I received an A plus grade for my efforts.

I then drove them north to the town of Sligo, to visit Yeats' tomb in the protestant churchyard where Yeats' grandfather had been rector for many years.

The drive was arduous, with twisting roads, clogged with trucks, sheep, cows and bicycles. Intermittent rain fell from gloomy looking skies.

Sligo seemed like a pit hole of a town to all of us. The restaurant we picked had inedible meat and no vegetables or even Coca-Cola.

Ryan stared through the rain in the graveyard, with Mt. Ben Bulben towering behind us, reading aloud the engraving on a simple headstone: "Cast a cold eye on life, on death; Horseman, pass by." He hereupon threw up his hands and said "Dad, I don't believe it. You drive us over a horrible road to get to this awful town to look at a gravestone in the rain, with words that make no sense to me. You get an F minus for this."

Years later, when he was a senior at Duke University, Ryan took a final course in his English major, one on the life and works of William Butler Yeats. He showed me his last essay in the course, entitled "Casting a Cold Eye on Yeats' Tomb." In the paper, he reflected upon that day when he was 15 years old, and again seven years later, with a semester of Yeats permeating his Irish blood.

At the top of the paper was a grade - an A! I felt vindicated.

*John Davis Cantwell, M.D.*

**Summary**

I am occasionally asked what propels me to travel to remote regions of the world, dealing with the inconveniences of third world countries, enduring seasickness, foods teeming with coliform bacteria, and high altitude illness. Why do people climb mountains, other than that "they are there?"

Maybe René Daumal said it best:

"You cannot stay on the summit forever,
You have to come down again…
So why bother in the first place?
Just this: what is above knows what is below,
But what is below does not know what is above.
One climbs, one sees. One descends.
One sees no longer: but one has seen."

My family and I have fortunately seen some incredible things: the ink-black sky and radiant stars, with snow-capped Himalayan peaks soaring 25,000 feet or more on either side of the Glacier; the first view of the Matterhorn through our hotel window in Zermatt; Masai warriors, trekking up to our game park in Kenya to view the placenta of a newborn elephant, an act said to bring good luck; the little wave of an Israeli shepherd boy, as our van followed a twisting road beneath his pastureland; the breathtaking view of the illuminated Parthenon, as I sipped red Boutari wine from a rooftop restaurant; the harbor of Portofino, the walled city of Dubrovnik, the fiords of Milford Sound, Chateau Pontet Canet in Bordeaux.

*Adventures on Seven Continents And Other Essays*

I have seen. And I plan to keep seeing, whenever the opportunity arises. I share the spirit T.S. Eliot wrote about in "Little Gidding:"

"We shall not cease from exploration,
And the end of all our exploring
Will be to arrive where we started
And know the place for the first time."

*John Davis Cantwell, M.D.*

# 64

## SEARCHING FOR VAN GOGH IN THE SOUTH OF FRANCE

Peter Mayle spent a year in Provence. I only had a week, but what a wonderful week it was.

My main interest was to get a feel for what Vincent van Gogh saw, when he lived there over a century ago. I also wanted to visit some of the quaint hill towns (including Menerbes, Lourmarin, Roussilon and Gordes) and to enjoy prolonged lunches and dinners with my wife and three other couples.

Through a Toronto-based company, Vacancies Provencales, we rented a restored 17th century stone farmhouse outside of the town of Viens, 16 kilometers east of Apt. It was said to easily accommodate four couples (they didn't mention that one couple had to pass through another's bedroom during the night to use the bathroom) and to have a solar-heated swimming pool, alas under reconstruction, another point not mentioned.

We still had a terrific time. We rented three cars so there was a lot of flexibility in choosing the events for a given day. We had a schedule of the market days for the nearby hill towns, and a list of good restaurants. Each evening, over wine, cheese, and fresh garden salads, we would gather to recount our various adventures.

Our rented farmhouse in Provence

## Van Gogh

Vincent van Gogh was Dutch by birth. He came to Arles, seeking the "luminous colors like the ones in Japanese prints." While living in Paris he had been stimulated by the colors of the Impressionists and subsequently "… abandoned his dreary Dutch palette and developed his own virtuosity with color."

His life up to that point had seemed a failure. He was fired by an art dealer for "arguing too much," and didn't last long as a book store clerk. He took piano lessons but when he told the teacher that the notes "range from dark blue to yellow" the teacher thought him crazy and dismissed him. He worked as a lay preacher for a while, following in his father's footsteps. Assigned to a region in Belgium along the French border, he did evangelistic work among the poor, giving away

*John Davis Cantwell, M.D.*

most of his clothes and spending his nights nursing miners who had been burned in underground explosions. His neighbors felt that he was either mad, or a saint. His church supervisor eventually dismissed him "for lack of eloquence." Jobless, at age 26, he decided to become an artist. He studied art for a time in Antwerp, where one teacher dismissed his work as "petrified dogs". He failed art classes "because he refused to follow instructions."

**Letters to Theo - and Mental Illness**

A lot of what we know about van Gogh is based upon his 650 letters to his younger (by four years) brother, Theo, beginning when Vincent was 19. Theo was a branch manager of an art gallery, who bought all of Vincent's paintings that the latter did not trade or give away, sending him 150 francs per month. People often laughed when Theo showed them Vincent's works, so little was he appreciated in his time. Only one of his paintings was ever sold in his lifetime.

He was a different sort from early childhood, said to be "sorrowful yet always rejoicing," and had difficulty mingling with others. During 1882 and 1883 he lived with a prostitute and her two children. He wanted to marry her, but Theo managed to discourage him.

At Theo's suggestion, Paul Gauguin came to Arles to live with Vincent in the famous "yellow house." Gauguin managed the cooking and the finances. The relationship ended after only two months. Vincent had burst into Gauguin's room one night and wrote on the wall "I am the Holy Spirit, my spirit is whole," while laughing madly. Van Gogh later supposedly threatened Gauguin with a razor. Gauguin subsequently moved out. The following day van Gogh cut off part of his right ear, wrapped it in cloth, and presented it to "Rachel," at a local brothel.

He eventually asked to be admitted to St. Paul de Mausole, once a monastery in the 11th century and subsequently a mental hospital in St. Remy, 15 miles from Arles. He was there for about 12 months. For three and a half of those months he was too ill to paint, but he made up for it thereafter in a flurry of productivity, with over 100 paintings including "The Starry Night."

His room in the hospital is still in use, so a facsimile was made to satisfy the many tourists who visit.

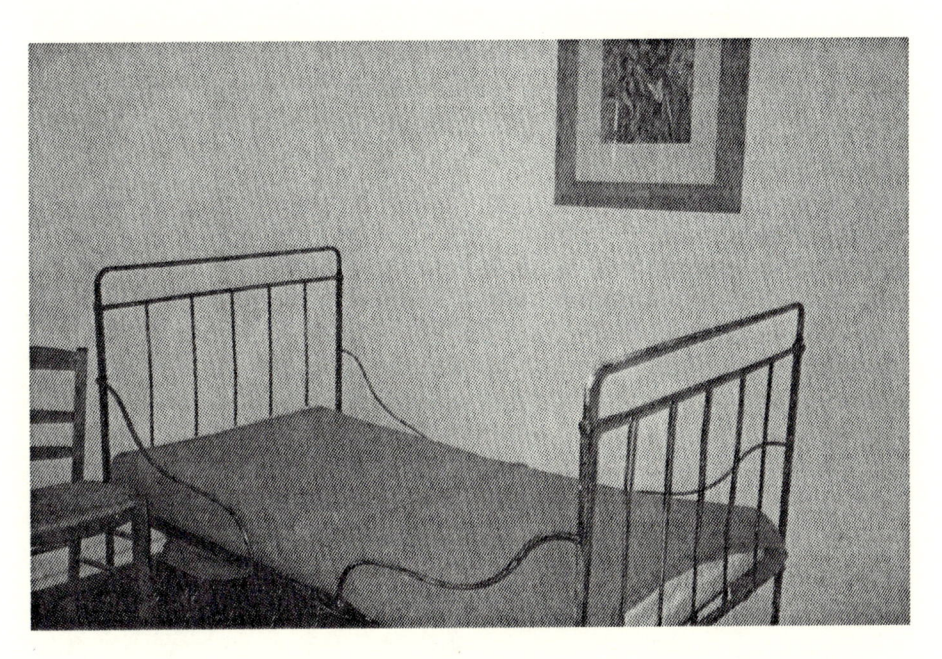

**Facsimile of van Gogh's hospital room in St. Remy**

*John Davis Cantwell, M.D.*

Across the hall is another room, containing the hot and cold baths which were used to treat his condition, felt to be acute mania, general delirium and epilepsy.

Van Gogh tried to "look upon madness as a disease like any other," a rather mature approach for his day.

**Dr. Gachet in Auvers**

Upon his release, van Gogh came to Paris, but "took fright at the noise and bustle." He left for nearby Auvers, where he would be under the medical care of 62-year-old Paul Gachet, M.D., a semi-retired homeopathic physician and art lover (also a friend of Pissarro, Cezanne, Renoir, and Manet).

Van Gogh found Dr. Gachet to be eccentric, with nervous troubles "at least as serious as mine," and felt it was like "one blind man leading another blind man." When Gachet expressed discouragement about his job as a doctor, as van Gogh did about his job as a painter, Vincent suggested that they swap jobs, to no avail.

In the 70 days van Gogh lived in Auvers, he painted about one masterpiece a day, worth over one billion dollars today. In 1990, his "Portrait of Dr. Gachet" sold for 82.5 million dollars, breaking his own record of 53.9 million dollars for "Irises".

Still mentally unbalanced, van Gogh borrowed or stole a gun one day and went out into the countryside where he shot himself in the abdomen. He walked back to his room. Besides the doctor, his brother Theo was summoned, and spent 12 hours at Vincent's bedside until his death on July 29, 1890. He was only 37, and had been a painter for 10 years. In his pocket

Theo found one last letter, that his brother had not mailed yet, which said "there are so many things I should like to write you about, but I feel it is useless."

## Possible Diagnoses

Speculation as to van Gogh's underlying illness has ranged from acute digitalis intoxication and acute intermittent porphyria to Geschwind's syndrome. Biochemist W. N. Arnold seemed to make the more sense to me. He proposed that van Gogh had Thujone poisoning. Thujone is a terpene, like camphor, which van Gogh took for his insomnia. It is a subclass of ketones that is found in wormwood, which in turn is a component of absinthe. Absinthe drinking was a social problem in the 19th and early 20th centuries, a cause of gastric irritation, mental deterioration and seizures. It was finally banned in France in 1922. Van Gogh was known to partake of this substance.

Even in death, van Gogh seemed in the grips of Thujone. Dr. Gachet had donated an ornamental tree for the grave site. The coffin was moved in 1905 to a larger plot that would also accommodate Theo's grave. The tree's roots had wrapped around Vincent's tomb. The tree, on closer inspection, was a Thuje tree, "a classic source of thujone."

*John Davis Cantwell, M.D.*

*Adventures on Seven Continents And Other Essays*

# FAMILY

*John Davis Cantwell, M.D.*

## 65

**BRAD**

Like E.T., he was funny-looking, emitted weird noises, drank and ate whatever he got his hands on (beer, wooden balls, plastic bananas, sponges), and brought out the best - and occasionally the worst - in those he encountered. Unlike the Extra-Terrestrial, he had a double row of teeth, repeatedly voided on his mother's best carpeting, and was not obsessed with phoning home, for he lived there for most of his life, within the warmth and security of a close-knit family.

Bradley arrived on a night I was to quarterback the Mayo Clinic residents' team against a squad of Rochester construction workers (affectionately known as the "cement heads"). It was cold and rainy, a miserable night for football, so I didn't mind accompanying my wife to the labor and delivery area of St. Mary's Hospital. I was hoping for a future all-American, a Rhodes scholar, or at least an Olympic candidate.

The birth was uneventful, but within several days my tearful wife told me (a mother's intuition, I guess) that Bradley was defective. I couldn't be sure, and neither could his pediatrician. The diagnosis was finally made several months later by a six-year-old boy in one of the waiting rooms of the Mayo Clinic: "My, what a tiny brain," he observed, after peering at Brad for a few minutes. He was right on target, for the infant had mild microcephaly and would be severely mentally retarded and epileptic.

*John Davis Cantwell, M.D.*

We moved to San Diego so I could study cardiology under Eugene Braunwald. My wife spent much of her time working with our son, feeling that it would make a great difference in his development, and expected me to do likewise. I rather resented this, as my studies were hard and my free moments all too infrequent. I didn't think my time with Brad was very productive. Once, however when I was home alone with him, I heard gurgling sounds from his bedroom. I rushed in and found him in the midst of a grand mal seizure. When it persisted, I carried him to the car and headed for San Diego County Hospital, where I worked. En route, he became cyanotic and, shortly thereafter, stopped breathing. I administered cardiopulmonary resuscitation, as best I could under the circumstances, while racing to the emergency room.

*Adventures on Seven Continents And Other Essays*

**Bradley and Marilyn**

*John Davis Cantwell, M.D.*

Their staff took over upon my arrival, and I was asked to sit in the waiting room. I heard a Code 99 page and saw the cardiac arrest team dash into Brad's room. I wondered if he would make it. I had some conflicting feelings at that point, for he seemed like such a bother and had little to offer (or so I thought).

He did survive and, months later, seemed to make some progress. He would scoot along the floor after his pacifier, and we were encouraged that he was learning to crawl. We eagerly awaited our next appointment with the pediatric neurologist to show him how much Brad had improved: "That's not really crawling," the neurologist said. "He's just making some primitive swimming-type motions on the floor." Our spirits were dashed, but received a lift when another neurologist, one a little more sensitive to people's feelings, explained: "Yes! He really is beginning to crawl - commando-style."

We moved to Atlanta for my military service and additional cardiology training. A daughter had been born in California, and, in Georgia, another son followed. I developed a keen appreciation for their rather routine development and looked forward to spare moments when I could take them on neighborhood walks, balancing with them delicately on stone ledges and searching diligently for the troll who allegedly lived beneath the little wooden bridge in a nearby park.

Twenty-nine years passed quickly. Helped by a combined family effort and the discipline, love and encouragement of a former nun (who directed the special school he attended), Brad learned to walk and feed himself and became partially toilet-trained. Through him, I discovered the Special Olympics and soon became one of the team doctors for Georgia, complementing my other role as a team physician for the Atlanta Braves. I find similarities between both groups of athletes, namely, the importance of doing one's best with whatever abilities one has and striving always to improve.

There were light moments. A little boy inquired as to what was wrong with Brad. When told that Brad's brain didn't work real well, he advised us to take him right back to the hospital and have it fixed. The daughter of a friend kept her distance, later telling her mother that she didn't want to catch whatever it was he had. Our other children took a cardiopulmonary resuscitation course and were advised to put in extra time practicing on "Annie." As they explained this to me, their eyes simultaneously rested on their older brother and mischievous smiles appeared on their faces. "Don't you dare!" I admonished them. Instead, my linebacker son occasionally used him as a tackling dummy, pouncing on him as Lawrence Taylor, the Giants ferocious player, would.

We became accustomed to the embarrassing moments: the piercing shrieks in fast-food places, the telephone caller who asked, "Did you get a new dog? I hear barking in the background." (No ma'am, that's just my son.)

I no longer feel that the time I spent with Brad was wasted. On the contrary, he became my favorite snuggling partner for weekend afternoon naps. He exuded a lot of love and tended to bring forth the best of qualities in those who encountered him. He opened my eyes to the satisfaction of volunteer work with children like him.

*John Davis Cantwell, M.D.*

Finally, he enhanced and matured my appreciation of his two siblings. I recall a moment when I was coaching third base in a Little League game. My younger son, a switch-hitter, came to bat, the last chance for our team to salvage an important victory. The opposing pitcher, who looked considerably older than 12 (maybe it was the mustache), was throwing bullets as the last rays of an afternoon sun gradually disappeared beneath the horizon. Ryan managed to foul off a pitch, took a called strike, and refrained from nibbling at several fastballs beyond the strike zone. I called time and discussed the situation with him. The final pitch came in at his knees. He swung hard, as I taught him to, and missed. The game was over.

I walked with him to the car, my arm around his shoulders. He can talk, he can run, and he can slide headfirst into second base like Pete Rose. I smiled, whispered a prayer of thanks, and told him that everything would be okay, for even Dale Murphy (his favorite Atlanta Braves player) occasionally went down swinging.

*Adventures on Seven Continents And Other Essays*

Ryan with Dale Murphy

*John Davis Cantwell, M.D.*

# 66

## A VERY SPECIAL OLYMPIAN

> ...while in your pride ye
> contemplate
> your talents, power, or wisdom,
> deem him not
> A burden of the earth!
> - Wordsworth

Three boys burst from the starting line and covered the distance in less than 10 seconds. Another lad, the blond in the middle lane, commanded all my attention. The starting gun made him laugh, and he was so limp from the heat he could barely take the first step. With his sister's help, he finally started walking by himself at the 25-yard mark. As he approached the finish line, the cheers of the onlookers reached a crescendo: "Come on Bradley! You can do it! You can *do* it!"

I cried as my son stumbled across that line into the arms of a teenage volunteer, for I could only think of the hours and hours his teachers, my wife and my other two children spent getting him to take that first step. One of the Atlanta Braves' outfielders pinned the ribbon on his shirt. Brad had finished fourth in the 50-yard "race" for his age group in the Georgia Special Olympics.

I have experienced the joy of winning consecutive state high school basketball championships, the Atlantic Coast Conference basketball title, of reaching Mt. Everest, and of completing the Boston Marathon. None of

*Adventures on Seven Continents And Other Essays*

these gave me any greater satisfaction than did the performance of my little boy.

*John Davis Cantwell, M.D.*

**Bradley and Me**

*Adventures on Seven Continents And Other Essays*

Bradley was mentally retarded. In a broad sense, mental retardation refers to a subnormal intellectual function that might be associated with impairments in learning, maturation, or social adjustment. Three percent of the children born annually in the United States are retarded. The social stigma of the condition, formerly an enormous problem, has gradually given way to the more positive approach of maximum use of whatever talents and capabilities retarded children possess. In the Special Olympic Games, for example, one's normal children are usually ignored while the retarded one gets all the attention, a switch from the usual situation.

The painfully slow progress of a retarded child can be discouraging. I was helped immensely by a poem I had read in sophomore English at Duke University. In "The Old Cumberland Beggar," William Wordsworth revealed the beauty of a seemingly helpless person who managed to draw our the goodness latent in each person:

> *"No-man is dear to man;*
> *the poorest poor*
> *Long for some moments in a*
> *weary life*
> *When they can know and feel*
> *that they have been,*
> *Themselves, the fathers and*
> *the dealers-out*
> *Of some small blessing: have*
> *been kind to such*
> *As needed kindness,*
> *for this single cause,*
> *That we have all of us one*
> *human heart."*

*John Davis Cantwell, M.D.*

I saw this goodness in the eyes of the bearded "counterculture" youth who patiently interpreted the events at the Georgia Special Olympics to a severely retarded and physically deformed child. I see it daily in the staffs of special education centers as they struggle against formidable odds to teach children to walk, feed themselves and use the bathroom.

Bradley gave my life an added dimension. He opened my eyes to the tremendous challenge of helping the mentally retarded in whatever way I can, as a former athlete serving the Special Olympics, and as a physician. My experience with him gave me a vast appreciation of the rather routine development of my other two children (as mentioned in ch. 65). I would still holler at Kelly, as a teenage daughter, when she tied up the telephone in endless conversations with her boyfriend; I got on Ryan when he spent too much time playing video games and not enough time working on his jump shot. But my occasional criticisms were always tempered by the joyful realization that they were happy, healthful children, able to dance to the beat of Michael Jackson's music, to sing, to play and to join us for family adventures - a hike along the Inca Trail to Machu Picchu, an excursion into Hezekiah's tunnel in Jerusalem.

Sharing Bradley's joys, sorrows, and frustrations has created a deep bond of love between my wife and me as we shared the various stages of his life. This involved angry exchanges with the local school board, multiple letters and meetings, and an encounter with their attorney. Our only option, it seemed, was to enroll him in a special school in Florida. The school was clean, the people were nice, and the other children seemed to look out for Brad. I wondered, though, if anyone tickled him during one of his silly little moods, causing him to laugh almost uncontrollably. Did they snuggle with him on the sofa on a Sunday afternoon, or swing with him in a hammock under a canopy of pine tree shade? Did anyone hold him tightly, whispering in his ear that he was a sweet, dear boy who was deeply loved, and never considered a bother.

My wife and I tried to meet whatever challenges arose, aided by the same kindness and concern that sustained Wordsworth's Cumberland Beggar: the one human heart.

*John Davis Cantwell, M.D.*

# 67

## LETTER TO A YOUNG SON

Dear Ryan,

In 1900 Amos Alonzo Stagg, a famous football coach, wrote a letter to his 14-month-old son telling him of some things about life that the father deemed important. As a young teenager I saw a copy of that letter; I was greatly impressed by the contents and have carried the reprint in my wallet ever since. It was my thought to write a similar letter if I were ever blessed with a son.

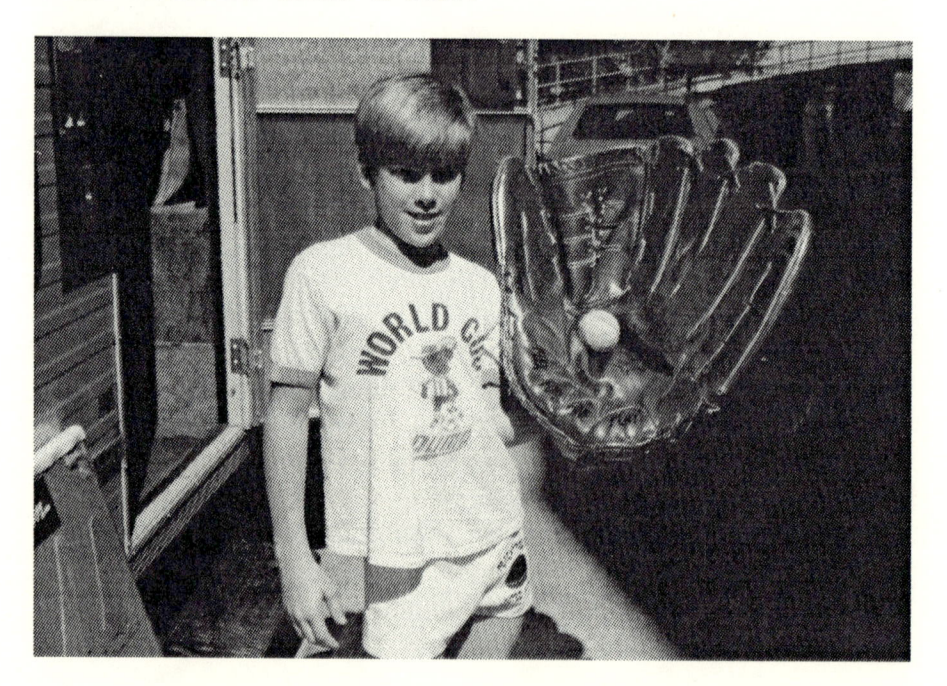

**Ryan at the Braves' spring training camp**

You are now six years old, a blond, rambunctious child. As Robert Frost would say, you are fast becoming a "swinger of birches." As you grow out of the stage of relative innocence and into that of manhood, your father would like you to think very seriously about the following suggestions:

1. Seek to strengthen your faith in God by practicing the Biblical guidelines on a daily basis. A good Christian, like a good athlete, does not get that way overnight. It requires a lifelong commitment of practice and study.
2. Be physically active all of your life. Learn the sporting skills in youth that you can enjoy forever. Remember - the true athlete remains a sportsman all of his life, not just during his school days.
3. In selecting an occupation, choose one that you thoroughly enjoy and one that enables you to do the most good. Consider, for example, the life of an artist or a fine craftsman. Their vocation is their avocation, an ideal combination; their work is enjoyed and appreciated by all who view it. Realize that the status of one's chosen occupation should be a secondary consideration; I have known happy and successful common laborers and some very unfulfilled wealthy professional people. I am biased toward the vocation of a physician, which (according to Stevens in 1848) "is the spirit of true Christianity in action. It consists not alone in healing the sick, in soothing the afflicted, and recalling the wandering intellect, but also in cherishing a love of peace and

*John Davis Cantwell, M.D.*

moderation amongst all men, and in promoting moral and intellectual improvement. The practicing of the healing art is an occupation intrinsically dignified."
4. Practice self-discipline, particularly regarding your thoughts and words, until you have learned to master yourself. You may never entirely succeed, but should strive toward that end.
5. Cultivate an interest in all types of people and in all aspects of life. Be a student all of your days. Know that it does not detract from one's manhood to appreciate the beauty of poetry, azaleas in full bloom, and the symphony. Your grandfather, a country doctor, had many diverse hobbies and interests such that he felt as much at home amidst farmers as he did with university professors. I would like you to develop this admirable trait.
6. Do not be motivated by the crowd; instead, step to your own drummer. If your peers decide to experiment with drugs, sex and the like, make your own decisions based upon your upbringing and stick to them. Keep abreast of current styles and thoughts and always be amenable to changes, but weigh each separately before modifying your life habits.
7. Give a part of yourself to a worthwhile cause without putting a price tag on the talent you offer. One such cause to consider is the affliction your older brother has, namely mental retardation. Love him dearly, do not be upset when your friends tease you about him, and

*Adventures on Seven Continents And Other Essays*

get to know some of the wonderful people who have been involved in his care. Search within yourself to find some way in which you can contribute.

These are only one man's thoughts. You will have to make the ultimate decisions. I have great confidence in you, my precious boy. I trust that God will always make His face to shine upon you.
With love,
Your Father

*John Davis Cantwell, M.D.*

# 68

## TO A TEENAGE DAUGHTER

Dear Kelly,

You have recently become a teenager, a milestone in your life. It seems like only yesterday when you were a little blond girl, excitedly pointing out boats to me at Lake Geneva and refusing to go down the slippery slide.

Words cannot express what a true joy you have been to your mother and me. I treasure the memories of our time together and of the various stages you have passed through. I look forward to sharing the forthcoming main events in your life, such as high school, college, boyfriends, marriage, career, and motherhood.

You have a wonderful role-model in your mother. Strive to imitate her combinations of sweetness and inner strength, her compassion and unselfishness.

*Adventures on Seven Continents And Other Essays*

**Kelly, in her teens**

(Do keep more heat on in your own house during wintertime, however, and stock a few more goodies in your refrigerator.)

We have tried to give you a good Christian upbringing, a base upon which you can build. You are cute, sensitive to the needs of others, and smart enough to become anything you so choose. Dare to be great, yet strive for happiness. Pass on your strong sense of values to your own children.

Set high standards for your future husband, as I did for my wife. Make it a permanent relationship, not a passing fancy as so many do these days.

Be physically active all of your life. At the same time, enjoy the many other facets of life such as good literature, music and art. Dig deep to expose your own creative talents, and pursue them to the fullest extent.

Travel the world, if the occasion occurs, learning from people of various nations. I

*John Davis Cantwell, M.D.*

cherish the experiences I have had, and hope you can do the same.

Finally, continue to study the Bible and use it as a guideline, along with prayer, when you are faced with important decisions in future years. Don't hesitate to use your faith as a "hiding place" in turbulent times.

I have great confidence in you, my precious daughter. Remember always that your parents love you, just as you are.

Your Father

Adventures on Seven Continents And Other Essays

# 69

## LETTERS FROM A YOUNG MAN AT WAR

In his book, *The First World War*, Martin Gilbert concludes: "All wars end to being reduced to statistics, strategies, debates about their origins and results. These debates about war are important, but not more important than the human story of those who fought in them."

To me, that human story is preserved in a packet of letters I came upon, letters my father wrote from military training camps and from the battlefields of France, 84 years ago. His mother had saved all of them, as mothers are sometimes want to do.

My father was just 18 years old, fresh off the football fields of his high school days, when he enlisted in the army. Years later he never talked much about his war experiences, and I wasn't mature enough to ask him about them in greater detail. Perhaps he would not have said much even if I'd asked, as men of that era (and even today) tend to put memories of war experiences in the closet of their minds.

As Gilbert recounts, the war was triggered by the assassination of the heir to the Austrian Hapsburgs, Franz Ferdinand, in Sarajevo, by the 19-year-old Serbian, Gavrilo Princip. The winds of war had been blowing for a few years prior, however, and even in 1905 Germany developed a plan to attack France, coming through Belgium and Holland.

My father's letters begin from Waco, Texas, where he was sent for military training. One

473

*John Davis Cantwell, M.D.*

can sense in his letters a deep feeling of patriotism, a certain bravado that youth are blessed with, a sense of fatalism, and a longing for things and people near and dear to him.

**My father, Arthur Cantwell, in 1918**

*Adventures on Seven Continents And Other Essays*

*December 12, 1917* (Waco, Texas)

I have some news to tell you, which will no doubt cause you to worry, but I hope that you will take it the way I do. We are to leave for regions unknown:

...We are the first bunch of Guards to go, because we have proven ourselves soldiers, and the government has picked us to go first. Troops will be moving right along and the plan is to have two million there by April...I will write four times per week in order that some may reach you.
...I am leaving with the knowledge that mother will get $20.00 per month and that I am insured for $10,000. That makes me feel good, to think that I am worth something.
...I sure am glad that I am able to take part in the greatest of all wars, because it's always been my ambition to be a soldier.

*January 19, 1918* (From Jersey City, N.J., after a train trip from Waco)
...We are in one of the largest camps in the U.S...We are supposed to be ready to go to France and the next step is boarding the boats.

*February 17, 1918* (From Ireland and England, after his troop ship "Tuscania" was torpedoed and sunk)
...I suppose you folks were mightily worried about me. I got off the "Tuscania" in fine style, did not even get wet...I kept cool and that is why I got off. I now feel able to hold my own at any time.
...The British Army is made up of fine fellows. Every one of them are men and are helping us as much as they can. Our two

*John Davis Cantwell, M.D.*

countries have been knit together by this war and the two armies act like brothers.

We have been filmed and if you see any of the pictures, look for a fellow with a heavy red beard and mustache. Am growing a good red chaplin that would do credit to Dad.

How is my horse, cat and chickens? Take good care of them and trusting that I will be back before many moons.

...Tell Dad that his parents left a mighty fine country (Ireland). In fact, the prettiest that I have ever seen. Am going back there if I ever get the chance.

*March 27, 1918* (Somewhere in France)

...I have not seen one good-looking French girl. Those Arabian night tales in the States are all bosh. We are in a great game now and in order to win we must leave both wine and women alone. And I want to win!

*May 12, 1918* (Mother's Day, Somewhere in France)

Today, as you no doubt know, is Mother's Day. Every soldier in the A.E.F (American Expeditionary Forces) is *asked* to write to his mother. ...Remember, Mother, if I fail to come back, I only did my duty, and someone has got to pay the price. I was a volunteer, as I thought it was my duty to go, and I'll always think the same...I would like to get back home again, but if fate wills different, I paid the price for democracy. But I will get back, if given half a chance.

*June 16, 1918* (France)

...The Hun is a regular wolf, brave with a big bunch but yellow when he meets an equal foe. The Yanks will push him back across the Rhine when they once get started.

...Shawano must be real quiet since all of the "toughs" have gone to war.

*Adventures on Seven Continents And Other Essays*

*June 23, 1918* (France)

...Dad, my two brothers learned many things while at school, but I have learned a few lessons in the bitter school of army experiences. They are to appreciate a good home, to save money, how to meet all kinds of men, how to avoid temptations, but the best one is HOME, and when I return I'll never cross the county line again. This game has been a great one for me and I never would be contented to go back to school again. That's too tame for me; I want to get into some line of business as soon as I get back and my sole object will be to make money.

*July 22, 1918* (France)

...I saw in today's paper where the people of New York want Teddy (Roosevelt) for Governor. He sure is a great man and his sons are chips from the old block. He has reason to be proud of them all, and his youngest died like a hero, and that's the easiest death of all. We are all fatalists over here, and are all waiting to take a crack at old Bill (Kaiser Wilhelm) and then go back home.

We expect to make another trip and do not, of course, know the date or the destination. But the old war holds no terrors for me now, and all of the boys are anxious to get to Chateau Thierry, because that's where the big fight is on.

You talk about thrills. Nothing beats riding along a camouflaged road, because you are well aware what the camouflage is for. With the barrages at night, the aero flights in the day time and our steady work, you can well imagine how the time flies. I hardly ever know the day or date.

*John Davis Cantwell, M.D.*

If you will send me Bill Wallrich's[*] address, I will try and locate him or at least write to him. If I know the number of his division I will be on the lookout for him.

*August 29, 1918* (France)

I picked up a casualty list yesterday and saw where Bill Wallrich was killed in action. Seemed hard to believe and I can well picture what (sadness) it will cause in Shawano.

When such things appear you folks back home are excited, etc., but imagine us fellows at the front. We take it as a matter of fact, because our time is taken up chasing the Hun and the days of sorrow must be put off. We are downhearted when such news comes, but we are in a stiff game.

It is getting colder here and reminds a fellow that winter is coming. The boys are fighting like tigers and we hope to have them across the Rhine before winter.

*September 4, 1918* (France)

...I suppose you have read General Pershing's order of the day, citing the divisions for their work during the 2nd Battle of the Marne. The old 32nd has done her bit and will continue too, until it is finished.

...I don't know how Dad is on politics nowadays, but I think the sun rises and sets on Roosevelt. He is a dandy fighter and game to the core. Teddy is one great man, in my opinion, and it's too bad that he can't grab a gun and help the boys in the line.

*September 9, 1918* (France)

...As you well know (I saw in a paper where General March announced that the 32nd was the unit operating north of Soissons and the one that took Juvigny and Terny), we have been

---

[*] *Another soldier from Shawano, Wisconsin.*

where the fighting was the thickest. The 32nd is one of the best (we call it the best division in the army) and when they want real fighting done they call on the 32nd.

...You asked about church services. Well, Mother, they are hardly needed at the front. Our one thought and action is the fight and we have not time for anything else. We are all fatalists and it fits in fine. When we get back to a rest area we can attend services at the YMCAs, but they are not up at the lines. You see (as always), I have some excuse for not going to church.

You wrote about that drive for Fismes. Well, it was our old F Company that took it from the Hun and they did great fighting at the Marne and also at the Aisne. Both are called rivers, but although quite deep are not as wide as the pond at home. The Hun blew up the bridges, but the allied engineers built pontoon bridges and later some stationary ones. It won't be long before we bridge the Rhine, either.

...I am still driving the car and it has stood up fine under the conditions. The roads at the front are usually bad (shell holes, etc) and such bumpy roads are not very good.

...Chateau Thierry is quite a place now. When we first entered, it was almost a pile of ruins for the Hun had just left. But when we pulled through again on our way to this front it was quite a place again. The French are great at reconstruction. It must have been a swell place in its day, sort of a summer resort.

*September 22, 1918* (France)

...The Hun is getting an awful trimming, and it seems like fate, the different Allies seem to be taking turns. Soon, it will be ours on the Western Front again, and when the Allies

*John Davis Cantwell, M.D.*

hit the line (it will be like the old football days), it will crack and we will go over, not for a touchdown but for victory.

Dad, you remember how crazy I was about baseball and big leaguers, don't you? Well, I don't give a whoop for the game and the players either. It makes me sore to hear of them playing the World Series,* and joining the Steel League, when they ought to be over here fighting. About the only big league star over here (who was not drafted) is Hank Gowdy, and he is the only *real sport* of the bunch.

...I have seen many beautiful women of late, but they don't bother me at all. Have no use for this at this game. The results would be too much. I don't use tobacco either - shows that I am holding on to myself.

...One thing the Yanks don't like is the efforts of some people to make the States dry in their absence. With the big jobs we have before us, any quabbling about booze makes us tired. England and France both issue liquor to their troops and are the leaders in all of the battles. The boys say that they will vote the States wet again (in case they go dry) when they come back, or they will stay in France. Not for me, as our old well produces the best liquid that I have ever tasted.

*November 1, 1918* (France)

As you well know, tomorrow at eleven, Marshall Foch demands an answer. While we all hope for peace, if the Hun plays the bullheaded stuff, well-enough, for the Allies will then give them an awful trimming.

*November 11, 1918* (France, in a letter to his brother, Rog.)

---

* *Babe Ruth was the pitching star for the Boston Red Sox, winning two games against the Chicago Cubs.*

Well, old Boy, the war is over and the Huns are beaten. I figured they would give in and at the present writing the armistice is in effect.

...I'll bet the States are putting on some celebrations and I sure would like to be there. But with good luck we will figure in on a few good times of our own.

Dad and Mother must be happy and they are probably worrying about me still. But I am okay and have gone through some bad stuff, Rog, and will take good care of myself until I return.

*November 24, 1918* (Letter to father, overview of war experience. On way to Germany)

The whole A.E.F. celebrates by writing to their dads, and it is with great pleasure that I write for your work on the Draft Board has been the real stuff. You helped back the "boys" here, and did it without a murmur.

Censorship rules have loosened up a bit, and I will attempt to give a short diary of my life abroad.

It was 10 months ago that the good ship Tuscania pulled from New York Harbor. We boarded January 23rd from Hoboken, N.J., and it sure was cold when we left. We were not allowed on deck but I managed to see the old "Goddess" (Statue of Liberty) when we left. Sure will be glad to see her again.

We had a fine trip across *while it lasted!* To make the story short, we were met by the Kaiser's sub on February 5th. We landed (from a destroyer) in Ireland and were treated royally. We went to Dublin (on the rocky railroad) to board our steamer for England. Stayed in England about six weeks.

*John Davis Cantwell, M.D.*

We reached France about the 20th of March...I then drove the Captain's Dodge and to date have covered about 11,000 miles.

We left for Fontaine (Alsace) the 12th of May, stayed in the vicinity until the 24th of July when we left for stations unknown - which later turned out to be Chateau Thierry. Entered the city the 8th of July and the division went into battle on the 30th. The 32nd Division went 18 km in six days and the bunch covered themselves with glory. We were stationed at Mezy - across the Marne - near where Bill Wallrich is buried.

While at Mezy we got the first taste of real Hun bombing (they bombed a Red Cross Hospital nearby). I never thought a fellow could get so scared as I was that night, but my pride overcame my fear and I wouldn't run from any Hun, aviator or not. Bunches of fellows were running for dugouts but I stayed in the car. We have had many such entertainments since and I never ran either (don't think I'm bragging because I'll admit that I almost lost my jaw - it was on the verge of rattling off). We were at Vic Sur Aisne - and fought with the French under General Maugin, who commanded the 10th French army. We lost Eli (Elefson)[*] this time.

We left here to join the 1st American Army and were stationed at Chevillon about September 12 where the army went into action. We were in the rear (for a change), left for Fleury Sur Aire, then moved to Dombasle - for the battle of Argonne. Moved near Montfavion, then to Boutheville and finally to Dun Sur Muse when the armistice went into effect. Some relief, too.

---

[*] *The star halfback on the high school football team.*

*Adventures on Seven Continents And Other Essays*

The 32nd has had her share of the battles and now is marching on to the Rhine.

*December 17, 1918*

Well, Mother, we have crossed the Rhine and are now at the end of our journey...I am billeted in a German house and am almost part of the family. There is a piano in our room and the head of the house (it's a man here) plays for us...The German people now hate the Kaiser and they realize how they were duped. They are a good class of people and it would be a good country to live in if they had a good government.

*December 25, 1918* (Marienrachdorf, Germany)

On this glad day I address my family greeting to you. Last evening everything looked gloomy, but after helping the German lady trim her tree for her kids I went to bed. Christmas morning I woke up and found about three inches of snow on the ground and that looked better...We had pork roast for dinner and after our eleven months of Bully Beef you can well imagine how swell it tasted. Also had mashed spuds with brown gravy, pickles, bread and butter, applesauce and Lowny chocolates.

*January 13, 1919* (Marienrachdorf, Germany)

...We have heard that Teddy R. is dead. He sure was a great man and I have all but worshipped him since joining the A.E.F. Surely was too bad he did not live to see the new Col. Roosevelt (of the 1st Division) and his other son return to the U.S. Of all fighters, Teddy was the best and I can well picture the States in mourning for the man who first stated "100 percent Americanism." *May 21, 1919* (Camp Morrison, Newport News, Virginia)

At last, after almost 16 months of foreign service, I am back in God's country, and to try to express my feelings is impossible. I

*John Davis Cantwell, M.D.*

walk around feeling better than any king and I will soon be home.

We had a hard trip across as the battleship, Virginia, is a tub. I telegraphed to you the minute I got off the boat, thanks to the Red Cross women who met us at the pier.

...I had my first ice cream (real stuff) yesterday on the way out here, a good 5 cent cone.

Don't plan on meeting me, except at the old depot, as I want to drop in as if nothing happened and be home with you folks. I am going to stop in Chicago and take a good Turkish bath and then, after leaving the mud, etc., of Europe behind, will speed homeward.

Your son,
Arthur Allen Cantwell

**Comment**

Other participants in the war, besides my father, included Adolf Hitler, Charles DeGaulle, Douglas MacArthur, Ernest Hemingway, Mustafa Kemal Ataturk, Joyce Kilmer, Alvin York and Erwin Rommel, plus a cast of millions.

The United States declared war on Germany on April 6, 1917, about two months after Germany instituted unrestricted submarine warfare against all shipping in the Atlantic. Over one million American troops were brought across the Atlantic in convoy between May 1917 and November 1918. Only 637 drowned as a result of German submarine activity, including 210 in the sinking of my father' ship, the Tuscania.

At the 15-year reunion of the Tuscania survivors, each person was given a little medal which is a treasured family keepsake now.

*Adventures on Seven Continents And Other Essays*

The United States lost 48,000 soldiers in the war, including my father's boyhood friends, Bill Wallrich and Eli Elefson. Sixty two thousand other American soldiers died of influenza.

Overall, the Central Powers lost 3.5 million soldiers, mainly Germans and Austrians. The victorious Allies lost 5.1 million, with Russia (1.7 million) and France (1.38 million) being the heaviest losses. About 5600 soldiers were killed each day of the war. In the Battle of the Somme, the British had 20,000 deaths the first day. The war contributed to the fall of the Romanov dynasty, the Hapsburgs, and the Hohenzollern kings.

In his letters home, my father indicated that after the war his sole object was to get into business and make money. He apparently did not find this to be very satisfying, for he eventually went to medical school and practiced OB-GYN in his hometown for 37 years, until his sudden death at age 71.

He didn't travel much after the war, convinced that "home" had all that he needed - friends, family, a nice house on the river and a farm and cabin less than two miles away.

He never did get back to Ireland.

*John Davis Cantwell, M.D.*

# 70

## THE MAN AT THE WINDOW

    The rain splattered off my head, while tears streamed down my cheeks, as I waited for the car that would take me to the Florida hospital. The phone call had awakened me from a sound sleep. He had suddenly toppled out of his chair, while visiting with friends. An ambulance had been called, but there were delays because of the bad weather. I knew he was dead.

    A flood of memories. A busy small-town physician, he always found time for his children. Once, just before the start of a high school football game, played in bitter cold and snow flurries, I glanced at our side of the field before kicking off and saw a solitary figure in the stands. I knew immediately who it was. At my age then - 18 - he had gone from the football fields to the battle ground in France (see chapter 69), surviving a direct torpedo hit on his troop ship. He came back from the war, got a degree in business and sold ice cream for a while, before finally deciding to follow his father and brother into the medical profession.

    I must confess, he was a bit of an eccentric. He once made a deal with an in-law from Montana, a bonafide cowboy; if the cowboy died first, Dad would fly out to the funeral, make sure there weren't any flowers, and provide ice cream and cake for all the children in town. If Dad was the first to go, the cowboy would put Dad's aging horse to sleep and have them buried side-by-side.

*Adventures on Seven Continents And Other Essays*

He encouraged me in sports, and was pleased when I expressed an interest in medicine: he never pushed, however. According to Mother, when we were small, he used to grumble whenever called out on night duty. She mentioned once that it might discourage one of his children from following in his footsteps, and thereafter never heard another complaint.

When I later complained about how hard I had to study that first year in medical school, he reminded me that early in his practice he had evening hours, 6-10 p.m., six nights a week. I asked him if he didn't have guilt feelings about not having office hours on Sunday nights, and he gave me a playful cuff on the ear. Upon my graduation from medical school he presented me with a used 1965 red Mustang convertible.

*John Davis Cantwell, M.D.*

**Dad and me, with my medical school graduation present**

He had a wide variety of interests, ranging from collecting silver dollars to riding horses. His friends were from all walks of life - farmers, Harvard professors, former Chicago Bear linemen. He was very strict, and felt that the only thing worse than a spoiled dog was a spoiled kid. He wouldn't allow us to sleep late or to talk back, and was good about finding work for us to do, feeling that it helped build character.

His first heart attack was probably the day of my wedding. He had a low-grade fever and felt a little "punk." While I was getting into my tuxedo, he asked me to give him a shot of penicillin; I refused, telling him that he needed proper cultures first. I relented when he threatened to have the maid do it. He still wasn't up to par the following weekend, when one of my brothers got married. He finally had a physical examination and ECGs which confirmed the diagnosis. He later said that taking two blonds into the family in successive weekends was enough to give any man a heart attack.

He and Mother stayed with us in Atlanta for several days before our final trip to Florida. I was training for my first Boston Marathon, running 2.5 mile loops, each of which took me past the bay window of our rented home. He would anticipate my arrival, stand at the window in his bathrobe, and wave me on for another lap, with a big smile on his face.

Our last day together began with stimulating conversation over a leisurely breakfast. I went for a long run, enjoying the flat Florida terrain and the refreshing ocean breeze. We saw a preseason baseball game that afternoon, the Baltimore Orioles versus the Washington Senators. Ted Williams was one of the managers. David and Julie Nixon Eisenhower sat several rows in front of us. Dad liked the swing of an Oriole rookie outfielder, and correctly predicted that the young man would have a successful career. That evening we had dinner with friends, topped off by hot apple pie a la mode (he always said it was a crime to serve pie without ice cream). I asked to be dropped off at our hotel room, fatigued by the 15-mile run, while the rest headed up the coast to the friends' condominium. I sometimes wonder, had I been along, if the outcome of the ensuing cardiac arrest might have been

*John Davis Cantwell, M.D.*

different. I suspect not, because prompt defibrillation would still not have been available.

Dad had died three weeks before what was to be my first Boston Marathon. I forgot all about the race. Just before my return to Atlanta from his funeral in Wisconsin, Mother called me into her study. Always a quiet steadying influence throughout my life, she asked me to resume my training, reminding me how proud Dad had been of my athletic ventures as well as my scholastic ones. I did as she wished and struggled through the cold rain to the finish, thinking of my father a lot during the last five miles.

Thirty-two years have passed. A blond grandson, born several months after Dad's death, became a strapping middle linebacker on the high school team and is now a physician. A granddaughter, whom he only knew as an infant, is now a mother of two, expecting a third.

He would have been proud of them both. I still walk the same neighborhood circuit, which takes me past the house we used to rent. I can almost visualize his image at the window, a grin on his face, waving me on for yet another lap. I always dig into the upcoming hill, my arms pumping hard, my respirations synchronized with my footsteps, grateful for the man and the memory.

# 71

## MR. MAGOO

Other than one hospitalization for a sport-related concussion, five episodes of atrial fibrillation, squamous cell and basal cell skin cancers, a ruptured lumbar disc, a bout of depression and benign essential blepharospasm (BEB), I've been blessed with excellent health, good enough to jog (or rather limp) to the finish line of the 1996 Boston and New York Marathons.

Unlike my earlier maladies, which were just transient obstacles to overcome, the most recent condition, BEB, is likely to be with me throughout the rest of my life.

It began at an inopportune time, early in my Olympic medical work, but then again diseases take no prisoners, follow no particular schedule, spare neither kings nor paupers.

The initial symptoms were subtle, as they are in so many diseases. I seemed to be squinting a lot, blinking excessively. Did I need a new prescription for my eyeglasses? Were the sunglasses shaded enough?

I mentioned the symptoms to an ophthalmologist. He did a thorough examination and did detect a mild change in my vision. New lenses were ordered. The symptoms increased.

I told my dermatologist about the symptoms, while seeing him for some actinic keratoses. He suggested that I dip Q-tips in baby oil and roll them up and down the eyelids and eyelashes, to cleanse any possible irritating debris. I did this religiously. It didn't help.

*John Davis Cantwell, M.D.*

I was referred to another ophthalmologist, who performed an additional examination, and thought as did the dermatologist there might be a mild inflammation of the eyelids. Antibiotic drops were tried, to no avail.

One of his partners suggested another type of antibiotic, again without appreciable results. I tried a pair of trifocals, without any benefit.

I began to read about my symptoms. Could it be iritis? Uveitis? In my reading I came up with a disorder called benign essential blepharospasm, a disorder which may begin in my age group and is frequently very subtle in its early phases, and elusive to even the best of specialists. It seemed the most likely diagnosis to me.

I consulted a neurologist. It was a possibility, he said, even though I didn't display any obvious manifestations of blepharospasm in his office. Perhaps he could call one of my colleagues, I suggested, one who sees me virtually every day at the office and can describe her observations to him. He agreed, and based on what he was told, referred me to a neuro-ophthalmologist, who confirmed the diagnosis.

I work as one of the team physicians for the Atlanta Braves. Typically during night games, I am the only person in the stands, other than Jane Fonda, to be wearing dark glasses. This seems appropriate, since the disease has a prevalence of one in 50,000. The cause isn't known. A genetic predisposition is suspected, maybe a defect in the basal ganglia of the brain. My mother's side of the family, originally from Wales, seemed prone to some unusual diseases. They were also right-brain types - musicians, professors, writers.

Perhaps I picked up some of the good and some of the bad.

I contacted the head of a famous clinic, an eye specialist who once was a medical resident with me during the formative years, and who had written about BEB. He would be changing planes at the Atlanta airport in several weeks, and would be happy to discuss aspects of the disease, along with therapeutic options, with me.

In brief, his main recommendation was botulism toxin injections, to temporarily weaken the orbicularis oculi muscles and reduce the blepharospasm. I have been doing this for several years now, with modest temporary benefit. Some associated facial grimacing has developed, perhaps the beginning of Meig's syndrome. Patients with this variant tend to respond less readily to "bo-tox" injections than those without.

My neuro-ophthalmologist is appropriately empathetic and very supportive. I hope the changing healthcare scene will allow me to continue under his care.

The facial component can look like a smile to some, a wince to others. There are light moments. I move to the front of the fast-food restaurant to order lunch. The waitress tells me I must be an insurance salesman. "Why?" I ask. "Because you are always smiling," she says, "and someone trying to sell you insurance does that." "No, I'm not an insurance salesman," I state. "Well, what do you sell?" she asks. "Nothing." "Well, what do you do?" "I'm a physician," I add. "What kind?" "Heart." "Oh good," she comments, "I've had this problem..." "Look," I say, "I don't mean to appear abrupt, but I'm in a hurry and

*John Davis Cantwell, M.D.*

would just like to order a grilled chicken sandwich."

A patient was telling me about her chest pain. "Why are you smiling?" she asks. "It is really a bothersome problem, not a laughing matter." "I'm sorry," I state. "I wasn't smiling or laughing at you. I have this condition of the eyes and face, and it sometimes appears as if I'm smiling."

At a planning meeting for Olympic medical care I sip a Pepsi. A doctor across the way says "you really must hate that drink. Do you have Coca-Cola stock or something?" "No," I respond, I have this condition of the eyes and face…"

Walking down the hall of the hospital, after leaving a patient's room, another patient passes me and remarks, "It must be a private joke." It dawns on me, back in my office, that he must have thought I was smiling to myself about something. One could do a lot worse, I guess, than to have a disorder that causes one to smile, or even to wince.

Patients deal with disorders in different ways. I liked Bobby Jones' approach to his syringomyelia (an Everest compared to my Stone Mountain). He held a press conference, described the condition, and said he believed in playing the ball where it lays, and never mentioned it again. Edith Wharton, in **A Backward Glance**, advised us that to better cope with illness or sorrow, and to "…remain alive long past the usual date of disintegration," one could strive to be "…unafraid of change, insatiable in intellectual curiosity, interested in big things, and happy in small ways."

I am reminded about a cartoon character from my childhood, Mr. Magoo, who breezed through life, despite his visual handicap, seemingly protected by some unseen benefactor. In a way, I see myself as the embodiment of Magoo, well-meaning, perhaps a bit crotchety at times, negotiating my way through the maze of life, handicapped just a little, uncertain of the future coarse of the disorder, but guided by an unseen hand.

*John Davis Cantwell, M.D.*

# 72

## A FAMILY OF NURSES

Kelly Cantwell Myers, R.N.

*Adventures on Seven Continents And Other Essays*

To Kelly Cantwell Myers, R.N.

Dear Kelly,
On the occasion of your 30th birthday, I wanted to tell you about the two nurses who preceded you in the family, namely your great-grandmother and your grandmother. They left you a rich legacy.

**Katherine Lee Davis, with her first three daughters, (including my mother, center)**

This picture was made 90 years ago, in Bozeman, Montana. Your great-grandmother, Katherine Lee (Davis), is on the right. Your grandmother, Alice Davis (Cantwell), is in the middle, about age four.

Katherine's given name was Elisa Katherine Lee, born to Mr. and Mrs. Frederick E. Lee in Somerset, Kentucky, in 1878. One of 10

John Davis Cantwell, M.D.

children, she came to Belgrade, Montana, (near Bozeman) at age two as the Civil War had ravaged their Kentucky area. Her mother died three years later, of typhoid fever.

The childrens' father "was a typical wild western product with vices and virtues mixed in proportion suitable for Bozeman in its palmiest days." The family "grew up in a little log cabin in the days of Indians." Frederick Lee "would go off on a three-day toot, and the little kids would be all alone. Sometimes the Indians would come in and take their food." Their mother's family, the Cowans, "would look in on them once in a while."

Katherine dropped her first name, Elisa, when kids started teasing her, calling her "Lizzy Lee." She decided to go by Kate. She grew into a strong, big, good-looking woman, "afraid of nothing or nobody." She "would bang away at anything with her shotgun."

In the late 1800s, Kate went to Salida, Colorado, for nurses' training, and worked temporarily at the Denver and Rio Grande Railroad Hospital.

William Owen Davis, From Racine, Wisconsin, went west with a friend on the railroad around 1900 for health reasons (he had a tendency to lung congestion). The railroad was also heavily recruiting young men with promises of a land that greatly exceeded reality. Will enjoyed singing, especially church hymns, and while in Bozeman went to the Baptist Church, where he met Kate. On his return to Racine, he corresponded with her and they were eventually married in Chicago in 1902. They lived in the old homestead near Racine, but Kate missed Montana a great deal so they bought a farm in

*Adventures on Seven Continents And Other Essays*

Bozeman. After several years there, it was Will who became homesick for Wisconsin and he returned for a year with Kate and the three children in the picture. The strong-willed independent Kate "did not feel that she fit in well and decided she would return to Montana, with our without her spouse." The family moved back west, intact.

Kate never returned to nursing, to my knowledge. An ideal mother, she reared eight children. One died of appendicitis at age 15. All of the others became college graduates, quite a feat at that time, eventually married and had children of their own.

Alice Davis was Kate's and Will's third child. Her older sisters tended to be sickly, so she bore the brunt of the farm work, milking six cows before going to school in the morning and helping her father with other chores.

She attended public school in Bozeman, across from the present Historical Society. At age 18, she came to Chicago and entered Evanston Hospital as a student nurse, completing the course in four years. She did some private nursing and then worked as a night supervisor, at both Evanston and Passavant Hospitals.

She met a medical intern, Arthur Allen Cantwell (your grandfather), at Evanston Hospital and they were married in 1933 at her uncle's home in Wilmette, Illinois.

Like Kate, Alice gave up her nursing career after marriage to rear four children. When Sally developed bulbar polio in 1948, Mother drew on her nursing skills. She and Dad literally moved to Madison during Sally's

*John Davis Cantwell, M.D.*

hospitalization, providing around-the-clock medical and nursing care as best they could.

You knew Mother later in life. She was always a hard worker, a trait from her childhood. Totally devoted to Dad and to us, I couldn't have asked for a better mother. She would invariably find something positive to say after one of my athletic events even if I had an off game and our team had been soundly trounced. She was especially nice to new people moving to Shawano, and they remembered her and her kindness in her later years.

I sent her a card before her 82nd birthday, and tried to call her a night or two after. It was around 9 or 9:30 p.m., and nobody answered. I assumed that she was visiting with my brothers, Bill or Art. In truth, she was lying on her bedroom floor, her speech destroyed by a stroke. Art found her the next morning and, in carrying her to his car, ruptured a disc and wound up in the same Appleton hospital that Mother was in.

When I received the news about the severe stroke, my main prayer was that she wouldn't be taken away in a flash, like Dad was, so that I could express to her all that she meant to me. That prayer was answered. Although she never was able to speak again, in the seven remaining years of her life she could understand, and knew how much we all loved her, because we told her so, over and over again.

Two women, both big-boned, strong, good-looking and rock-solid. Nurses by training, they were products of their times, and used their nursing skills, among other talents, to be wonderful wives and mothers. They would both be so proud of you today, for being a successful nurse, wife and mother. And wouldn't they have adored little Sarah Carson and Blair.

Love,
Dad

*John Davis Cantwell, M.D.*

# 73

**REFLECTIONS ON A 38TH WEDDING ANNIVERSARY**

Greg Maddux once said about pitching that "it ain't always as easy as it might appear." The same can be said about a marriage. Thirty-eight years after my wedding day, I don't have all the answers (as I'm still learning), but as Robert Frost said, "I do know the questions."

*Adventures on Seven Continents And Other Essays*

**Marilyn and me on our wedding day**

One question pertains to what makes a successful marriage. I would list the following answers:

1) A realization that our concept of love evolves over time.

    Some people, especially around middle-age, get divorced because their love doesn't seem like it once was. Tolstoy wrote, however, that "each time of life has its own kind of love." I have an elderly woman patient, severely crippled with arthritis. Her husband always comes with her, and attends to her needs. I'm sure their relationship is different that it once was. I'm also sure that their love is deeper than it has ever been.

2) A mutual trust in God.
    Things might occur in a marriage that are difficult to resolve, given human imperfections. By trusting in a higher power, and following Biblical guidelines, one can successfully negotiate the minefields of life.

3) Affair-proof your marriage.

    An elderly minister once advised the young Billy Graham to avoid three big pitfalls, namely problems with money, sex and pride. Regarding sex, he advised Graham to avoid any one-on-one encounters with a person of the opposite sex, to both remove temptation and the

*John Davis Cantwell, M.D.*

>threat of a perceived impropriety. A certain president might have benefitted by such an approach.

4) Having the ability to forgive and move on, if mistakes are made and the offender is truly contrite.

I recently attended the remarriage of friends, 11 years after he ran off with a younger woman. The new wife, in turn, eventually left him, for a younger man. "What comes around goes around," according to the old saying. Fortunately for my friend, his first wife was forgiving and he, in turn, has learned to dearly appreciate her virtues.

Some of the happiest people I know are elderly couples, who, at family reunions, are surrounded by their children and grandchildren, and who have given the latter a living example of the joys of maintaining the marital vows and bonds.

*Adventures on Seven Continents And Other Essays*

**At the millennium sunset**

*John Davis Cantwell, M.D.*

# 74

## A FATHER'S FAREWELL TO HIS SON

From the hills west of the city, General Joe Johnston and his Confederate troops could view downtown Atlanta. One-hundred- and-thirty-three years later I stood at the same site, with a panoramic view of Atlanta's skyscrapers. I was there for a different purpose, however, namely to select a grave site for my oldest son, Bradley.

Unmarked Confederate graves and weathered infantry trenches are "poignant reminders" of past events. The region is now called Crestlawn Memorial Park, a euphemism for cemetery, and has the remains of Ms. Daisy Werthan, (of "Driving Miss Daisy" movie fame), Rabbi Jacob Rothchild, former Congressman Dr. Larry McDonald and countless others. One day my wife and I will be there as well, joining our son.

Bradley's esophageal cancer probably manifested itself just before the 1996 Olympic Games, when he developed anemia and black stools. Esophagogastroscopy revealed just mild erosive changes then. When repeated six months later, just after Christmas, a mid-esophageal mass lesion was noted. The biopsy revealed adenocarcinoma, probably triggered by chronic reflux and changes in the cells lining the esophagus (a so-called Barrett's esophagus).

The cancer was too extensive to consider surgery. Radiation was carried out, in hopes of slowing the bleeding. My wife and I elected to treat him at home, each working half-time, she as a speech therapist and I as a cardiologist. In discussions with our other two children, a physician and a nurse, we chose to do reasonable things (feeding him as best we could, transfusing him when his hemoglobin level dropped below 7 grams, and keeping him comfortable) and to avoid aggressive and invasive measures. It was a sad irony that the one thing Bradley could do well - eating - became so difficult toward the end. We spent large sums of money on baby food, such that the clerks at Kroger must have thought we were overzealous grandparents.

Our support systems were incredible. Friends called, wrote, dropped off hot dishes, planted rhododendrons in our backyard, invited us (along with Bradley) for dinner, babysat, and offered prayers and encouragement. Their kindness greatly eased our burden.

I spent each afternoon with Bradley, enjoying together the unparalleled beauty of spring as we rocked in the hammock and listened to the songs of the many cardinals.

Some things needed to be done in preparation for the end that could come at any time. In addition to picking out the grave site, I selected the type of casket, wrote his obituary, and picked out some favorite Biblical verses for his service. Among the verses were I Corinthians 15:42 to 44, read by Dr. Edward Atkinson, in Antarctica, in 1912, at the service for Robert Falcon Scott and his colleagues, who perished on their return from the South Pole. I also chose Psalm 103:15, which was read at Margaret Mitchell's funeral.

Our minister didn't know Bradley very well and asked that I jot down some favorite memories of him. My notations included the following:

*John Davis Cantwell, M.D.*

    —was born at the Mayo Clinic, on a night when his father was to have quarterbacked the Mayo Residents' touch football team.

    —had silly moods where anything you did to him (like gently pinching his nose and giving it a playful shake) elicited laughter.

    —never scored a touchdown, made a basket or hit a triple, but once won a Special Olympics medal for walking 50 yards, a greater feat.

    —liked going to Wendy's on Saturdays with his dad, for a chocolate Frosty and a hamburger.

    —couldn't have been loved more, or cared for better by his mother, who often left a trace of lipstick on his cheek each morning.

    —held on long enough to attend his younger brother's wedding.

    —lived 29 years, and was always considered a joy to his family, and never a burden, even in the most difficult of times.

    —made one appreciate the normal everyday things we too often take for granted.

    Bradley had an estimated I.Q. of less than 20, but he taught us a lot in his short lifetime. In living, he taught us the beauty of unconditional love, and of how much one gets back in return. In the process of dying, he taught us about the ravages of cancer, the challenges and rewards of care giving, the love of our friends, and the preciousness of each moment.

*Adventures on Seven Continents And Other Essays*

The last picture of Bradley, at his brother's wedding

*John Davis Cantwell, M.D.*

## **REFERENCES**

*References for quotes used in the essays are available in the original journal publications or can be provided by the author (fax 404-355-1977).*

*John Davis Cantwell, M.D.*

# ABOUT THE AUTHOR

Dr. John Cantwell is a third generation physician from Wisconsin. He is a cardiologist with Cardiology of Georgia P.C., medical director of the Homer Rice Center at Georgia Tech, and director of Preventive Cardiology and Cardiac Rehabilitation at Piedmont Hospital, He is editor of the Journal of the Medical Association of Georgia.

He attended Duke University where he majored in English, participated in varsity basketball, and was a member of Duke's first ACC championship team. After graduating from Northwestern Medical School, he interned at the University of Florida and obtained a medicine residency at the Mayo Clinic. Post-doctoral fellowships in cardiology were served at the University of California, San Diego, and Emory University.

He served as Chief Medical Officer for the 1996 Olympic Games, ultimately responsible for the care of over 10 thousand athletes and 1.5 million spectators.

Dr, Cantwell holds fellowships in the American College of Cardiology, the American College of Physicians, and the American College of Sports Medicine. He has been a consultant to the President's Council of Physical Fitness and Sports, and is a team physician for the Atlanta Braves and the Special Olympics, He was president of the Association of Major League Baseball Team Physicians in 2000.

The author and co-author of seven books, (including *Stay Young at Heart, Modern Cardiology, Medicine For Sport, and From the Heart to the Himalayas*), Dr. Cantwell enjoys creative writing, reading, distance running, and participation sports with his wife and two children, one a physician and the other a nurse. He is an active member of the Explorers Club and has enjoyed adventure travels to all seven continents. He is a charter member of his high school's Sports Hall of Fame for his football, basketball, and baseball exploits, and still holds the school's career basketball scoring record.

Awards and honors include the Atlantic Coast Conference Honor Roll for Scholarship and Athletics, the Aven Cup (highest award of the Medical Association of Atlanta), and the Morehouse Medical School Award of Excellence (other recipients include Archbishop Tutu, Jane Fonda, Lennie Wilkens, and Edwin Moses).